Interrogating Muslims

Islam of the Global West

Series editors: Kambiz GhaneaBassiri and Frank Peter

Islam of the Global West is a pioneering series that examines Islamic beliefs, practices, discourses, communities, and institutions that have emerged from "the Global West." The geographical and intellectual framing of the Global West reflects both the role played by the interactions between people from diverse religions and cultures in the development of Western ideals and institutions in the modern era, and the globalization of these very ideals and institutions.

In creating an intellectual space where works of scholarship on European and North American Muslims enter into conversation with one another, the series promotes the publication of theoretically informed and empirically grounded research in these areas. By bringing the rapidly growing research on Muslims in European and North American societies, ranging from the United States and France to Portugal and Albania, into conversation with the conceptual framing of the Global West, this ambitious series aims to reimagine the modern world and develop new analytical categories and historical narratives that highlight the complex relationships and rivalries that have shaped the multicultural, poly-religious character of Europe and North America, as evidenced, by way of example, in such economically and culturally dynamic urban centers as Los Angeles, New York, Paris, Madrid, Toronto, Sarajevo, London, Berlin, and Amsterdam where there is a significant Muslim presence.

American and Muslim Worlds Before 1900
Edited by John Ghazvinian & Arthur Mitchell Fraas

Anarchist, Artist, Sufi
Edited by Mark Sedgwick

Amplifying Islam in the European Soundscape: Religious Pluralism and Secularism in the Netherlands
Pooyan Tamimi Arab

The British Muslim Convert Lord Headley, 1855-1935
Jamie Gilham

Islam and Nationhood in Bosnia-Herzegovina: Surviving Empires
Xavier Bougarel

Islam and the Governing of Muslims in France
Frank Peter

Islam as Critique: Sayyid Ahmad Khan and the Challenge of Modernity
Khurram Hussain

Sacred Spaces and Transnational Networks in American Sufism
Merin Shobhana Xavier

Interrogating Muslims

The Liberal-Secular Matrix of Integration

Schirin Amir-Moazami

BLOOMSBURY ACADEMIC
LONDON • NEW YORK • OXFORD • NEW DELHI • SYDNEY

BLOOMSBURY ACADEMIC
Bloomsbury Publishing Plc
50 Bedford Square, London, WC1B 3DP, UK
1385 Broadway, New York, NY 10018, USA
29 Earlsfort Terrace, Dublin 2, Ireland

BLOOMSBURY, BLOOMSBURY ACADEMIC and the Diana logo are
trademarks of Bloomsbury Publishing Plc

First published in Great Britain 2022
This paperback edition published 2024

Copyright © Schirin Amir-Moazami, 2022, 2024

Schirin Amir-Moazami has asserted her right under the Copyright,
Designs and Patents Act, 1988, to be identified as Author of this work.

For legal purposes the Acknowledgments on pp. vi–viii constitute an
extension of this copyright page.

Series design by Dani Leigh
Cover image © Brian Stablyk

All rights reserved. No part of this publication may be reproduced or transmitted
in any form or by any means, electronic or mechanical, including photocopying,
recording, or any information storage or retrieval system, without
prior permission in writing from the publishers.

Bloomsbury Publishing Plc does not have any control over, or responsibility for, any
third-party websites referred to or in this book. All internet addresses given in this
book were correct at the time of going to press. The author and publisher regret
any inconvenience caused if addresses have changed or sites have ceased
to exist, but can accept no responsibility for any such changes.

A catalogue record for this book is available from the British Library.

A catalog record for this book is available from the Library of Congress.

ISBN: HB: 978-1-3502-6637-7
       PB: 978-1-3502-6641-4
       ePDF: 978-1-3502-6638-4
       eBook: 978-1-3502-6639-1

Series: Islam of the Global West

Typeset by Integra Software Services Pvt. Ltd.

To find out more about our authors and books visit www.bloomsbury.com
and sign up for our newsletters

Contents

Acknowledgments vi

Introduction 1

1 Genealogies of *Islampolitik* and Integration 29
2 Integration and the Emergence of a "Muslim Question" 47
3 Measuring Integration: Governing through Knowledge 61
4 Dialogues with Muslims: Governing through Recognition 87
5 Blood, Race, Religion: Governing through Discipline 111

Conclusion 141

Notes 151
References 170
Index 187

Acknowledgments

This book is the result of a long journey across various institutions, across various scholarships, and especially across various encounters and conversations that have contributed to its emergence.

I would like to thank the *Bundesministerium für Bildung und Forschung* (BMBF) for the funding of a joint research project "Muslims in Europe" and the fruitful conversations with colleagues at the Institute of Comparative Cultural and Social Anthropology at the European University Viadrina in Frankfurt/Oder and the *Zentrum Moderner Orient* (ZMO) in Berlin. My main gratitude goes to Dietrich Reetz, the spokesperson of the research group, and to Werner Schiffauer, the mentor of my project.

I am also deeply indebted to my colleagues at the Institute of Islamic Studies at *Freie Universität Berlin* as well as the *Graduate School Muslim Cultures and Societies* for offering me a generous space for developing my own teaching and research profile of *Islam in Europe*. I am especially thankful to Gudrun Krämer for her tireless support and for her openness for unconventional research and teaching perspectives. I thank Sonja Eising and Angela Ballaschk for their amazing help and for keeping the institute together. I cannot thank the students enough for their energy and curiosity to engage in complex and sometimes uncomfortable issues and for their thoughtful questions and discussions.

I benefitted a lot from the inspiring intellectual environment at the University of Bristol during my *Benjamin Meaker* guest professorship. I would like to thank in particular Tariq Modood for his invitation and for many thought-provoking conversations, and Aleksandra Lewicki for her intellectual company and friendship.

My gratitude also goes to my colleagues at the Cluster of Excellence *Contestations of the Liberal Script (SCRIPTS)* for ongoing inspiring conversations, and to the *Deutsche Forschungsgemeinschaft* German Research Foundation for their generous financial support.

Many of the ideas and perspectives developed in this book have emerged from extremely inspiring discussions with colleagues and friends of the network *Configurations of Muslim Traditions in European Secular Public Spheres*, funded by the Netherlands Organization for Scientific Research. The same is true for the network "*Unfolding the 'Muslim Question'. Towards a genealogy of religious freedom and the minority question in Western European nation states*," funded by the *Blankensee-Colloquium* at the Institute for Advanced Studies in Berlin. For the latter I am particularly grateful to my co-organizers Nadia Fadil and Sarah Bracke for numerous fruitful exchanges.

I am incredibly thankful to Ruth Mas for her generous feedback on all chapters of the book, for her sharpness and intellectual spirit, and for the many wonderful hours we spent together during her different stays in Berlin.

I would like to thank the series editors Frank Peter and Kambiz GhaneaBassiri for having read all chapters carefully and for their extremely helpful comments. Likewise, I am thankful to the two anonymous reviewers, who gave me very productive feedback on earlier versions of the manuscript. Lalle Pursglove and Lily McMahon from Bloomsbury have also been of tremendous support.

Finally, I would like to express my gratitude to my family. First and foremost, I thank my mother Renate Amir-Moazami who left us far too early but whose strength and love will continue to accompany me. I am thankful to my dear father Behjat Amir-Moazami for his trust, love, and warmth. My gratitude to Barbara Witton's energy, support, and generosity can hardly be expressed in words. I thank my sister Susann for always being there for me, and I thank my niece Kimia for many inspiring conversations and fresh thoughts. My deep gratitude goes to Mika Hannula for his intellectual rigor, for his endless encouragements, for his love, and partnership during the (too) long process of getting this book done. Our beloved children Yuri and Aila have been a constant source of joy and they also helped me to put things into perspective.

Parts of Chapter 3 were first published in:

2018 "Epistemologien der 'muslimischen Frage' in Europa" in Schirin Amir-Moazami (ed.): Der inspizierte Muslim. Zur Politisierung der Islamforschung in Europa, Bielefeld: transcript, 91–123.
2021 "Epistemologies of the 'Muslim Question' : On the Politics of Knowledge Production in a Minefield", in Amélie Barras, Jennifer A. Selby and Melanie Adrian (eds.): *Producing Islam(s) in Canada: On Knowledge, Positionality, and Politics*, Toronto: Toronto University Press, 27–49.

Parts of Chapter 5 were first published in:

2016 "Zur Produktion loyaler Staatsbürger: Einbürgerungstests als Instrument der Regulierung von religiös-kultureller Pluralität in Deutschland", in Aleksandra Lewicki (ed.): *Soziale Bewegungen*, Special Issue: Bürgerschaft und soziale Bewegungen in der Einwanderungsgesellschaft, 29 (2), 21–34.

Introduction

Muslims and Islam in Europe are on the spot. No debate about religious plurality, immigration societies, or "refugee crises" passes without the evocation of Islam as the central target. This discursive incitement is coupled with a whole set of political measures and interventions of which *integration* has turned into a master paradigm. In the intertwined processes of securitization and recognition, calls for integration revolve around debates on Muslim populations and the institutionalization of Islam (Brunn 2012; Mavelli 2012; Schinkel 2017; Tezcan 2012). Proclamations such as "naturalizing Islam,"[1] turning Muslims in France into "French Muslims" (Fernando 2014), or creating a "Euro-Islam" (Mavelli 2012) are its most pertinent political-rhetorical devices.

Integration can, of course, mean many different things. The term "integrate" derived in the seventeenth century from the Latin word "*integrat*"—"make whole," also based on the sixteenth-century use of the term *integer*—"intact, whole" (*Concise Oxford English Dictionary*). When employed in contexts of immigration today, integration imposes itself as a remedy for a seemingly fragmented, non-cohesive, and therefore deficient society *because* of immigration. Integration can be oriented toward the enhancement of equal opportunities in educational institutions or in the labor market to achieve the social equality of immigrant populations. It can also be directed at the recognition of cultural or religious practices considered minoritarian. And it can involve attempts to remodel these very minoritarian practices according to majoritarian rules, norms, and lifestyles. While thus mobilizing a variety of—partly contradictory—political practices, integration is centrally about managing the segregation of what is considered particular and exceptional from what is considered as general and normal.

In short, the demand for integration is expansive and little contested. Its operations are rarely laid bare, and its normative underpinnings are largely taken for granted, even if there is no consensus whatsoever regarding its concrete implications. In this book I suggest moving a couple of steps sideways. Rather than joining the chorus on the critical importance of improving integration in order to create a more cohesive society, I seek to denaturalize the very quest for integration. Instead of asking if what Muslims are doing, saying, or thinking is indicative of their integration into immigration societies, I interrogate the conditions of this very interrogation, the discursive patterns that it takes, its liberal and secular presuppositions, and also the aporias running through the very promise and quest for integration. I interrogate the grounds on which the politics of integration are justified and reasoned upon, and how they consolidate rather than disrupt divisions between seemingly unmarked majorities and marked minorities. I ask what the discourses and practices of integration do, whence their salience derives, and why Muslims have become their central focus. I interrogate the language that organizes the grammar of integration. I ask what contours the liberal-secular matrix of state power gain when specific minorities—in this case Muslims—are interrogated as subjects of integration. And I ask how the paradigm of integration in its ambition of inclusivity navigates between universalistic claims and particularistic—racial and religious—reenactments of a secular nation-state framework. Addressing this set of questions in this book I centrally argue that integration directed toward Muslims as a "religious minority" in Europe is indicative of the problems that it purports to resolve. I therefore do not so much ask how the integration of Muslims into the social fabric of European nation-states could be improved. Instead I take integration seriously as a political program which is imbricated in, and productive of, complex operations of power and its functions to secure the authority of the secular nation-state.

To unfold this argument, I take Germany as my point of departure. In Germany public, political, and academic discourses on integration have exploded in the last two decades as an answer to the seeming absence of a coherent policy that would respond to the fact that Germany has become a country of immigration. In light of the cyclically reemerging "refugee crises," the call for integration has gained further salience since 2015. The "law on integration" (*Integrationsgesetz*), implemented in August 2016,[2] has endowed this program with an additional—legal—dimension. Migrants settling into Germany can now be obliged to take integration classes in which they must learn German, and become acquainted with the basic rights and principles of German society.

Very similar to other European countries, integration discourses in Germany have increasingly centered on the governance of *religious* plurality, generally, and of Muslims in particular (Brunn 2012; Fülling 2019; Schlerka 2021; Tezcan 2012). Its associated slogan "Demand and Support" (*Fördern und Fordern*) has been put forward in state-led integration programs and in the Immigration Act of 2005[3]. This slogan shows that this paradigm is driven by the ambivalent goal of assisting immigrants or people marked as such in settling and participating in society, while at the same time signaling the conditions and limits of this endeavor. Immigrants generally, and Muslims in particular, are requested to "do" something in exchange for the support they receive by the state or by society at large.

Precisely because political authorities consistently denied that Germany had become an immigration society, scholars of migration often praised the move toward integration as an overdue step (Bade 2007, 2017; Heckmann 2014; Joppke 2010). Many had already called for the social and economic integration of migrant workers from the late 1970s onwards, when "guest workers" were not adjusting to the rotating system of a cheap labor force and to the logic of the labor market, and instead permanently settled in Germany (Bade 2007; Fincke 2009; Heckmann 2014).[4] Calls for the integration of Muslims in particular have been endorsed as the overdue acknowledgment that Germany has turned into an immigration society (Foroutan 2010; Heckmann 2014; Laurence 2011).

Raising the question of how integration could gain this largely uncontested status for addressing the presence of Muslims in Germany, I expand the scholarship of critical migration studies (Castro Varela 2013; El-Mafalaani 2018; Ha 2007; Hess, Binder and Moser 2009). These scholars have critically examined the normative premises of integration discourses, and the power dynamics involved in the one-sided request for certain populations to integrate. They have shown that integration programs are largely unable to address social inequalities on a structural level and instead treat immigrants paternalistically with a mission to pacify and civilize them.

On a conceptual level Willem Schinkel's monograph *Imagined Soceities. A Critique of Immigrant Integration in Western Europe* (2017) stands out as the most relevant for my own analysis. Schinkel couples his critique of integration with a critical inquiry into social theory. He argues that integration fulfills the function of imagining "society" in holistic terms by constructing immigrants as subpopulations that are set apart. Social theory itself, Schinkel claims, has been epistemologically complicit of this binary. With their conceptualizations social theorists provided the ingredients for the social imaginary of "society" as a bounded entity. People considered in need of integration into "society," conceived of in such holistic terms, are necessarily constituted as "people apart." In the very moment in which these "people apart" are addressed distinctively from what is considered the norm, this very norm takes shape, which in turn secures the notion of a totalized society. Schinkel shows at length how social science knowledge production has been productive of this operation:

> Precisely because inside and outside are at the same time a consequence of the working of "society" they cannot be regarded as separate terrains that conform to a realist opposition between "society" and its "outside." And so … when the sociology of immigrant integration opposes "society" to groups and individuals that are "not (well) integrated," it contributes to the imagination and thus the very formation of "society," even though it claims to describe as given the object and its environment, its transformations and its identity. The same goes for social theory more generally: it has itself been part of a more encompassing social imagination.
>
> (Schinkel 2017: 37)

This performative function assigned to sociological knowledge can thus be understood as a form of governing social reality by constructing it through knowledge. While Schinkel has convincingly analyzed how integration works as an enabling force of an allegedly holistic core of "society" by constituting immigrants as eroding society's margins, the role and function of the nation-state therein still require more careful attention. Schinkel, moreover, has observed an increasing culturalization of integration discourses across Europe. This has entailed an asymmetric focus on Muslims as being encompassed by a distinctive "culture." Schinkel, however, does only marginally discuss the question of how, when, and to what end "culture" has become almost univocally equated with "Islam." Similarly, the question of how the politics of integration sit on a longer legacy of interrogating "problematic" racial or religious minorities still needs more careful attention.

I therefore expand and complicate Schinkel's approach in two important ways. First, I suggest a slightly different temporality: Despite their current rise to prominence in dealing with immigration as an irreversible reality, integration discourses are not unprecedented in German history. Their legacy is located in the formation of modern nation-states and their simultaneous production and inclusion of national, religious, or cultural "minorities." To show this, I do not provide a historiographical analysis. I rather build my argument on Zygmunt Bauman's conceptual elaborations on the paradoxes of assimilation as a technique of power closely related to what Bauman has called the "gardening forces" of the modern state (1991: 28; 178), and its specific manifestation in the assimilation of Jews in Germany (see also Arendt 1951; Aumüller 2009; Jansen 2013; Markell 2003: Chapter 5). Bauman understands assimilation as a technique of governing a disturbing cultural and religious plurality in the course of nation-state formation and its ambitions for homogeneity and order. Assimilation, Bauman argues, works as a trap: while promising inclusion into a national community, assimilation marks, manages, and transforms incompatible difference into something familiar.

I do not claim that integration is the same as assimilation or that the Jewish minority in the nineteenth and early twentieth centuries could easily be equated with the situation of Muslims in Germany today. I rather follow Ann L. Stoler's suggestion to think of repercussions of past events or processes in terms of "recursions" (2016). "Recursions," according to Stoler, are not simple repetitions of historical, social, and political processes: "Rather, they are processes of partial reinscriptions, modified displacements, and amplified recuperations" (Stoler 2016: 27). Throughout the different chapters, and most notably in Chapter 1, I argue that integration today operates as such a reinscription of assimilation. I therefore lay emphasis on the complex reworkings of the trap that is entailed in the dynamics of the conditional state-offered support for minoritized groups.

Assimilation revolved around somatic metaphors of organic "cultures," or the "nation" as an imagined body (Volkskörper). In the paradigm of integration instead, somatic aspirations are both inscribed and concealed in the frequent request for Muslims to be loyal to the liberal-secular contract by bracketing their religious sensibilities and opening up to allegedly abstract liberal principles. I therefore locate political programs of Muslim integration in Germany in the genealogy of the *secular* nation-state and its production of (religious) minorities. I raise the question of how in a consolidated liberal-secular nation-state the presence of Muslims brings to the fore distinctions between established citizens and outsiders (not yet or not quite citizens), and how a liberal and secular lexicon conceals the embodied contours of these very distinctions.

It is in this vein that I secondly expand Schinkel's view on the relationship between integration and secularism. Pertaining to this connection, Schinkel writes that "secularism operates in the same plane as religion, as a program that allows for the attribution of inside/outside values through topics debated with a view to the secular and the religious. Secularism is part of a larger self problematization of 'society'" (Schinkel 2017: 32). Throughout the different chapters I show that the politics of integration in liberal-secular nation-states do not merely work through distinctions made between "inside/outside values." The integration of Muslims rather operates by conditionally embracing religious difference, while at the same time transforming it to make it compatible with contingent understandings of religion's legitimate place in public life. To show this requires more careful attention to the *secular* state in its enabling and monitoring functions. And it also requires attentiveness to the distinctive liberal commitment to accommodate religion while guarding the borders between the religious and the political. I thus argue that projects that organize the institutionalization of Islam and the social integration of Muslims in Germany are animated by a contingent liberal-secular matrix through which the sovereign state, in close connection with civil society, is empowered to decide what counts as proper and improper religion.

Furthermore, my genealogically informed reading of contemporary discourses on the integration of Muslims is inspired by the postcolonial scholarship that has put emphasis on the colonial patterns prevalent in today's governance of Islam and Muslims in Europe, most notably France (Davidson 2012; Fernando 2014; Mas 2006; Scott Wallach 2019; Silverstein 2004). These approaches have challenged the recurrent assumption that Islam and Muslims would have been discovered unprecedentedly as a problem after 9/11.

Arguably, 9/11 reinforced the racialization of Muslims by an expansive security apparatus or by the quasi-natural categorization of immigrants as "Muslims." However, the deeper rootedness of these discourses and the related emphasis on integration have to be located prior to 9/11 and even prior to post-Second World War migration.

Recently, scholars have started to account for this deeper rootedness in Germany. They denoted analogies between Islamophobia and nineteenth-, early twentieth-century anti-Semitism (Keskinkılıç 2019; Shooman 2015) and observed that contemporary discourses on Muslims and Islam in Germany echo Orientalist tropes (e.g. Attia 2009; Keskinkilic 2019; Shooman 2014). The complex question more rarely posed is how these tropes are translated into *liberal* projects of accommodating difference and managing minorities today. Integration projects which govern Muslims with the incentive of according Islam its legitimate place within German society, and sometimes in explicit rejection of enmity and segregation, thus tend to escape from view. Sometimes, Muslim integration even figures as a counter-strategy to Islamophobia and is celebrated as paving the way for "Muslims' emancipation" (Laurence 2011). These shortcomings derive from a narrow analytics of power, which does not account for the powers of liberalism. But they also stem from the fact that secularism as a structuring feature of religious plurality has not been taken seriously into account in the scholarship on Islamophobia or anti-Muslim racism in Germany.

The intimate intertwinement between integration and politics of Islam in contemporary Germany in its partly tacit operations of power cannot be fully grasped if we do not recall the older legacies in which Islam has been conceptualized as subordinate to Christianity, and subsequently, as subordinate to political secularism. This also implies recalling the imperial and colonial legacy of a "spatialized knowledge regime" (Jackson 2019) in which Islam was constructed as the external friend or, more frequently, the enemy of European Christianity (Marchand 2010; Salvatore 1999; Stauth 1993). It is in this context that the notion of "politics of Islam" (*Islampolitik*) as a specific mode of governing Muslims was coined by Orientalists such as Carl Heinrich Becker when German imperialism was endangered. In Germany today, politics of Islam is frequently coupled with approaches to Muslims as subjects of integration (Fülling 2019; Tezcan 2012). It is therefore necessary to ask under which conditions *Islampolitik* has acquired a renewed salience in political discourses on Muslims in Germany in today's context of institutionalized liberal freedoms, and given that Muslims have become an intrinsic part of German society. And we have to ask how these complex legacies and functions of the integration paradigm geared toward Muslims are played out in relation to reconfigured epistemologies of "religion" as a modern notion of classification and distinction.

Distancing ourselves from the immediate present can help us to understand the exclusionary patterns of inclusion in its epistemological underpinnings, which the discourse on integration in its liberal grammar itself tends to conceal. One of these patterns, which is central for my analysis, pertains to a seeming paradox, which Aladin El-Mafaalani has elaborated on (2018). Al-Mafaalani claims that the more a minority associated with its immigration background gets settled and rooted in a society, the louder the call for integration is voiced (El-Mafalaani 2018). Pertaining to the different operations and functions of integration discourses throughout the chapters in this book, I argue that this is only seemingly a paradox: integration is advocated as the sole remedy for pluralistic nation-state contexts at moments in which the internal and external borders of these very nation-states crumble. If integration functions, generally, to fix the borders of the nation-state, the liberal-secular framework in which the integration of Muslims is called upon functions to demarcate acceptable versions of religion (liberal, secular, moderate, etc.) against the background of unacceptable (i.e. excessive, political, radical, etc.) ones within these very borders.

I therefore put forward the argument, in Chapter 3 especially, that "religion" functions as a significant category of ordering majorities and minorities in secular nation-states. What Schinkel has called the "moral monitoring" of integration through the production of sociological knowledge in Europe gains a specific momentum in state-commissioned studies which measure and correlate Muslims' degrees of religiosity with their degrees of integration into society. If integration of immigrants is morally monitored by modern techniques of knowledge production, generally, the integration of Muslims, more specifically, is monitored, measured, and regulated by classificatory regimes of knowledge that are provided by the liberal-secular nation-state.

By problematizing "religion" as an epistemic category of both ordering and ordaining, I suggest expanding our scope beyond the recurrent observation that Muslims in Europe have been increasingly racialized (Aguilar 2018; Davidson 2012; Meer 2013; Tyrer 2013). While race has been rightly problematized as being reinscribed in terms of "culture" or "values" (Balibar and Wallerstein 1988), "religion" figures rarely as a problem of classificatory and hierarchical systems of knowledge and power. The production of Muslim subjectivities in Germany and Europe more broadly, however, works through acts of internal classification in which race and religion often operate in tandem. It is through this coupling that a distinctive Muslim "population" appears as the margins of the embodied contours of the liberal-secular nation-state. My analysis in this regard contributes to the growing scholarship that has problematized "religion" in its intertwinement with "race" (e.g. Anidjar 2008; Jansen and Meer 2020; Kalmar 2016; Topolski 2018; Vial 2016). I engage in this scholarship by asking how the *liberally* constituted nation-state governs *religious* plurality, which requires particular attention to the relationship between liberal and secular governance.

Integration as Liberal Governmentality

Turning our view to the productive force of integration discourses in their liberal and secular underpinnings has analytical implications. The inquiry into the functions and operations of integration demands responsiveness to the regulations of sensibilities and conduct of life to which people marked as minorities are exposed in the call for integration. More importantly, it requires expanding our analytical lenses and not merely focusing on manifestly racist discourses, or discriminatory laws and practices, or overtly repressive forms of governing Muslims. It has to account for the tacit interrogations that are geared to measure, diagnose, and eventually transform Muslim's social life and religious practices. Scrutinizing the polyvalent powers of discourses of integration is particularly salient because integration in the case of Muslims is often motivated by liberating these very populations, either from their religious constraints or from their marginalized positions within society. Because of this liberal incentive integration tends to be considered unproblematic or devoid of power.

Michel Foucault's elaborations on governmentality (*gouvernementalité*) are particularly useful in answering the question of how integration discourses are rationalized in a liberal vocabulary (Foucault 2006 [1977–79]). In his studies of governmentality, Foucault is mainly concerned with liberal forms of governing, and the shifting functions of state power that emerged with the formation of modern nation-states. Two interrelated presuppositions of governmentality will guide my analysis in this book: the intimate relationship between governance and knowledge, and the focus on the powers of liberal freedoms.

In his lectures on governmentality, Foucault traces a path to account for the productive force of liberal freedoms enabled by the emerging liberal state in the eighteenth and nineteenth centuries, and its neoliberal components in the early twentieth century. He carves out the shifts in the reflections on *how* to govern, and the related effects of liberal governance on the political rationalities of state power. The governmentalization of the state engendered the accumulation and dispersion of governance through the enhancement of bureaucracy, security techniques of control, surveillance, and scientific knowledge production. The liberal doctrine of the nineteenth and twentieth centuries aimed at limiting state power.[5] The self-limiting liberal state, however, simultaneously enlarged liberal freedoms and established new technologies of bio-political control, measurement, and surveillance of individual bodies and of the "population" as a newly emerging segment of governance. The liberal state's incentive to protect life, accounting for, managing, regulating, educating, controlling, and disciplining bodies and souls has essentially been tied to processes of selection and distinction. The governmentalization of the state has therefore been productive of divisions and hierarchizations (e.g. the healthy from the pathological, the mad from the normal, licit sexual practices and pleasures from illicit ones, or the docile from the criminal subject). The governance and production of the "population" have occurred within the production of specificities and particularities, which are constituted as bearing either unbridgeable differences or as those that need to be disciplined, educated, or erased (see Dean 2001; Hindess 2001).

As a pertinently self-reflexive art of governing, governmentality entails an inseparable linkage between governing and knowledge, and most notably knowledge of the subjects of government. Relevant instruments in the governmentalization of the state were no longer the apparatus of justice and the threat of death but rather the regulation of life that was attached to a growing apparatus of knowledge. Scientific knowledge became a central element in the process of rational calculation and categorizing subjects, for example, in the domains of medicine, psychology, criminology, or pedagogy.

At the heart of the distinctly liberal power-knowledge-nexus stood the ideal that governing should be structured only to the extent that subjects are enabled to govern themselves. This idea of the "conduct of conduct," that is to say enabling the subjects' self-conduct became of major importance of governance, and freedom served as its motor. Foucault's diagnosis of the genealogical shifts in state power necessitates an understanding of freedom and power as intimately attached to each other. Governmental power presupposes *free* subjects, or strives for subjects to be freed from constrains. In his seminal exegesis of Foucault's concept of governmentality, Thomas Lemke contends that this intimate nexus of modern-state formation and subjectivation resulted from a complex combination of political and pastoral power:

> While the former derives from the Greek polis, and is organized around rights, universality, public space etc., the latter is a Christian religious concept that focuses on the comprehensive guidance of individuals ….The difference between this and Ancient Greek and Roman ideas of government is that the Christian pastorate developed methods of analysis, techniques of reflection and supervision that intended to secure the knowledge of the "inner truth" of the individuals.
>
> (Lemke 2010: 34)

Pastoral care, Lemke goes on, in its secularized translations, was constitutive for the modern state which relies on the "production of rational knowledge about the individual and the population" (Lemke 2010: 34). The related forms of governance are no longer the law but the norm. In another article Lemke even goes so far as to claim that the security technologies of the modern state stand in opposition to the legal normativity which codifies norms through the law: "The technologies of security represent the very opposite of the disciplinary system: whereas the latter presumes a prescriptive norm, the former takes the empirical norm as its starting point, which serves as a regulative norm and allows for further differentiations and variations" (Lemke 2011: 47).

It is important to remind that these divergent forms of power should not be understood as having linearly replaced each other (Foucault 2008 [1979]: 26). Despite institutionalized shifts in state power and in the different rationalities of reflecting and critiquing these shifts, it would be misleading to speak about an age of sovereign power, an age of disciplinary power, and the current age of neoliberal governmental power. More importantly, for my analysis, a sharp distinction between a prescriptive and an empirical norm is misleading. Rather, in programs of the integration of Muslims a prescriptive norm is not only coupled with an empirical norm, but also often enabled through it.

This intimate relationship is particularly salient in the epistemologies and methodologies of knowledge production about Muslim forms of social life and religious practices as indictors of the success or failure of integration. As I will show in Chapter 3, research on minoritized populations addressed as Muslims in Germany has flourished throughout the last decades. The prescriptive norm of how a legally backed and institutionalized "religion" should look like in the context of knowledge production operates through the empirical norm of what is studied and categorized as religion. It is enabled by empirical data-gathering and its related classificatory methods. Focusing on the scientific measurement of Muslim integration, I analyze knowledge production as an instance of how the secular state gets reproduced as the unmarked seeing subject that is invested in "religion" as a distinct unit of analysis. These forms of knowledge production both reveal and enact built-in epistemological structures that reproduce normality and deviance through classificatory knowledge orders. They are predicated on a longer legacy that predates the contemporary social-scientific investigation of Muslims and the degrees of their integration. I locate them in the rise and naturalization of statistics as a means to represent and "make people" (Hacking 2002), in the claim to objectivity as well as in the scientific study of religion as a distinctive field of analysis.

In Chapter 4 I discuss another inflection of this knowledge order which can be found in the recurrent narration of the democratic roots of Christianity and Christianity's gradual acceptance of its subordinate and yet democratizing function in the liberal democratic state. Such narrations perform what Theodore Vial has called "prototypes" of religion (Vial 2016: 123), which provide the template against which Muslims are empirically measured and prescriptively transformed into compliant citizens. Analyzing integration through the lens of governmentality will thus allow me to examine how particular politics of knowledge production and their related epistemologies work as governmental practices. Knowledge here not only inhabits the instrumental function of "serving" power. It inhabits a significant part in ordering and shaping society.

While governmentality as an analytical lens pertains to the tactics of governing beyond the state as the embodied sovereignty representing the people, I follow the scholarship which has emphasized the necessity of bringing the state back into the picture (Bröckling, Krasmann, and Lemke 2012; Brown 2006: Chapter 4; Butler 2006; Dean 1999; Purtschert, Meyer, and Winter 2007). The call for the integration of Muslims in Germany has been saliently fostered on the state level. It has been evoked as response to the challenges posed to state sovereignty by Muslim movements and their quest for participation and for the institutionalization of Islam. The state is thus neither absent nor a minor player in the interrogations of Muslims as subjects of integration. On the contrary, it acts as a regulatory and managing force in integration discourses and programs and it is intimately related to civil society such as the church, the media as well as experts.

I am mostly inspired here by Wendy Brown's seminal work on tolerance discourses in the United States, and her analysis of the interconnection between governmentality and state sovereignty (2006). Brown argues that tolerance operates centrally as governmentality in that it is primarily paralegal, yet not extralegal. Governing through tolerance discourses works with a range of tacit social powers, and employs and infiltrates a number of discourses conventionally conceived of as being detached from political power, such as scientific discourses (2006: 81). Brown cautions that this dispersion of power, pertinent in governmentality, should not underestimate the disciplining features of state power in discourses of tolerance. She even argues that the deployment of tolerance was partly an answer to the state's legitimacy deficit, and to its "historically diminished capacity to embody universal representation" (2006: 84).

As one example, relevant for my analysis, Brown focuses on the state's call to be tolerant toward Muslims, and the simultaneous enhancement of measures that have targeted people who are marked and interpellated as Muslims as potential security threats in the aftermath of 9/11. The parallel hailing of subjects as unified in a multicultural *nation* through "tolerance talk" (ibid.: 102) and the marking, racializing, and disciplining of the same subjects as suspicious and in need of special treatment are, according to Brown, characteristic of the complex project of state legitimacy in late modernity:

> But here is how the legitimizing logic goes: defined against the unfree, intolerant peoples who menace us, a tolerant citizenry is a virtuous and free citizenry; and it is precisely this virtue and freedom that license security. The virtue and liberality contrast with the direct racialized violence of the state; however in conferring the virtue of tolerance upon the people, in calling for tolerance, the state allies itself with virtue, regardless of what it actually does or incites.
>
> (ibid.: 103)

Integration works similarly to the way tolerance does according to Brown, that is, as paralegal practices that are largely distributed in different spheres of civil society. At the same time, integration discourses serve the strengthening and legitimizing role of the liberal-secular state whose sovereignty has been weakened in the domain of the religious and cultural pluralization of society precisely because of its commitments to liberal and secular norms. Throughout this book I argue that the discursively evoked need to regulate cultural and religious plurality via the integration of Muslims into society significantly increases the governance of populations deemed to be in need of being governed in order to better govern themselves. In contrast to Brown, however, I offer a more empirically grounded picture regarding the different instances of the relationship between governmental power and state sovereignty.

A Foucauldian-inspired analysis of power departs from the conception of the (liberal) state as an already constituted ensemble of institutions and actors, and instead conceptualizes the state as an *effect* of various, partly contradictory techniques of power. I thus start from an understanding of statehood as put into effect by the very discourses and practices prevalent in the specific governmental practices I investigate. While a lot has been written on governmentality as productive of Muslim subjectivities in Europe (e.g. Bracke 2011; Fadil 2011; Fernando 2014; Mas 2006; Peter 2021; Tezcan 2012) my analysis contributes to the question of how governmental techniques simultaneously produce particular understandings of the liberal-secular state and its means of governing the religious lives of specific populations.

Looking at integration in terms of governmentality therefore does not mean neglecting the state, but rather asking what kind of state integration discourses and programs *perform* in a liberal-secular order that is formally committed to individual freedoms and to state neutrality vis-à-vis religious plurality.

More appropriately, I argue that state sovereignty in integration measures is enacted through different forms of governmentality and that the state that is thereby effected varies according to these forms. The state that is effected by the scientific and especially statistical measurement of the integration of Muslims into society, which I will look at in Chapter 3, differs from the state that is effected when integration is rationalized as the conditional recognition of minorities, which I will investigate in Chapter 4. Finally, as I will show in Chapter 5 which looks at regulations of citizenship through naturalization tests, state sovereignty in integration programs can also occur through the investigation of individual minds and bodies and through the threat of sanction (see Tadros in Caldwell 2007: 114). In this case, state bureaucracy reveals its disciplinary functions vis-à-vis subjects that are to be turned into German nationals by eventually denying them the passport.

State sovereignty enabled by governmental means in the case of citizenship tests reveals the connections between modern state bureaucracies and biopolitics, for which Eric Santner (2011) has coined the notion of "biocracy" (2011). According to Santner the vacuum of power caused by the transition of the king's sovereignty to the sovereignty of everybody—the people— represented by the democratic state has been compensated by technologies of surveillance and control by bureaucratized institutions such as schools, universities, hospitals, prisons, etc. that are in charge of producing docile, law-abiding, and democratically minded citizens. The new bearer of sovereignty that is entitled to represent "the people" is, accordingly, the modern nation-state along with its bureaucratic apparatus as well as the "new kinds of power and authority wielded at least to a very large extent by medical and social-scientific experts authorized according to secular protocols of knowledge production" (2011: 11).

While Santner's reading of the metamorphoses of monarchical sovereignty into modern technologies of power is conventionally Foucauldian, what is more intriguing for my analysis is his emphasis on the corporeal dimensions of these transformations. Santner centrally argues that the "royal" part of the king's body has been dispersed into the bodies of new bearers of sovereignty: the people. The "flesh," that fattened monarchical authority, and "a type of excessive materiality" (ibid.), which was horizontally redistributed among citizens in a polity, furthered by democratic revolutions, has become the object of "new sciences of the flesh" (2011: 5). The reference to power as an "empty place," as an absent center that is the defining feature of democratic societies, in Santner's view, thus did not get rid of the problem of the carnal or corporeal dimension of political representation but rather made it more difficult to delimit and locate it:

> What I believe Foucault has drawn attention to here without being fully able to name it is, precisely, the mutation of the King's two Bodies into the People's Two bodies: the migration of royal flesh—that strange material and physical presence endowed with a peculiar force—that supplants the merely mortal body of the king into the bodies and lives of the citizens of modern nation-states. This mutation calls to the scene the "experts" charged with managing the sublime somatic substance of the new bearer of the principle of sovereignty.
>
> (Santner 2011: 10)

The path to modern liberal democratic orders, Santner argues, is thus not driven by moral progress, rationality, or disenchantment, but rather by the metamorphosis and displacement of an enchanted "royal materiality" that, despite its elusiveness, is held to inform the very structure of our political life. Santner is thus explicit in underlining that it is precisely the looseness of the transformed sovereign power, which makes it difficult to grasp and identify. In his engagement with Hannah Arendt it becomes clear that what he calls the "flesh of the social bond" gained a new form of representational corporality in the national community (2011: 50). The medicalization, control, and surveillance of the body of the population, and of individual bodies, have thus been coupled with the scrutiny and production of particular subpopulations that are considered unruly and in need of civilization, who don't belong to the nation by function of their ascribed "nature."

Santner's examples of biocracy are however limited for my purpose in that they are mainly taken from Arendt's investigations of excessive racist bureaucracy in totalitarian regimes. In contexts of institutionalized individual rights, the state under the rule of law and individual freedoms biocracy is not limited to a bureaucratic apparatus that operates through making life by taking life, and that is justified by a formally racist state that divides and hierarchizes people into different races. In integration measures like citizenship tests biocratic power operates much more subtly: It is justified with abstract liberal principles instead of with recurrence to national or racial purity or superiority. Moreover, mechanisms of selecting, inspecting, and disciplining lives of people framed as potentially illiberal are intertwined with the promise to incorporate these people by rendering them liberal. Oriented at the transformation of Muslims into compliant liberal citizens, biocracy is simultaneously productive of divisions between appropriate and inappropriate forms of religiosity ("liberal," "enlightened," "European" vs. "traditionally Islamic," "conservative," "overtly religious").

Focusing on the relationship that is created between state bureaucrats and Muslims as subjects of integration, I read citizenship tests as "zones of contact" (Linke 2006), where the biocratic state both reveals and conceals its corporeal groundings. When integration is rationalized as a formal procedure of testing the constitutional loyalty required for citizenship, it reveals the explicit juridical and disciplinary rationality that underlies this endeavor. At the same time, this rationality functions as a means of casting Germany as being constituted by liberal, secular, and law-abiding nationals against the backdrop of an illiberal, exhaustively religious, and potentially unruly Muslim counterpart.

To answer the question of how state power is effected in and through various forms of liberal governmentality in integration programs, I track the political rationalities of these practices. When speaking about political rationalities, I dwell on Mitchell Dean's elaborations on governmentality as a methodological device to prioritize questions that look at the "practices of government that form the basis on which problematizations are made and what happens when we govern and are governed" (Dean 2001: 39). The central question is then not in the first place *who* rules, what is the source of ruling, or what is the basis of its legitimacy. Instead the focus on *how* people are governed "then arises from a rejection of the political a priori of the distribution of power and the location of rule" (Dean 2001: 40). This understanding of political rationalities alludes to a thicker texture of state bureaucracy and the governmentalized state than the term rationality would suggest, if detached from a Foucauldian archive.

Political rationalities thus understood direct us to the ways in which various forms of embodied and rationalized sentiments are ingrained in political reasoning and practice. It follows that the visceral and affective underpinnings of political reasoning need to be taken seriously not in abstraction but rather in concrete operations. My task is then not so much to look at how actors, institutions, or particular parties "enact" power on Muslims by governing them through integration. I am more concerned with the rationalities—meant as reasoning—that undergird these practices, and I ask to what extent these reflect broader webs of power anchored in and productive of liberal forms of governmentality.

I read integration measures geared toward Muslims as symptomatic of the *productive* forces of liberalism in imagining and shaping liberal subjects. Practices of integration put into motion a juridical rationality (as exemplified by the threat of sanction) that is coupled with the performance of a liberal nation, staged as having unanimously incorporated gender equality, liberal tolerance, and individual freedoms. This benign mode of shaping and transforming subjects into docile citizens is even prevalent in citizenship tests (Chapter 5). While such tests display a renewed version of Germany's exclusivist notion of nationhood, I read them as the simultaneous effort to overcome its racist legacy by performing the achievements of an inclusive and liberal constitutional order.

Understanding integration as a tool of liberal politics that accommodates, and, at the same time, reshapes difference, also involves critically investigating these built-in predicaments of political liberalism, and asking how these are played out in concrete political measures. It is precisely because powers of freedom work differently from powers of discipline, coercion, and constraint that they tend to escape from view or that they are considered oppositional to coercion and constraint. The liberal powers of integration programs operate with a set of partly divergent rationalities that range from scientific inspection, civic pedagogy, to control and discipline. In line with Foucault's and Nikolas Rose's (1999a, 1999b) further elaborations on the contingent powers of freedom, it is therefore important to go beyond the valid but limited assumption about the "Janus-faced" nature of individual freedoms (Berlin 1958; Gray 2000; Saar 2007: 38), especially in its claim that illiberal politics are justified with recurrence to liberal ideals. This understanding of liberalism in one way or another presumes that there was a purer liberal core to be distilled from its misuses. Rather, as Rose reminds us, we should be attentive to the *productive* forces of liberal freedoms and their governance, and the ways they function through various modern technologies of power. Rose reveals how modern notions of freedom constitute one of the backbones of the modern civilizing process, and how this process has entailed emancipating, normalizing, and disciplining components. Seemingly paradoxical freedom and coercion operate as twins according to Rose:

> […] the programmatic and strategic deployment of coercion, whether it is in the name of crime control or the administration of welfare benefits, has been reshaped *upon the ground of freedom*, so that particular kinds of control of justification have to be provided for such practices. These might include, for example, the argument that the constraint of the few is a condition for the freedom of the many, that limited coercion is necessary to shape or reform pathological individuals so that they are willing and able to accept the rights and responsibilities of freedom, or that coercion is required to eliminate dependency and enforce the autonomy of the will that is the necessary counterpart of freedom.
>
> (Rose 1999a: 10, emphasis added)

Quite similar to Elias's macro-analysis and longer-term historical perspective on the civilizing process in France and Germany (Elias 2000 [1939]), Rose demonstrates how the emerging ideals of freedom as something to be taught, cultivated, learned, and embodied were coupled with specific practices that targeted sensibilities and norms of sociability (Rose 1999a: 10/11). More concretely, he points to the ambivalences entailed in the efforts to shape subjectivities by enabling subjects to govern themselves. Situating liberal ethics in what he calls practices embedded in a "pedagogy of civility" (Rose 1999a: 73ff.), Rose thus concretizes Foucault's work by emphasizing the extent to which regulating norms of freedom became the key technique of government (1999a: 76) throughout the late nineteenth and early twentieth centuries: "Normality was natural, but those who were to be civilized would have to achieve normality through working on themselves, controlling their impulses in their everyday conduct and on habits, inculcating norms of conduct into their children, under the guidance of others" (1999a: 76). Looking especially at nineteenth-century liberal political thought, Rose analyzes how liberal freedoms were coined as something to be learned and achieved through developmental notions of discipline and training. The significance of these technologies lies less in the fact that they extend domination than in the way they function as practices that enable freedom coupled with the "obligation to be free" (Rose 1999b: 258). The "obligation to be free" has encouraged particular practices of governing subjects by encouraging them to govern themselves.

Rose therefore conceptualizes modern notions of freedom as normalizing practices tied to institutions of knowledge production, such as prisons, asylums, schools, the university, or the family (1999a: 72; see also Danzelot 1997 [1977]; Mahmood 2015). While the domains of privacy and intimacy were declared to be outside of the political and the public domains in liberal thought, the practices of shaping subjects to govern themselves targeted precisely these domains. Even if Rose does not explicitly mention it, the domains scrutinized by his "pedagogy of civility" centrally concern gender, sexuality, and the family. Feminist theorists have shown the extent to which liberal notions of selfhood, conceptualized as universal, were modeled on particular understandings of a rational, masculine, white, Christian subject (Haraway 1988; Hirschmann 2003; Scott Wallach 1997).[6] Contrary to what much of liberal thought has taught us, liberal freedoms therefore by no means escape bodily techniques and conventions. What Rose calls "civilized sensibilities" (Rose 1999a: 78), the strife to become free from norms and constraints, centrally concerns manners and habits that are inscribed into techniques of the body.

In integration programs these bodily techniques mainly push themselves to the forefront through the depiction of Islamic bodily norms as deviating from social conventions inscribed into liberal principles. The quest for the constitutional loyalty of Muslims as a precondition to their inclusion into the social fabric of the German nation thus centrally revolves around the suspicious body of the other. In consequence, the formation of liberal subjects chiefly depends on counterparts that are either constituted as illiberal per se, or as not yet ready for freedom. Such "dividing practices," as Mitchel Dean has called it (Dean 1999: 157ff.), are instilled into liberal thought and practice. Its developmental approach to human subjects is anchored in an imaginary time whose underlying teleological aim situates the achievement of human progress (through conversion, discipline, or training) in the future.[7] More concretely, despite the promise of liberal freedom's abstraction, inclusiveness, and universality that are replicated in contemporary discourses of integration, the embodiments and social conventions of these very freedoms come to the fore *through* the marking of certain people and their practices as not being in compliance with normative notions of freedom. This enactment through division is, however, not generic but contingent. It is therefore important to investigate its concrete workings in concrete times and spaces. I therefore take governmentality as an analytical lens to study, on a microscopic level, how individual freedoms are governed and, by means of regulation, necessarily restricted but also produced in different integration practices.

Such an analytical lens renders obsolete attempts to detect benign versions of liberal practice as devoid of power, because any notion of freedom presupposes forms and techniques of governance that mediate ideals about *how* to act as a properly free subject.[8] Lending these analytical lenses to the liberal politics of governing religious and cultural plurality in Europe, and in Germany more specifically, also goes beyond the argument made by critical migration studies that the primary functions of integration consist in depoliticizing global social inequalities by attributing responsibility to the yet-to-be-integrated individual (Castro Varela 2013; Hess, Binder, and Moser 2009; Schinkel 2017). I claim instead that it consists in immunizing the liberal and secular function of the state from critique.

In the case of Muslim integration conceptions and conventions about how to be properly free are simultaneously coupled with presumptions about how to be properly religious in a political order that is organized by a liberal and secular grammar. The powers of liberal freedoms in the domains of governing religious plurality are therefore coupled with secular powers, and thus require a more explicit engagement with secularism. To understand how Muslim forms of social life, bodily dispositions, and religious practices are addressed in the discursive realm of integration politics as either incommensurable with secular society or as practices that need to be accommodated within it, we therefore have to broaden our analytical scope. This is what I reference as the "liberal-secular matrix" of integration.

The Liberal-Secular Matrix

Speaking about a liberal-secular matrix does not imply treating secularism or liberalism as fixed norms. Rather, this matrix enables and impedes certain kinds of questions, it constitutes a discursive framework in which religious plurality is debated, and it simultaneously provides and constrains spaces for action. The liberal-secular matrix operates with specific modes of inclusion and exclusion, and it is productive of normality and deviations. These modes are neither fixed nor homogeneous, but contingent and dynamic. Understanding integration measures as symptomatic of a broader process of governmentalizing religious plurality and Muslims in Germany thus allows me to study the operations and dynamics of the liberal-secular matrix in a concrete context and on a micro-level.

My analysis here builds up on Talal Asad's approach to secularism as an organizing principle through which the state manages and regulates religion, and governs the borders between the public and the private. Secular governmentality in this understanding also pertains to a set of norms, sensibilities, and practices of conduct. The secular thus understood implies studying secularism beyond the formal, that is, legal, division between church and state, or between religion and politics, and focusing instead on the discursive practices that regulate these separations and interactions. Secularism is historically closely tied to the emergence and implementation of the modern nation-state in charge of administering the religious realm and hence deeply indebted to the post-Westphalian principle of *cuius regio, eius religio* (Asad 2006: 499).

The commitment to, or impediment of, particular religious practices by state institutions is significantly related to the establishment of the nation-state as the main source of authority in charge of the worldly care of the population, regardless of the latter's concrete religious practices (Asad 2006: 499). Asad even speaks about the state having turned into the "transcendent as well as a representative agent" (Asad 2006: 499). As many scholars have pointed out, this double function of the secular state entails a set of inherent tensions (Agrama 2012; Fernando 2014; Mahmood 2015). Among the most salient for my purpose is the observation that while the modern secular nation-state is formally confined as neutral and remote from religious matters, its authority is dependent on its capacity to determine what kinds of religious expressions and practices are legitimate and which are not. It is through this mandate that the state, in close connection with civil society, is authorized, and at times even compelled, to judge the contents and limits of religious practices in public institutions (see also Sullivan 2005). The unending legislation on various forms of veiling across Europe serves as a case in point for political secularism's capacity to shape religious practice by deciding which forms of religiosity in public spaces are legitimate and which are transgressive (Amir-Moazami 2013; Asad 2006; Fernando 2014).

This conception of secularism disrupts progressive narratives of the secularization thesis in which secular rule succeeded a premodern age of religious rule, and the assumption that a depoliticized form of religion could be uncovered in a secular conception of state neutrality (Asad 2003: 25). Asad instead proposes tracing the emergence of the category of the secular genealogically by looking at historical ruptures and rearrangements of discursive structures, and by asking how boundaries between secular and religious realms were drawn in the course of the project of modernity in general, and of modern nation-states in particular. The historical narrative of secularizing progress itself has to be understood as the result of a normative structure that undergirds and puts into effect the rule of the modern nation-state by defining the proper "place" of religion and religious subjectivities, that is, in their spatial and temporal opposition to the secular. The narrative of secularization is prominently evoked in the interrogation of Muslims as subjects of integration in Germany. I analyze this historicist narrative in its function to constitute an idealized secular society. Muslims can become part of Germany under the condition that they translate their religious practices to turn them legible within this contingent secular grammar. This understanding of secularism guides us toward recognizing the prevalence and powerfulness of the secularization paradigm, without taking its normative assumptions for granted.

Dismantling the powers of secularism in my analysis of integration politics in Germany does not mean declaring that secularism is a myth or claiming that closer scrutiny reveals that the boundaries between the religious and the political are more blurred than is usually acknowledged. Rather, it means looking more closely at the concrete practices and technologies of power intrinsically tied to the liberal nation-state through which these boundaries are governed, and how, as a consequence, Muslim subjects are also compelled to situate themselves within the same grammar that organizes liberal and secular orders (Mas 2006).

Borrowing from this conceptualization against the background of the questions I address in this book implies problematizing the ways in which Muslims are interrogated as *religiously* exceptional and in need of closer scrutiny in measures of integration. And it implies asking what the structure of these interrogations tells us about the epistemological and normative underpinnings of religion and its legacies within a specific arrangement of state, church, and the nation. This does not mean ignoring the variety of arguments in the various constitutional debates, which the Muslim presence in Germany has currently triggered, or claiming that the secular has become a coherent or repressive norm. It means, instead, problematizing the very framework of interrogations in such debates and the discursive structures that enable them.

While it is important to be cautious about the contingencies within the liberal-secular matrix, I do claim that its discursive structures and the framework of questions that this matrix enables interpellate Muslims to situate themselves and their religious practices in ways that have substantive effects on their subjectivities and ways of being Muslim (Bracke 2011; Fadil 2011; Fernando 2014; Mas 2006; Peter 2021). While not focusing my analysis on this interrelatedness, I use the discourse of integration as one such form of interpellation.

With the claim that this form of interpellation brings to the fore aporias that are in-built into the secular nation-state I do not reject the liberal-secular matrix as a reference point for the ways in which religious plurality is dealt with. I also do not offer an alternative matrix capable of stepping out of the productive functions of secularism. Instead, I explore the complex epistemological and normative conditions, including their affective attachments and sensibilities, that is, their bodily dispositions, emotions, and social conventions that are present in the discursive operations of the regulation of religion in a liberal-secular order.

On a more specific level, I built up my arguments on the scholarship on Muslims in Europe, which has critically investigated operations of secular powers in the formation of Muslim subjectivities in Europe (Birt 2006;

Bracke 2011; Fadil 2011; Fernando 2014; Jouili 2015; Mas 2006; Peter 2021; Sayyid 2014; Winkler 2017). Based on a Foucauldian analytics of power, these works share a critical perspective on state power and on its postcolonial rearticulations in dealing with minorities. They also explore the pervasiveness of secular governance in shaping religious subjectivities. This scholarship has been pioneering in developing an analytical framework that extends the focus of national juridicio-political orders across Europe, organized through individual rights, including the formal separation between state and church.

Emphasizing the pervasive, subtle, and partly violent capacities of the secular rule, I expand this scholarship by focusing more explicitly on the corporeal components of secularism. In this regard, I borrow from Saba Mahmood's analytical distinction between *political secularism* as the political and legal regulation of religion and *secularity* as a set of sensibilities, emotions, social conventions, and habituated practices of liberal-secular couplings. "Secularity," Mahmood specifies, constitutes "the epistemological and cultural ground on the basis of which religious claims can be authorized and validated" (2015: 206). In this book I am mostly concerned with the intimate connection of these two dimensions of secularism. For it is only by taking seriously how secular rule is complicit with, and dependent on, these more tacit and often unmarked inscriptions of formally liberal and secular societies that we can fully understand the conundrums for religiously marked minorities living in liberal democracies.

In Chapter 4 I provide a concrete example for the interweaving of secularism and secularity in discussing the controversies about mixed sports and swimming classes in state schools. This issue was raised in the course of the German Islam Conference (*Deutsche Islam Konferenz*, DIK), one of the most capacious measures of the integration of Muslims in Germany since 2006.[9] I use this example to show how, through the dialogical encounter between the state and Muslims, Muslims were circumscribed into a normative notion of gender equality that was coupled with expectations of specific modes of behavior and bodily conduct. The demarcations of the body politic into which Muslims are asked to integrate are deeply embodied. They constitute themselves through the depiction and marking of religious corporeal practices, which are considered not yet compatible with secular assumptions ingrained in liberal freedoms.

Beyond this example, integration as dialogue has been significantly characterized by calls to foster the emotional attachments to the communal order by adjusting to normative ideals of religiosity modeled by a secular imaginary. In the DIK, this coupling of rights and values has been framed as "Constitution Plus." With the "Plus" attached to the constitution, Muslims have been authoritatively invited to declare their inner loyalty to Germany by adopting social conventions that are closely tied to assumptions about how to behave as a properly secularized citizen.

I read this quest for the constitutional loyalty of Muslims as a precondition to their inclusion into the social body less as an atypical byproduct of integration when conceptualized as recognition. Analyzed against the political-theoretical scholarship that has critically investigated the politics of recognition in liberal/ or late-liberal democracies as a means to handle cultural or religious plurality (Markell 2003; Povinelli 2002), integration by definition starts with the premise of a clearly demarcated subject needy to be integrated. Here I ground my analysis in Patchen Markell's argument about the intertwined problematic between the sovereign agency of the subject to be recognized and the recognizing instance that is represented by the state. Markell goes beyond the commonsense critique of a Romantic, essentialist understanding of identities (cultural, religious or otherwise) to be recognized. He situates the politics of recognition more fundamentally in a problematic caused by the production of state sovereignty by liberal nation-states within which recognition is distributed as a "good," and which therefore produces sovereign subjects by recognizing them. The very position of having to turn into a candidate for legal recognition freezes complex and dynamic religious practices, while the state enhances its sovereignty by turning into the distributor of the good of recognition. Religious minorities are thereby faced with the requirement to exhibit the signs of their difference—"presenting oneself as knowable" (Markell 2003: 31)—in order to gain legal protection. At the same time, they are compelled to transform their difference in accordance with an existing framework, in our case made up of specific arrangements of church, state, and the nation. This arrangement is paradoxically contoured by the gesture of integration via recognition itself. The minority is thereby both subjected to an inspecting gaze and required to adjust to an undetermined abstraction.

One last word on the politics of my analysis: throughout this book I do not question the sincerity of the political rationalities of integration, nor do I propose more inclusive ways of interrogating Muslims. It also goes without saying that a critique of integration is not to be conflated with a plea for segregation or misrecognition. In this book I do not develop a normative argument that puts forward better or more efficient models for integrating Muslims. I rather take the aims of integration seriously as political practices that are embedded in and productive of the liberal-secular constitutional state and its regulations and formations of (religious) minorities. My task is to unpack their reasoning as well as their normative presuppositions and functionalities. This analytical labor is all the more salient because the conditions of integration, its one-sided focus on populations deemed unruly, infantile, inadequately religious, or otherwise abnormal, and the powers involved in these interrogations are often concealed in hasty efforts to draft new models for the "harmonious coexistence of diversity." This critical inquiry, is, however, neither innocent nor devoid of normative presumptions. Suffice it to say at this stage that one central task that I will unfold throughout the different chapters is to suggest a shift of the gaze from the "Muslim minority" to the conditions that constitute this very minority as minor and that make the liberal-secular matrix of integration appear to have no alternative.

1

Genealogies of *Islampolitik* and Integration

Integration is a two-way process. It is not a one-way road. It requires, on the one hand, that immigrants feel at home here. If they do not want to live like one lives in Germany but maybe according to ideas of some people in the Islamic world, then the necessary requirement for integration is missing [...]. In turn, we do not only have to want that immigrants feel at home, but we also need to know that our conditions of life and also we ourselves will change to a certain degree. We are changing, our country is changing, if three and a half Million Muslims live here. This is a different country than if no Muslims lived here. To know and accept this is also part of the integration.

(Schäuble 2006a)[1]

Throughout the last two decades, the German state in close interaction with civil society began to foster the regulated institutionalization of Islam and the social and cultural integration of Muslims into society. Devices like making "immigrants feeling at home" are common discursive iterations of this trend. The proclaimed incorporation of Muslims into the social fabric of German society and the related structured institutionalization of Islam are part of a more general turn to integration as a remedy for increased immigration as well as the management of religious and cultural plurality.

Given that Germany's immigration policy has often been characterized as a "laissez-faire" structured programs of integration have routinely been embraced as a necessary and overdue step in coping with the growing cultural and religious plurality in Germany (e.g. Bade 2007; Fincke 2009; Heckmann 2014; Joppke 2010). In these first two chapters I complicate these analyses by suggesting a different temporality and by problematizing the ambivalences

---

[1] Wolfgang Schäuble (2006b), former Federal Interior Minister and founder of the Deutsche Islam Konferenz (German Conference on Islam), author's translation.

of the integration paradigm in the context of Muslim and Islam of Germany. That integration generally and that of Muslims in Germany pushed itself onto the political agenda in the aftermath of 9/11 should however not lead to the conclusion that its patterns were entirely unprecedented or even primarily related to Muslims in the first place.

To begin, let us look at the statement quoted above from the inaugural speech at the German Conference on Islam (*Deutsche Islam Konferenz*, DIK), by the then Federal Minister of the Interior Wolfgang Schäuble. This statement is characteristic of the political rationalities that integration measures in Germany share: they govern through dialogue and recognition, rather than overt sanction, discipline, or exclusion. The benevolent statements such as "our conditions of life and we ourselves will change to a certain degree," however, rarely exist without consequences. Rather, the behest to make immigrants feel at home and the affirmation of the lasting, as opposed to temporary, presence of Muslims in Germany is frequently coupled with a whole set of conditions. These simultaneously mark, contour, and reenact the borders of the nation. Precisely because the conditions for integration are flexible ["live like one lives in Germany and not according to the ideas of some people in the Islamic world"], the line between inclusion and exclusion is much thinner than it appears at first glance. The requested and supported integration as a flexible instrument characterizes mechanisms of the constant reproduction of majorities and minorities more fundamentally.

What is more, Schäuble's conflation of Muslims and immigrants as the main target of integration politics symptomatically reveals the strong connection between politics of Islam and integration programs (Brunn 2012; Fülling 2019; Tezcan 2012). Let us bear in mind that the DIK has been designed exclusively for Muslims and as part of a wider program to structure the institutionalization of Islam in Germany as expressed in the notion of politics of Islam (*Islampolitik*). It was initiated in parallel to the national integration forum (*Nationaler Integrationsplan*) established in 2005. I will return to the DIK in Chapters 3 and 4. But I first want to lay the ground for dismantling the implications of the intimate connection created between politics of Islam and integration programs.

To consider the history of the present I suggest recalling the intertwined legacy of how Islam and Judaism have been discursively addressed and ordered as problematic "religions" or "world-religions," both inside and outside of nation-state borders. I therefore, first, embed current state politics of Islam (*Islampolitik*) in Germany in a colonial and imperial legacy and its related knowledge orders. This helps me to situate integration politics directed at Muslims as grounded in discursive repertoires of classification, hierarchization, and remodeling of populations along religious and racial categorizations. Second, I argue that integration, both as a concept and as a state practice, needs to be understood as a reconfiguration of assimilation. For this, I dwell on Zygmunt Bauman's chapter on assimilation in *Modernity and Ambivalence* (1991). Bauman has provided an analytical lens to uncover the functions of assimilation to secure majoritarian rules by both incorporating minorities and rendering them invisible. I thus read the seemingly different archives of politics of Islam and assimilation together as a matter of knowledge production and state-regulated minority management. Doing so, I locate the ongoing disproportionate emphasis on Muslims and Islam as a problem of integration in a legacy that is internal to the functioning of the German nation-state and informed by the imperial entanglements that exist beyond its borders.

To be sure, when recalling these legacies, I do not suggest to write a proper history of the present. My endeavor is centrally inspired by the genealogical incentive to put to the fore historical legacies, which usually remain opaque, mostly because their patterns are tacitly inscribed into the present. I thus do not suggest a linear or undisrupted continuity between the past assimilation of Jews and the present integration of Muslims in Germany. Nor do I claim that politics of Islam in their imperial ambitions are the same as politics of Islam directed at Muslims as subjects of integration in contemporary Germany. Instead, I emphasize that current politics of integration entail deep-seated patterns that are ingrained *and* reworked in the contemporary discourses on Muslims as subjects of integration. This genealogical aim is meant to put to the fore those legacies of Germany which are inscribed into present inequalities, legacies that are conventionally considered "historical" and hence concealed with reference to a remote past that has been overcome by consolidated institutionalized liberal freedoms and equality. I therefore do not employ a proper historiographical methodology. Rather my aim is to highlight how the legacy of colonial and imperialist categorizations of race and religion is intertwined with assimilatory forces of modern nation-states and how these reemerge in a distinctive liberal grammar in present integration programs directed at Muslims in Germany.

The Legacies of Current Politics of Islam

Let us bear in mind that the very notion of *Islampolitik* is not entirely without precedent in German and European history (Franke 2012).[1] Levent Tezcan's (2012) preliminary attempt to historicize the current "politics of Islam" in Germany is useful in this regard. Tezcan locates the notion within Germany's colonial politics. He recalls how the scholar of Islamic Studies, Carl Heinrich Becker, first popularized a German *Islampolitik* during the First World War, even if the "problem" that Islam posed for German expansionist ambitions had of course already emerged by the late 1880s with the uprisings in the German colonies (Habermas 2014: 233 and 246; Marchand 2010). According to Tezcan, the current interrogation of Muslims as a *religious* population is thus predicated on the colonizer's and political authorities' understanding of Islam as both a resource and a problem to be addressed within and outside of the colonies and the declining Ottoman Empire. This endeavor was most explicitly spelled out in the various Colonial Congresses in 1902, 1905, and 1910.

To fully grasp the epistemological ground paved by Becker's program for a German- or European-driven *Islampolitik* it is important to understand the implications of his politico-scientific investigation and hierarchization of religions in their intimate relationship with race as a co-constitutive category. It is in this vein that my analysis differs from Teczan's reading of the antecedents of current *Islampolitik*. While Teczan continuously seems to be troubled by the excessive focus on Muslims as a "religious" community, he neither conceptualizes this focus as a form of racialization, nor does he investigate the epistemic framework that undergirds the ranking order into which Muslims are circumscribed.

In this regard Becker is only one amongst other symptomatic figures for a wider discursive formation. What renders him particularly important for my analysis is that he coupled the project of *Islampolitik* with the ambition to reorient knowledge on Islam in Germany's Orientalist scholarship into a more policy-orientated endeavor. The "scientific" knowledge of Islam, Becker contended, should be invested in the project of remodeling Islamic societies through conviction, education, and diplomacy instead of force and violence. Becker's goal was to gently foster what he called a "European" version of Islam. The normative ideal of a "Euro-Islam" will in fact reappear in contemporary projects of integration with a distinctive emphasis on European Enlightenment that stands in as a model for the integration of Islam into German society. The idea of the Europeanization of Islam, in other words, was imagined by both colonial authorities and scholars who laid the epistemological foundations of the colonial project.

Most importantly, the "problem of Islam," as Becker framed it, was inherently modeled by a Christian imaginary (Becker 1909, 1916). Grounding his analysis of Islam as a threatening "civilization" in a reading of Christianity as a tamed and secularized "religion" Becker emphasized the difficulty of Islam to turn into a "proper," that is, "good," religion. Because Islam was intrinsically political, Becker contended, it failed to function outside of the political realm, and its intrusive characteristics rendered it unable to distinguish between society's different subsystems. Becker promoted the need for education to handle this perceived deficit. In his seminal article *Islampolitik*, which was written during the pressures of the First World War, he stated:

> Of course, the Orient in education and the press has been under the influence of the Occidental, especially the French, mental life (*Geistesleben*), and this wave of European thought can no longer be dismissed with the flow of modern-oriental thinking. Nonetheless, awareness is gradually finding its path that the healthy turn towards modern development is only possible by connecting with the transmitted cultural values and not through their import. It is particularly important for schools to strengthen the study of worldly topics and to thereby "de-clericalize" [*Entklerikalisierung*] the school. This development has already started. Cultural-religious and secular [*weltlich*] education, each in its own position, will continue to be necessary in the future, but one should try to separate these two spheres as much as possible. Wherever we look, we see that in terms of its internal policy, Turkey addresses the problem of Islam. The medieval identity of church and state is gradually being replaced by modern thought, but the state as such remains Islamic.
>
> (Becker 1916: 105–6 translation, mine)

There would be a lot to deconstruct only in this short passage most notably in regard to the Christian-theological and temporal vocabulary through which Becker reads the "problem of Islam."[2] My aim is yet to emphasize only one particular aspect: Becker's juggling between a paternalistic, benign, and disciplinary approach toward Islam is symptomatic of a broader discursive formation which is reconfigured in contemporary politics of Islam and underwritten by a distinctive liberal grammar. His navigation between outright aversion to Islam and a pedagogical aspiration to remodel it along ideals of a tamed and internalized religiosity is symptomatic of deeper-rooted epistemologies which are ingrained in the politics of integration in Germany vis-à-vis Islam and Muslims: On the one hand, Islam is considered substantially incompatible with "modern thought" (liberal values, for that matter). On the other hand, it is slotted into a teleological project of modernization, which is modeled by a Western European Christian vocabulary and its contingent legacy of the connection between worldly and theological authority. Becker offered a program that should tame Islam by gently educating Muslims in the colonies and in the decaying Ottoman Empire, while preserving Christianity's epistemic and material superiority.

Even if Becker himself praised Europe's emancipation from the dominance of the church, his politics of Islam was centrally a collaborative endeavor between Christian missionaries, colonial administrators, and scholars of Islam of his time (Habermas 2014; Marchand 2010).[3] The pedagogical incentives for Becker and his interlocutors were driven by a normative understanding of reformed Christianity that constituted the backbone of reeducation projects. Suzanne Marchand has pointedly called this project a *"Kulturprotestantismus* for Muslims" which she described as: "The making over of Islam into mere cultural glue, its detachment from centralized institutions and hierarchies, and, crucially, the secularization of the educational system. Islam did not have to disappear as a system of belief, but it did need to subordinate itself to European ideas and practices" (2010: 358).

Becker's paternalistic tone is thus part of a wider epistemic framework in which the emergence and proliferation of discourses on "religion" throughout the eighteenth and nineteenth centuries was linked to Europe's self-understanding as being driven by a gradual secularization of Christianity (Anidjar 2008; Asad 1993; Masuzawa 2005; Vial 2016). The conquering violence that drove colonial and imperial interventions was thus attached to a benevolent and pedagogic project toward the not-yet-reformed populations of Muslims. It was largely motivated by a Christian ethos and the conviction that ever since the Reformation, Christianity had reached the highest rung in the ladder of all "world religions" (Masuzawa 2005). Becker thus popularized the project of *Islampolitik*. His discourse was, however, embedded in a broader epistemic framework that justified Western European Christianity as superior and hence as the legitimate model for colonial interventions and imperial expansion through acts of comparison. This framework was animated by an intimate connection of race and religion as modern categories of knowledge and hierarchization.

Tomoko Masuzawa's analysis of the discourses of "world religions" is seminal in understanding how the epistemic order of dividing and ruling therein was played out on a European scale beyond the borders of the emerging German nation-state. Masuzawa locates the first salience of the concept of world religions (originally "religions of the world"), and the discourses that developed from it, in the institutionalization of academic disciplines that produced comparative knowledge on religion (Religious Studies, Sociology of Religion and Oriental/Islamic Studies). Analyzing the texts of European scholars of Oriental Studies, Philology, or the newly emerging discipline of Comparative Religion, Masuzawa shows how Christianity, *by way of* comparison with other world religions, gradually turned into a universal category, or the implicit scale with which non-Christian world religions were measured. Christianity served either as the explicit analytical toolbox for comparisons, especially for the emerging disciplines of comparative religious studies, or as the unexpressed foil, most notably for Oriental and Islamic studies. The practice of comparison hence functioned as a means to contour the modern understanding of religion as a universal (yet particularly Christian) category supported by the emerging paradigm of secularization. It was centrally advanced by the discipline of the Sociology of Religion (Masuzawa 2005: 20; see also Salvatore 1999: Chapter 6).

Masuzawa carves out how the construction and hierarchical arrangement of different world religions were strongly inspired by the racialized construction of language groups in the discipline of comparative philology. Subsumed within the category of Semitic language groups, Islam and Judaism were constituted as world religions mired in ethnic origins and hence not really apt as candidates for universalization. Judaism, because of its fragmented dispersion throughout the world, gradually turned into a "diaspora," and then, throughout the late nineteenth century, into a biologically defined "race." Meanwhile, its biblical heritage was considered as having merged with, and refined by, Christianity. Islam, in turn, was conceived of as the inherent political and backward counterpart of a tamed, reformed, and self-critical Christianity. The mixture of Europe's nineteenth- and twentieth-century imperial ambitions, and the simultaneous fear of Islamic expansion, provoked a widely shared understanding that Islam was the most recent of the three monotheistic religions and therefore always lagging behind modern developments. The statement by the German theologian Otto Pfeiderer (1839–1908) blatantly summarizes this view, and simultaneously brings to the fore the functionality of such contrasts based on the coupling of race and religion:

> Islam, the religion of Muhammad, is the latest among the historical religions, a later after-impulse of the religion-forming power of the Semitic race. Founded by the prophet Muhammad under Jewish and Christian influences among the half-barbaric Arabic people in the seventh century, Islamism shares the monotheistic, rigidly theocratic and legalistic characteristics of Judaism, without its national limitation; with Christianity, it shares the claim and propagating impulse of world-religion, but *without the capacity for development* which belongs to a world-religion. It might be maintained, probably, that Islamism is the Jewish idea of theocracy carried out on larger scale by the youthful national vigor of the Arabians, well calculated to discipline raw barbaric peoples, but a brake on the progress of free human civilization.
>
> (Pfeiderer quoted in Masuzawa 2005: 199, emphasis mine)

Many of the scholars who Masuzawa analyzes thus constructed both Islam and Judaism as prototypes of religions based on attached racial, that is, "Semitic," ties, which lacked all the ingredients of a peacefully universalizing world religion. This historical shift in the construction of Islam as a Semitic religion emerged primarily during colonialism with its scientific innovation, economic trade, and exploitation of human and natural resources. This massively shifted the balance of power and sustained Europe's dominance. Islam as located in the "Orient" thus went from being conceived of as part of distant "Lands of desire," à la Hegel, to the "Lands of obstacles" (Masuzawa 2005: 183).

In turn, Christianity and Buddhism were constructed as close allies; the closeness of "Aryan" and "Asian" language groups was considered as their scientific proof. Both were granted the status of world religions due to their purportedly peaceful expansions throughout Asia and Europe, and their shared scientific and philosophical aspirations and standards (Masuzawa 2005: Chapter 4). The hierarchical and often analogous categorization of world religions and language families was thus deeply charged with discourses on human races, which were justified linguistically, for that matter, and not biologically. Semitic languages were constituted as grammatically imperfect and unrefined, Aryan language groups as grammatically sophisticated and complex. The higher sophistication of Aryan language groups and races was consistently associated with their civilizational superiority (see also Anidjar 2008: 32).

Even by constructing non-Christian religions as legitimate units of analysis and granting them the status of world religions, most acts of comparison ultimately contributed to the confirmation of Christianity's universality. As is well known by now, for example, Max Weber's enterprise of establishing the comparative sociology of religion was both based on Christian conceptual repertoires and it contributed to epistemologically shape the modernization of Christianity (Salvatore 1999: Chapter 2; Stauth 1993; Turner 1993: Chapter 4). A hierarchical impetus was also prevalent in more pluralist and inclusive discourses on world religions.[4] The production of knowledge that was implicated in the project of *Islampolitik* was by no means limited to Oriental or Islamic Studies (Marchand 2010; Masuzawa 2005; Salvatore 1999). Becker was in close conversation with a set of scholars from various disciplines (most prominently Max Weber) who, in one way or another, shared his ambition to *understand* Islam in order to govern or conquer it. The interrogative character of Becker's thoughts on the politics of Islam is the result of these conversations.

What needs to be captured from my analysis so far is that the coining of religion as a distinct subsystem in society and world religions as a concept of comparative and hierarchical ordering of the world was essential to the production of imperial knowledge and the discovery of the "Oriental and its religions" (Anidjar 2008: 27). Indeed, the fact that for Becker and his academic and political interlocutors Islam was simultaneously territorial, racial, cultural, civilizational, theological, philological, and philosophical reflects that it was considered deficient in its adjustment to the standards of a modern religion like Christianity. Becker's work is therefore symptomatic of the assertive creation of a "political fact": that Islam is a problem precisely because, unlike Christianity, it has not yet learned the modernizing lessons of how to distinguish what belongs to the sphere of religion from what belongs to politics.

As modern categories of knowledge and governance race and religion were thus intimately coupled and not detached from each other. Anidjar most pointedly summarizes this: "Figuring, at first, a linguistic division, Semites and Aryans quickly became racial markers, markers that also persisted in articulating a theologico-political difference, which Europe could locate as historically and geographically distant (the Middle Ages or the Middle East)" (Anidjar 2008: 30). This intimate relationship challenges assumptions, which by now have become commonly endorsed, that race, whether biologically or in cultural-linguistic terms, is a more problematic category than religion, or that religion predated scientific approaches to race, or was the more innocent category. "Religion," in other words, was coined as a concept, as a unit of scientific analysis, and as an object of political intervention at the same moment as race was turned into a structuring feature of nation-states and of their instruments of measuring populations and subpopulations. Race and religion, as Anidjar writes, are "*contemporary*, indeed coexistive and, moreover, co-concealing categories" (2008: 27, emphasis in original). These observations also require a word of caution regarding today's inflationary observations about the "racializing of Muslims" (e.g. Aguilar 2018; Meer 2013; Shooman 2014), as if Muslims existed as a religious category prior to the process which turned them into a racial one.

Another lesson to be learned from recalling Becker's and his interlocutor's "politics of Islam" is that we cannot reduce *Islampolitik* to the problematic of "representation," as many critiques of German Orientalism tend to suggest (Mangold 2004; Polaschegg 2005).[5] Rather, Orientalist knowledge orders were coupled with concrete modes of governance structured by a colonial and imperial order into the social and religious lives of the people to be conquered or pedagogically convinced of the superiority of Western European Christianity and its secularizing institutions. This order had emerged long before Becker and others began to rationalize its adequacy, and hence also before the foundation of the German Empire (1884–1914) (see Anidjar 2008: 34; Marchand 2010: Chapters 1–3).⁶ It is in this moment, however, that the term *Islampolitik* became a programmatic feature of German imperialism, and that the scholarly, missionary, and political discursification of Islam was first correlated with the formation and expansion of the German imperial nation-state.

The discursive repertoires nurturing early twentieth-century *Islampolitik* simultaneously reveal a twisted relationship between the constructions of Islam and Judaism as racialized and improper, "Arab" or "Semitic" religions. What Anidjar calls the "Semitic hypothesis," the lumping together of Jewish and Arab race and religion in much of modern scholarship, indeed also provides an entrance point to read together the seemingly distinct archives of minority regulation inside the nation-state and imperialism beyond national borders. Modern knowledge production coupled Jews and Arabs epistemologically under the rubric of one racial and religious category. In addition, the approaches to Islam and Judaism within German scholarship and by political authorities are characterized by the ambivalence of overt aversion and attempts to remodel both along idealized notions of tamed and secularized Christianity.

Today, Muslims and Jews are approached as distinctive, if not antagonistic racialized figures in Europe for a number of different reasons that go beyond the scope of this book (cf. Anidjar 2008; Hochberg 2016; Massad 2015: Chapter 5). The intimate linkage between race and religion as modern categories of academic knowledge and political intervention has yet remained in reconfigured repertoires in contemporary integration programs in Germany. This epistemic ground also played a crucial role in projects of assimilation to which I will turn in the next section of this chapter. *Islampolitik* with its distinctive orientation toward the remote external borders of the emerging German nation-state did not play a major role in the organization of non-Christian minorities in German territories. However, the performance of a particular model of Christianity as co-constitutive for the emergence of the German secular nation-state and its handling with "minorities" within German borders definitely did. Becker's pedagogical-civilizational approach to the "problem of Islam" outside the German state finds an analogy in the political strategy of emancipatory projects of assimilation in dealing internally with the "Jewish problem." To capture this mechanism as an antecedent of today's integration paradigm, in the next sections of this chapter I recall Bauman's seminal analysis of the paradoxes of assimilation (1991) in relation to the ordering forces of the modern nation-state.

The Traps of Assimilation

In his chapter on assimilation Bauman stresses that segregation and assimilation are two sides of the same coin and part and parcel of classificatory principles inscribed into the modern nation-state. Contrary to the conventional understanding of minority incorporation as the friendly inclusion, Bauman conceptualizes assimilation as inherent to modern nation-states and, more generally, as a technique of erasure of ambivalence that is key to modernity. Central to his analysis is the parallel structure of universalistic ideals, and the necessarily particularistic demarcations of belonging and membership in a territory defined by nation-state borders.

The notion of assimilation was first coined and adopted by the disciplines of the natural sciences during the sixteenth century. In biology, in particular, assimilation described the process of absorption of one organ or substance by another (Bauman 1991: 103; see also Aumüller 2009: 28). Given the emergence and proliferation of racist theories and of what Hannah Arendt termed "race thinking" (Arendt 2004 [1951]: Chapter 6) in the nineteenth century, which relied heavily on natural science epistemologies, it is not surprising that the notion of assimilation was quickly translated into human sciences and incorporated into national projects. The focus of assimilation, Bauman goes on, shifted in the late eighteenth and early nineteenth centuries from the converting organism to the "'absorbed material'—exactly about the time when an invitation (or, more precisely, *the command*) to assimilate was first sent around by rising nationalisms" (Bauman 1991: 103, emphasis in the original).

In accordance with the somatic metaphors used in national projects of assimilating subpopulations into an anticipated national body (*Volkskörper*), the term "assimilation" increasingly referred to the transformation of the foreign into the familiar, or the strange and deviant into the desired and normal.[7] As I will show in my analysis of contemporary politics of integration, somatic metaphors or rationalities have mainly disappeared. However, the excessive focus on Muslim corporeal practices as deviating from liberal norms, and the continued secular understanding of religion as internalized *belief*, have reintroduced these rationalities and translated them into vocabularies which conceal their violent characteristics.

According to Bauman, the somatic rhetoric of absorption went beyond the metaphorical. It was a functional mechanism of the modern nation-state. The "designing/ordering/gardening ambitions of modernity" (ibid.: 189) and their efforts to measure, classify, order, tame, segregate, or incorporate the abnormal have found their way into modern nation-state institutions such as the legal, educational, and medical systems or border regimes which regulate citizenship and belonging. More importantly, the quest for assimilation was never merely reduced to culturalist, *völkisch*, or outwardly racist understandings of nationhood. On the contrary, Bauman elaborates on the intimate relationship between discourses of "value superiority" (ibid.: 107) that dwelled on Enlightenment notions of equality, liberty, and tolerance, and the injunction to uniformity.

> What made the standing invitation particularly alluring and morally disarming was the fact that it came in the disguise of benevolence and tolerance; indeed, the assimilatory project went down in history as a part of the *liberal* political program of the tolerant and enlightened stance that exemplified all the most endearing traits of a "civilized state". The disguise effectively concealed the fact that the assimilatory offer must have tacitly assumed, in order to make sense, the stiffness of discriminatory norms and the finality of the verdict of inferiority passed on nonconformist values.
>
> (Bauman 1991: 107–8, emphasis in the original)

Bauman's assertion that assimilation was not only limited to nationalistic incentives but part of a liberal political program confounds attempts to distinguish soberly between particularistic, that is, nationalist, and universalistic aspirations of organizing difference within a nation-state framework. The indefiniteness and putative openness of the liberal project, indeed, turn the call for assimilation into a moving and never-ending target.

Unsurprisingly, Bauman discusses at length the example of Jewish assimilation in Germany in the nineteenth and early twentieth centuries.[8] This case assimilation aptly shows how the means for measurement of conformity to liberal and ideals were intimately tied to a civilizational project of remodeling: The gradual granting of citizenship rights for Jews and the simultaneous absorption of their differences were bound by the condition to become docile subjects. And yet, and hence the paradox, no matter how much Jews tried to overcome or hide their Jewish traditions and reveal markers of Germanness, they never reached the status of fully recognized citizens. However strongly they tried to erase their markers of Jewishness, they remained the "unregenerate Jew[s]" (Bauman 1991: 121).[9]

Assumptions about the (in)assimilability of minorities through the granting of liberal rights were thus at no point unconditional. Rather, assimilation was based on the assumption that these minorities should abstain from the particularities of their traditions and merge into ideals of the abstract human subject (Bauman 1991: 107, see also Aumüller 2009: 146).

Bauman therefore describes a deadlock in which Jews were trapped, however hard they tried to adjust to the requirements of the ruling elite. For these requirements remained simultaneously vague and dynamic. More importantly, the "*measures* of progress were not negotiable" (ibid.: 182, emphasis in the original). The shifting rules of assimilation rendered its success contingent to the evaluation of those who set the criteria for success. In regard to Jewish intellectuals in Germany,[10] Bauman observes:

> The assimilating Jews acted under the pressure to prove their Germanhood, yet the very attempt to prove it was held against them as the evidence of their duplicity and, in all probability, also of subversive intentions. The circle was bound to remain vicious, for the simple reason that the values to which the Jews were told to surrender in order to earn acceptance were the very values which rendered acceptance impossible.
>
> (ibid.: 121)

While Bauman is attentive to race thinking, and to the racialization of Jews that was prevalent also in assimilation projects, he does not spell out the close relationship between race and religion in the intrusive techniques of the ordering nation-state. For the purpose of my analysis it is, however, important to consider that the modern nation-state has since its inception been driven by gardening ambitions in relation to "religion" writ large and to non-Christian minorities, more specifically. What I referenced in the first section of this chapter as the discursive ordering of world religions into peaceful, universal (Christianity, Buddhism), and putatively political and ethnically confined ones (Islam and Judaism) needs to be associated with the modern nation-state as the arbiter of "religion." In her seminal book *How Judaism became a Religion* Leora Batnitzky states in this vein: "It is apparent here how the modern concepts of religion and the sovereign state were born together. While it may first appear that the notion of religion as a distinct and private sphere of experience is a fundamentally apolitical idea, it is actually predicated on a conception of state sovereignty" (Batnitzky 2011: 26).

This intimate relationship between modern religion and the modern sovereign state had severe implications for Catholicism (cf. Borutta 2011), and it had existential consequences for Jewish traditions. Focusing on eighteenth- and early nineteenth-century Prussia as a paradigmatic case, Batnitzky argues that instead of being rendered neutral toward "religion," the Prussian state had been deeply implicated in protecting a Kantian ideal of religion as rooted in the autonomous self. This was pitted against "any notion of religion as rooted first and foremost in public practice" (2011: 26). With her entwined intellectual and political history Batnitzky reveals how Protestant notions of religion as feeling (Schleiermacher) or as rationalized through the autonomous mind (Kant) were gradually adopted by Jewish intellectuals, partly as a program of renewal of Jewish thought and partly in the hope for emancipation.[11] The dictum of an internal reform was in part prescribed by political authorities and predicated on the prognosis that Jewish religion would be enlightened and thereby almost inevitably turn into some kind of Christianity.

Connecting this diagnosis to a conceptual analysis of assimilation, Jutta Aumüller (2009) therefore contends that assimilation was primarily based on the assumption that Jews should abstain from the specificities of *Jewish* normativity and practice in order to merge into a liberally informed conception of the abstract human subject. Liberally justified aspirations to merge Jewishness into a putatively abstract universal category of "the human" were centrally predicated on a liberal-Protestant understanding of religiosity. The legal and orthodox orientations of Jewish Rabbinic and Talmudic traditions were thus in tension, if not in a substantial contradiction with liberal-Protestant theologies and politics (Aumüller 2009: 147). Aumüller succinctly concludes: "From the point of view of antisemitism as well as from a liberal human rights position 'the Jew' is in a situation between Scylla and Charybdis: for the anti-Semite the Jew stopped being human; for the proponent of liberal human rights he needs, in order to be human, to stop being a Jew" (Aumüller 2009: 146, translation mine). In light of this conclusion it is necessary to specify Bauman's paradox and argue that no matter how much Jewish intellectuals exposed their willingness to merge into dominant ideals of religion, they remained "unregenerate Jew[s]" (Bauman 1991: 121). It is in this vein that Patchen Markell (2003) argues that Jewish emancipation (which he sometimes equates with assimilation) was principled on a process of reshaping Jewish religious practices in exchange for equal rights. Markell contends that this "signaled its intention to transform Jews from members of a *Volk* or *Nation* into individual subscribers to a religious creed" (ibid.).[12] What Bauman generically describes as the acts of sapping "social foundations of communal and corporative traditions and forms of life" by the modern state (Bauman 1991: 104), in fact involved substantial interventions into Jewish theological authority structures that increasingly resembled that of Protestant clergy (Sorkin 2019).

Markell notes that the very notion of "Judaism" emerged as a result of that transformation: Judaism, he clarifies, as a "mode of belief or as one faith among others—interchangeable, in that sense, with Christianity and equally representative of 'religion in general'—was itself in important ways a product of the initial work of political emancipation" (Markell 2003: 136). This modification of Jewish thought, practice, and of structures of authority had tremendous consequences, for it did "not just entrench Jewish religious consciousness by privatizing it, but transformed the meaning of Jewishness itself, working to convert it *into* a matter of religious consciousness, and doing so in the service of the project of nation-state sovereignty" (ibid., emphasis in the original).[13]

Such analyses of the historical circumstances underpinning processes of racialization through the tacit remodeling of theological traditions in exchange for assimilation are important for my analysis. They show that techniques of categorization, inspection, and exclusion coexist with the more benevolent mechanism of the slotting in of minoritized populations into the nation-state. The political language that structures assimilation marks minorities through inclusion and incorporation rather than overt segregation or exclusion. Critical investigations of assimilation, however, indicate that the inclusion of minorities into the nation-state meant first and foremost their absorption via internal transformation into a dominant and yet unstable framework. Assimilation therefore has to be understood as a modern technique of power inscribed into the operations of the secular nation-state and its regulations of minoritized religions. More importantly, they are infused with complex operations of powers, including the powers of secular orders to shape religion. Assimilation entails specific economies and functions, one of which is to keep intact or to recreate the nation and its associated components of language, religion, and culture by demarcating minorities as not yet truly part of the social fabric and in need to be interrogated.

Before leaping from these conceptual observations on assimilation and (conditional) emancipation to contemporary projects of Muslim integration in Germany, I want to make sure that my aim is not to draw linear causalities. The assimilation, emancipation, or conditional recognition of Jews in the eighteenth, nineteenth, and early twentieth centuries is, of course, not the same as the integration of Muslims in postcolonial contexts of migration in Western Europe today. Precisely because of its racist and intrusive legacy, assimilation is rarely invoked today as an intelligible political strategy to deal with the growing cultural and religious plurality in formally liberal-secular nation-states.

Some of its patterns have, however, reappeared in reconfigured ways. Jutta Aumüller is revealing in this regard:

> The problem with the model of gradual emancipation was that the end-result of that process of adaption was difficult to identify [...] This problem of the reification, the locking-up of social exclusion by way of the constant emphasis of deficient attributes that make inclusion impossible, finds an analogy in contemporary discourses on integration of immigrants and their children.
>
> (Aumüller 2009: 143, translation mine)

It is useful to remind that in social theory the term integration has also emerged from an organicist discourse, in which *society* works analogous to the human or the national body: "Society, in this logic, is constructed as a closed body that may be inhabited or invaded by foreign influences that remain essentially 'outside' of the social body" (Schinkel 2017: 5). I would not, however, claim that whenever integration is evoked, the social body is constructed as a holistic and homogeneous entity through the deployment of metaphors of invasion and foreignness. Rather, precisely because such metaphors have been discredited as contradicting the liberal incentives of the German nation-state after 1945 we need to be attentive to the distinctive *liberal*, that is, proclaimed disembodied vocabulary that is evoked, especially when it comes to the integration of Muslims.

The more compelling question than the comparative one ("what distinguishes assimilation from integration?") is why integration could step in as the master tool with which to organize Germany as a society of immigration under current conditions of institutionalized individual rights and liberal freedoms. With Stoler's idea of "recursion" in mind, we should therefore ask: which methods are used to present specific populations as being particularly in need of inclusion via inspection and transformation under the conditions of anchored liberal freedoms and formal equality, and which do so in a way which makes the violent nature of this inspective mode hardly discernible? How, despite formal equality, despite institutionalized freedoms and rights, to which Muslims can also appeal, have institutionally supported ranking systems continued to break new ground on the basis of political programs that are geared toward minority inclusion? These are the questions that preoccupy me in the next chapter. Therein, I turn to post-1945 Germany to show how integration emerged in immigration policies before it turned, after September 11, 2001, into a state-centered paradigm that was coupled with a renewed version of *Islampolitik*.

2

Integration and the Emergence of a "Muslim Question"

I started off the previous chapter with the quotation by Wolfgang Schäuble and his appeal to integration as a two-way process with a distinctly Muslim addressee. I have then moved backward to the emergence of *Islampolitik* in Germany as well as the assimilation paradox to show the deeper rootedness of the tensions in Schäuble's inclusionary exclusion. My main concern in this chapter is to analyze the conditions under which *integration* emerged as a discourse and as a political program in the course of postwar immigration and under which conditions it became increasingly attached to Muslims and Islam. To be sure, I will not write the history of integration from 1945 to the present. My focus is rather on the interrelation between the emergence of integration as a paradigm for ordering immigration and organizing cultural and religious plurality and its gradual focus on Muslims. I therefore put emphasis on the question of how race and religion reappeared as categories of classification in the aftermath of the guest-worker system.[1]

As many sociologists of migration have pointed out (Bade 2007; Bade and Bommes 2004), the guest-worker system in Germany produced an immigration regime that was more than simply restrictive in terms of border regulations and citizenship laws (see Chapter 5). Migrants were, more generally, treated as a mobile labor force commodity, serving "German" interests, first in the rebuilding of the country and later, more broadly, in the labor market and economy. Immigration in that sense was, indeed, regulated, even if merely along economical logics by the interests of the labor market. The guest-worker system paved the ground for two developments which had long-lasting effects in Germany's formation into an immigration society: First, it created the social category of the labor migrant with little social mobility, something which

Marxist inspired sociologist Marios Nikolinakos has called the reproduction of a new proletariat formed by foreign workers (1973). Through their gradual integration into the labor market, former "guests" were simply confirmed in their status as low-skilled and low-paid workers. This exploitive system was paralleled by legally backed up racialized distinctions between "Germans" vs. "guest-workers," later "foreigners" or "foreign co-citizens" (*ausländische Mitbürger*) as innately distinctive. Second, the guest-worker system paved the ground for a paradigm of integration which has been driven by a flexible "Demand and Support" (*Fördern and Fordern*) logic: Because of their low social and economic status, but also because of their "descent" (*Herkunft*) guest-workers as well as the following generation were constituted as deficient and in need of assistance. In return, they were required to do something for the support they might expect from the state. In both components, differentiating categorizations of race and religion became gradually reinscribed in a liberal language of rights and duties.

But when and under which conditions did integration move to the forefront of German immigration policies? A migration regime solely driven by the logics of supplying a low-skill labor force with foreign workers was in tensions with the adoption and appraisal of liberal principles—equality before the law, freedom of movement, the sanctity of the family (the "private sphere"), tolerance of cultural plurality, and so on. The utilitarian logic, more specifically, was at odds with Germany's self-fashioning as a liberal and democratic nation that had left behind Nazism and racism.[2] It is in this context that the quest for the integration of immigrants was voiced from late 1960s onward, especially by those who were in close contact with migrants—church functionaries, social workers, and some local politicians, as well as an emerging scholarship that studied them (see O'Brien 1996: 52). Think tanks (such as the German Youth Institute) and enlarged education programs were established and were mainly geared toward the "second generation" of former guest-workers who were increasingly considered in need of assistance and education (O'Brian 1996: 65–6). As Peter O'Brian compellingly shows, the gradually felt need to slot in immigrants while not necessarily granting them equal rights was part and parcel of the troubled self-understanding of Germany as a liberal nation, able to overcome its excessive nationalist and racist past (O'Brian 1996: 58).

At a more centralized political level, integration programs were drafted by the Social Democrats in the late 1970s. In 1978, the erstwhile Chancellor Helmut Schmidt (SPD) established the position of the "commissioner for foreigners" (*Ausländerbeauftragter*) who was in charge of the nation's measures of integration, with the SPD-politician Heinz Kühn as the first appointed commissioner. In his famous "Kühn-Memorandum" (1979), Kühn promoted wide-ranging measures toward the durable settlement of foreign workers and their families in Germany. He aimed at guaranteeing political rights and also articulated suggestions to reform the nationality code by granting children of immigrants the option to choose German nationality. The Memorandum also spelled out explicitly that Germany had turned into an immigration country and suggested to gradually turn foreigners into citizens. The Kühn-Memorandum is conventionally praised as the first milestone of a liberally minded national integration program (Rütten 2013: 33). What often remains silent in this appraisal is the culturalist entrenchment of the memorandum.

While Kühn discards the purely functional-economic logic of including "foreigners" into the labor market, he simultaneously employs a culturalist vocabulary which portrays "foreigners" as deficient subjects in need of special support. Integration for Kühn meant investing in pedagogical programs to assist foreigners and their children to bridge deficits that reside both in social status and in "cultures of origin" (*Heimatkulturen*). Interesting for my concern is also that "culture" is recurrently juxtaposed with "religion." For example, Kühn proposes to offer "ideologically neutral" religious classes to address religiously motivated fears of parents against the "cultural alienation" (Entfremdung) of their children (1979: 20) and to prevent "problematic self-help attempts (for example in 'Coran Schools' [*Koranschulen*])" (ibid.: 32). The first introduction of Islamic classes in state schools in the late 1980s can be seen as a direct follow-up to this goal of preventing Turkish migrants and their children from drifting toward Islamic extremism (O'Brian 1996: 74).

The Kühn-Memorandum is therefore significant for an inherent tension of the integration paradigm: universalistic, liberal aspirations on the one hand and modes of distinction between established majorities and deficient minorities in need of transformation on the other. It is interesting to note that many of Kühn's suggestions remained unrealized. This concerns in particular the quest for a change of citizenship laws as well as legal and political rights for immigrants. What has been implemented and kept alive, instead, was the political rationality of "demand and support" (*Fördern and Fordern*), which symptomatically foreshadows contemporary integration projects.

Culture, Race, and Religion

The different "culture" of immigrants had started to preoccupy politicians and public opinion from the early 1970s onward and it reappeared in repertories of integration prevalent prior to the Kühn-Memorandum (Chin 2009). "German" or "majority culture" was conventionally attributed with signifiers like individualistic, progressive, or modern, and contrasted with the "cultural circles" of guest-workers as traditional, rural, or communitarian (Chin 2009: 87). The thesis of an emerging conflict of cultures was particularly salient in the debates on gender and sexual morality within communities of Turkish backgrounds, which also figured in the first studies on the "culture" of migrants. Scholars of psychology contributed to this by coining the notion of a "conflict of culture" (*Kulturkonflikt*)—the assumption that children of immigrants were torn between holistic systems of culture. Pedagogical research seconded the "culture conflict" thesis (Hamburger 1984: 66ff). Julia Franz (2018) asserts that although this thesis proved to be both the condition and the result of knowledge production, its principle has been kept alive to date.

Historical lessons learned notwithstanding, a Herderian notion of culture was also reactivated in the more benign acknowledgment that the children of guest workers should be allowed to "maintain their cultural identity." Some of the early measures to acknowledge the "culture" of guest-workers, such as the "Day of the Foreigner" (*Tag des ausländischen Mitbürgers*), symptomatically expose the folkloristic and exoticizing take on preserving immigrants' "cultural identity." Churches initiated the event in 1975 as an integration measure. Immigrants, addressed as "foreign co-citizens" (*ausländische Mitbürger*), were asked to present for one day (later for one week) their culinary and cultural specificities. This initiative can be read as foreshadowing the *Karneval der Kulturen* that has been branded as a multicultural event, and has been organized yearly in Berlin since 1996. Parts of this pattern to recognize, compartmentalize, or celebrate cultural diversity—if abstracted from complex social realities or if consumable—will reappear in state organized dialogue with Muslims (in Chapter 4). It is not by accident that multiculturalism has been termed *Multikulti* in Germany. This trivializing gesture indeed captures well how multiculturalism was mainly reduced to commodification and never seriously engaged with as a political concept to deal with plurality.

As the critical race scholarship has shown at length, "culture" has often served as the more acceptable notion while disguising the persistence of the structuring category of race in postwar migration regimes (e.g. Balibar and Wallerstein 1988). While "cultural" racism and biological racism have coexisted already prior to racist biopolitics in the Nazi era, in the aftermath of the Second World War culture turned into the primary basis for explaining fundamental incompatibilities between immigrants and "Germans." Discussing the persistence of racism in German postwar immigration policies, Rita Chin locates the discarding and tabooing of race as a structural feature of discriminatory politics within the peculiarities created by the attempts to overcome Nazi outrages. The tabooing of race, however, did not lead to a discarding of racial politics and race thinking in Germany. Quite the contrary, the very tabooing and constant act of concealing race stabilized ranking systems which were now justified along ethnic or cultural lines. Chin observes a simultaneous reinscription and concealing of race and related justifications of social and economic inequalities in postwar German society:

> It was easy to assume that just because Germans had eradicated the word *race* from their vocabulary, they had also purged racism from actual conditions and practices. Ultimately, the postwar project of democratization denied the very category of race as un-German and therefore (mostly) unspeakable. Within this framework, it became possible both to idealize social and ideological distance from the Nazi past as well as to condemn overt forms of neo-Nazi violence in the present. But what this has left out are the more elusive forms of racialized thinking that have long surrounded the labor migration and ways of understanding difference in the Federal Republic.
>
> (Chin 2009: 101, emphasis in the original)

The introduction of integration as an acknowledgment of immigration as a social and political fact was thus from the beginning accompanied by the reintroduction of racial politics either through institutionalized differentiations between Germans and foreigners or through justifications of a hierarchical social order with reference to "cultural differences": Cultural deficits and backwardness of immigrants were often considered responsible for their deficient social integration. Instead of granting equal rights, as Kühn had suggested at least in parts, integration was predominantly oriented at the transformation of cultural barriers. The cultualization of social inequality produced by an institutionalized system of social segregation thus paradoxically served political authorities as the core argument for the refusal to grant equal rights. And it served as an argument to turn social inequality upside down by placing the burden to adapt properly on to "foreigners" (Chin 2009: 90).

I therefore interpret the "Demand and Support" logic introduced first in the Kühn-Memorandum as both a reconfigured expression of the teleological underpinnings of assimilation projects and a dictum that is now fully institutionalized[3]: The move from treating migrants as guests to a more proactive integration policy is predicated on the assumption that minoritized populations first need to be integrated socially and culturally before acquiring equal rights and hence becoming true German citizens. The criteria for measuring when social and cultural integration is achieved yet remain abstract and dynamic. This leads O'Brian to aptly conclude: "All the rhetoric to the contrary notwithstanding, integration was not a right guaranteed to migrants as human beings living in Germany, but a privilege they were to earn by learning to be a certain kind of being, *liberal* human being" (O'Brian 1996: 74, emphasis added).[4]

But how did the figure of the to-be-integrated Muslim move into the forefront of integration politics? In which context was "culture" almost by default equated with "Islam" and under which conditions has *Islampolitik* reemerged in new ways? The prevalence of "culture" as a marker of distinction and its concealing of race does not entirely explain how Islam as a religious signifier gradually turned into the central feature of culturalist integration discourses and programs.

Alarmed by global Islamic revival movements, and in particular by the Islamic Revolution in Iran, Islam started to reemerge as the core of distinctive "cultural circles" and as the main problem of "cultural conflicts" in the early 1980s, thus in parallel to the emergence of the integration paradigm. Islam also became the main explanatory cause for the "problematic" behavior of immigrants (see Chin 2009: 90). It was made responsible for the observed strictness in education, including parts of its non-egalitarian sexual moral codes, and the application of its strict gender norms and roles (cf. Binswanger and Sipahioğlu 1988; Elsas 1983; Neumann 1980; Thomä-Venske 1981).

Integration gradually turned into the master tool with which the German state in close interaction with civil society envisaged to remedy these deficits which were assumed to reside in "Islamic culture" (Chin 2009: 90). Integration gradually moved from a tool to structure immigration to a tool to manage religious plurality (Schlerka 2021: Chapter 7).[5] Because of global incidents like the Rushdie affair, the murderer of Theo Van Gogh, and terrorist attacks conducted in the name of Islam, throughout the 1990s and most particularly from the 2000s onward, integration became increasingly centralized. This mounted in the "National Integration Congress" (*Integrationsgipfel*) and in the DIK to which I will refer in the forthcoming chapters. The proliferation of the discourse on the urgency of integration, however, did not contribute in any way to a clearer contouring of the concept but even rendered it more elusive.

The unquestioned embracement of integration was paralleled by the slogan that "Multikulti has totally failed," first popularized by Angela Merkel in 2005, and repeated in 2010, and needed to be replaced by proactive integration politics.[6] Ironically, multiculturalism was thus sentenced to death before having seriously been considered as a program of institutionalized minority recognition (cf. Amir-Moazami 2005). In the domain relevant for my analysis, moreover, German *Multikulti* barely comprised the recognition of Islam as a "religion" on equal footing as Christian churches or more recently the Jewish community. The establishment of Islam classes in state schools or, more recently, the academization of Islamic Theology in universities is an indicator for the de facto institutionalization of Islam in Germany. However, they are not an indicator for the special treatment or for minority recognition. The institutionalization of Islam especially in domains of education resulted from the German basic law (*Religionsverfassungsrecht*) which attributes a privileged status to legally recognized religious communities in public domains, while at the same time granting the noninterference of the state into religious affairs.[7]

As a matter of fact, despite numerous attempts, none of the larger Islamic federations has yet achieved the status of a statutory body under public law (*Körperschaft des öffentlichen Rechts*) (cf. Spielhaus 2020).[8] Christian churches, in turn, benefit from a whole range of handed-down religious structures through this established status.[9] While they have increasingly come under pressure due to the decreasing numbers of members, the de facto and also de jure influential role of Christian authorities in Germany has not caused major contestations or controversies, even among confessed secular theorists like Habermas (2009). Nor did the codification of the moral mandate of Christian churches in local constitutions of the former GDR after the reunification process provoke wider public debates (Rommelspacher 2017: 169). Especially worth mentioning for my concern is the unquestioned moral function that the churches maintain in the German public sphere. According to the so-called "public mission" (*Öffentlichkeitsauftrag*), church representatives have the right and are even requested to intervene in public debates on issues like refugee politics, abortion, or reproductive medicine (see Klostermann 2000).

It is this public mission which has allocated a significant role to churches in advocating a renewed self-understanding of Germany as a country of immigration. At the same time, however, church representatives actively and successfully lobbied against the introduction of "religion" into anti-discrimination laws (Lewicki 2014: Chapter 6; Rommelspacher 2017: 169). Some church representatives have also been vocal in spreading the idea that Islam constitutes an obstacle for integration. In his monograph on church academies in Germany, Thomas Mittmann (2011) shows, for example, that already in the early 1970s, representatives of the Catholic academies paid particular attention to the emergence of Islam as a new religious force within Germany's borders. Mittmann illuminates the challenges that Christian churches faced with the loss of members, and the competition they received from alternative models of religious and nonreligious practices. Islam figured as one of the alternatives to established forms of Christianity and, as such, was regarded as a problematic competitor. Mittmann notes in consequence that the assumed "breakup of Islam emerged through the *re-coding* of foreign workers into 'Muslims,' not from remote countries anymore, but in front of one's own door" (Mittmann 2011: 176, translation and emphasis mine). This "re-coding," Mittmann argues, contributed to the contouring of the notion of modernized Christian churches through the contrast with Islam's and Muslim immigrants' cultural backwardness (ibid.: 176). This contrast was upheld even if the discrepancy between the alleged peacefulness of Christianity and the partly violent endeavors of Christian colonial missionaries, as well as the church's partial collaboration with the Nazi regime, caused strains on any claims about its uncontaminated moral superiority.

Simultaneously, however, church representatives were actively engaged in matters of diversity management. Church representatives started to promote measures of interfaith dialogue, first with Jewish representatives and gradually also with Muslim mosque movements. Tezcan suggests to understand these interfaith dialogue initiatives as a reconfigured version of Christian missionary movements, even if their ultimate goal was not necessarily conversion any longer. He furthermore observes that throughout the 1990s many of the hitherto locally and loosely structured interfaith initiatives in Germany gradually coupled their activities with normative and teleological goals by adopting the integration of Muslims as one of their central features (Tezcan 2006).

The state's attempt to institutionalize a structured conversation with Muslims for the "peaceful coexistence" of representatives of different worldviews meant that local grassroots and pluralistically structured interfaith dialogue initiatives also increasingly reoriented their agendas and acted as pioneers of integration. Not accidently, some of the more informal advisors to the *Deutsche Islam Konferenz* (DIK) were Christian theologians who translated their experiences of interfaith dialogue initiatives into this state-led integration measure (see Hermani 2010: 26). The gradual coupling of integration and *Islampolitik* can therefore not be understood without addressing church authorities justifying Christian privileges while simultaneously engaging in a structured conversation with Islam and Muslims.

This seeming paradox as well as the intimate relationship of church-organized dialogue initiatives in their paternalistic incentives is particularly well documented in "Clarity and Good Neighborliness" (*Klarheit und gute Nachbarschaft*). This widely distributed handbook (*Handreichung*) was published by the central Protestant Council of Germany (*Evangelischer*

Kirchenrat Deutschlands, EKD) in 2006. I want to end this chapter by focusing on this 128-page document because the Protestant Church, in particular, understands itself as an active advocate of Muslims' integration in Germany. Bishop Wolfgang Huber, then head of the Protestant church, states in this vein: "The government has started a dialogue with Muslims at the time of the publication of this handbook in order to advance integration. The EKD hopes that its convictions about the important questions set out here will support clarity and good neighborliness in our society" (2006: 9, translation mine).

Indeed, parts of the booklet read like a prelude to the documents published under state integration measures. It names in detail all the "problems" associated with the presence of Islam and Muslims in the country, and at the same time offers the church's mediating mission between the state and civil society. The text navigates between a benign approach that addresses Muslims as "new neighbors" and a paternalistic one that demarcates how these new neighbors should behave according to the rules set in advance. In this case these rules have an outspoken Protestant-theological underpinning and are subsumed under the voice of what the booklet interchangeably calls the "Protestant Church," "Protestants," or simply "Christians." It starts by underlining the communalities between Islam and Christianity, admitting the necessity to cultivate a "neighborly" encounter between Muslims and Christians in Germany. The neighborly tone, however, quickly dissolves. Christianity and Islam ultimately do not share much more than their monotheism. After stating that Sharia rules treat men and women, as well as Christians and converts to Christianity, unequally, the text clarifies:

> In the encounter with Muslims, critical questions which this handbook also poses, cannot be avoided out of love for the truth [...] Muslims who live in a Western society have to be attentive to critical questions concerning their tradition and culture, as well as certain interpretations of Muslim belief, in order to foster a constructive coexistence under a common value order [*Werteordnung*] [...] The Protestant Church is aware that it has learned through a long historical path to deal critically with its own tradition.
>
> (ibid.: 21, translation mine)

Emphasizing that "Muslim identity is rooted in a cultural world that in general has not fulfilled the transformations of a religion under the conditions of a scientific-technological age and a secular state order like the Occident" (*das Abendland*) (ibid.: 22), the handbook goes on to name all kinds of "critical questions" that Muslims in Germany should be able to answer. These range from freedom of speech, human rights violations in Islamic societies, lack of democratic norms, and gender inequality justified in the name of Sharia law, to the call that Muslim organizations in Germany should proactively condemn persecutions of non-Muslim minorities in Islamic societies.

More revealingly for my concerns, these "critical questions" are coupled with passages on integration. Reminding its readers that "Protestant Christians" want to be "pilots of integration" (*Integrationslotsen*) (ibid.: 47), the handbook notes that the common ground was the "recognition of fundamental constitutional principles of the secular, democratic and social rule of law ('legal loyalty') and the willingness to participate in civil society on the basis of democratic values" (ibid.: 47–8). Very much like what we will see in the state-led integration measures, the EKD substitutes this liberal constitutional order with a set of values that centrally concern rather unspecified ways of conduct. It states that because integration contains "political, social, and cultural dimensions, it is a continuous task" (ibid.: 47).

The handbook highlights over and over again that Christianity has already accomplished a modernizing process that Islam has yet to undergo. While the teleological impetus in this hierarchical ordering of Christianity and Islam echoes Masuzawa's critical analysis of the inception of the discourse on world religions in the nineteenth century, the EKD, for that matter, combines Christianity and Judaism by evoking the "Judeo-Christian" nexus. As is well known, this attachment, while having an anti-Semitic legacy, reoccurred in the aftermath of the Shoah as an attempt to recreate a positive narrative about Christianity's close relationship to Judaism—an attempt which has been critically interrogated as a gesture of whitewashing.[10] Most importantly, the attachment of the Judeo-Christian legacy has often been evoked as a referent to exclude Islam in this entangled past and future.

It is quite obvious that in the EKD text the embraced Judeo-Christian tradition fulfills exactly this function. Deliberating on the question of whether a teacher covered with a headscarf should be allowed to teach in a state school, or if a ban on female head coverings would violate the right of religious freedom, the authors conclude by giving up all previous attempts to balance their evaluation:

> Equal means to be treated equally, and unequal unequally. Therefore, a distinction is not only valid but even necessary. In regard to such a distinction, it is important to consider that the signs of expression of the Judeo-Christian tradition do not represent convictions that are in tension with the values of the German constitutional order. Rather, the Judeo-Christian tradition has contributed significantly to the basic cultural and mental principles of liberal democracy.
>
> (ibid.: 64–5)

It would definitely be problematic to subsume all kinds of interreligious dialogue practices under the rubric of the integration paradigm in which dialogue has ultimately similar functions to comparative religion, which is to openly or tacitly confirm Christianity's privileges and superiority. More research would be needed to better grasp the complex rationalities and practices of dialogue initiated by the Christian churches, especially at the level of local dialogues. It is, however, difficult to deny that what has reached the wider public and political approval are the paternalistic approaches similar to those of the EKD. To be sure, exclusivist truth claims and proclamations to superiority are not reserved to Christian theology but prevalent also in Islamic or other traditions. What is important to note, however, is that in this case the state has been aligned with church representatives in integration practices and that integration has a distinctively Christian political-theological orientation— even if not always as explicit as in the EKD handbook.

This material indeed reveals an interesting incident of Anidjar's observations that Christianity represents a model for modern notions of religion with clearly demarcated functions in society, and simultaneously upholds intrusive characteristics. Considering the Christian epistemological underpinnings of modern concepts of "religion" on the one hand, and Christianity's largely embodied and institutionalized status on the other, Anidjar notes that the (historical, epistemological, and governmental) pervasiveness of Christianity has become increasingly invisible (2015: 40):

> Everything is therefore as if the interrogation of the concept of religion did not unsettle our understanding of Christianity as a religion. A strange

essentialism. For what if Christianity were not a religion? Not exclusively so? What if, for two thousand years, it had been more than a religion? Or something else altogether? Christianity only became a religion (in the restricted, modern sense) latterly. Having learned what we could from and about the concept of religion—its novelty, its questionable disappearance, its containment—it may be necessary to reconsider what we mean by Christianity.

(Anidjar 2015: 41)

Even if Anidjar is mainly concerned with deconstructing intellectual history, his argument provides an intriguing starting point for me to understand current governmental measures oriented at the integration of different "religions" in Germany in their politico-theological underpinnings. Such a perspective opens up a path to see how the built-in structures of the close and ambivalent church-state relationship characteristic of the German secular state both affect the ways in which Muslims are addressed as subjects of integration, and consolidate this very intimacy.

To conclude the first and second chapters, let me recapitulate that I understand the current politics of integration as a reconfiguration and proliferation of older political rationalities of minority politics inside, and politics vis-à-vis Islam outside of nation-state borders. My inquiry here into the coining of *Islampolitik* and the paradoxes of assimilation also complicates the recurrent observations about a *recent* shift toward the "Islamization of Muslims," and the resulting one-dimensional focus on their religiosity. It also urges us to take the recurrent equation of ethnicity, race, or culture, *and* Islam seriously as not only animated by a racial regime but also by political secularism as a mode of governing "religion" in specific ways. Processes of addressing immigrants via their racialized difference as Muslims therefore must be understood as an instance of an intrinsic relationship between race and religion, in which specific populations are interrogated in specific ways.

If indeed we can observe a "discursive explosion" on Muslim forms of social lives and religious practices since the late 1990s, it is because this is predicated on an established and yet reconfigured discursive repertoire. If what Mittmann calls the "re-coding" of foreigners into Muslims was not visible to a wider public, including scholars of migration, then 9/11 and every further terror attack in the name of Islam contributed to placing Islam and Muslims massively to the fore. Thus, a shift occurred in that the state orchestrated and centralized the integration of Muslims, or people addressed and marked as such, at the very moment when Muslims have settled in Germany for several generations. Throughout the next chapters I will analyze how this tension between acknowledging a minority's long-standing presence while absorbing it like a strange organ into the nation-state's social body takes shape in different, partly divergent integration practices.

3

Measuring Integration: Governing through Knowledge

The flourishing of the political project of integration has stimulated a wide range of research on the successes or failures of immigrant integration (cf. Schinkel 2017: Chapter 3). In Germany, research that explicitly coupled integration and Muslims has gained a particular momentum at the inception of the DIK in 2006. One of the most immediate concerns was the observation that Germany lacked "reliable" and "representative" empirical data on Muslims living in the country.[1] Until today one of the DIK's explicit missions has therefore been to "expand knowledge about Muslim life in Germany and to ameliorate the availability of data."[2] As indicated, many of the loosely organized integration initiatives in which Muslims appeared as protagonists of the to-be-integrated population had been encouraged by specific events like the Rusdhie Affair, the murderer of Theo van Gogh or terrorist attacks. Precisely because these public debates on Muslims were often driven by shorthand deductions or speculations about the problematic nature of Islam as such, the call for academic knowledge appears as an important move at first glance. A closer inquiry into the political rationalities of the kind of research that has been requested and conducted, however, provides a more complicated picture. What centrally animated the goal to "ameliorate the availability of data" has been the measurement of integration through survey data on mentalities and social practices of Muslims as an instrument to provide recommendations for political action (Hermani 2010: 52 and 64).

This relationship between integration and its empirical measurement as a central tool of governmentality is by no means unique to the DIK or to Germany (cf. Schinkel 2017: Chapter 3).[3] Nor is it unique to knowledge production on Muslims and Islam more generally. In a short piece on knowledge production on Muslims in the United States, Hatem Bazian claims, for example, that the more Muslims have been studied, the less was actually known about them. Bazian continues this seemingly paradoxical observation by explaining that since 9/11, US think tanks had spilled millions of dollars for research on Muslims and Islam. These think tanks, driven by an empirical—if not imperial—problem-solving orientation, so Bazian contends, have investigated the Muslim subject within the framework of terrorism and Islamophobia. Bazian therefore concludes that unless the security and Islamophobic framework is not understood and dismantled, it will be impossible to "appreciate the uniqueness and complexity of the human being supposedly studied" (Bazian 2016).

In light of my analysis of the emergence of the integration paradigm and its assimilatory and civilizing inscriptions, the construction of Muslims as suspect religious communities that are "studied but not known" cannot be reduced to the effects of global terror and its discursive incitement (Bigo 2002; Bigo/Tsoukala 2008; Morsi 2017). Terrorism in the name of Islam has, definitely, contributed to incite discourse on Muslims and it also animated the proliferation of knowledge production, including entire new sections and programs such as "security studies" (Fadil, de-Koning, and Ragazzi 2019; Kundnani 2015; Morsi 2017; Schiffauer 2015). The hypothesis of suspicion has put Muslims under scrutiny by security offices and programs of prevention against radicalization (Qasem 2020; Schiffauer 2008a). It has also turned them into objects of scientific inspection (Müller 2018; Schiffauer 2015). This becomes particularly obvious in state-commissioned research on radicalization—a field that has triggered a whole research industry.

Empirical data gathering about Muslims is, however, not only driven by the focus on radicalization or animated by "Islamophobia," as Bazian seems to suggest. More generally, our analyses remain ahistorical, if we reduce the proliferation of knowledge about Muslims to the effects of recent processes of securitization, or even to postwar migration only. Precisely because the contours of integration are vaguely defined and diffuse, Muslims are studied both in their entire life conduct and in their religious practices, as well as in their heterogeneity. The inflationary use of survey data on Muslim social life and religious practices both in Germany and in other European countries with sizable numbers of Muslims is a case in point (Johansen and Spielhaus 2012).

The topics of these investigations have gradually expanded to encompass all kinds of spheres of life. Survey questions addressed to Muslims range from routines of religious practices in daily life, consumption habits, to attitudes toward liberal and/or democratic orders. They investigate questions of gender and sexuality, bodily practices in correlation with degrees of religiosity. In short, there is very little that escapes the statistical view. If political authorities invest in the integration of Muslims, they commission research to measure Muslims' degree and willingness to integrate.

Throughout this chapter I develop the argument that this "monitoring of integration" (Supik 2014: 124) in Germany operates within premises that go beyond the concrete object of study ("Muslims"). Instead, it brings to the fore and reconfigures inscribed epistemologies of knowledge production on "minorities" as well as on "race" and "religion" as classificatory categories of knowledge and/as governance. I show that the assumptions about what counts as proper knowledge in this field are intimately bound by assumptions about what counts as proper religion—bracketed and framed by liberal and secular aspirations.

A focus on knowledge production helps us to further redirect our attention to the historicity of the ways in which Muslims are governed by being studied within the paradigm of integration. It is important to note, however, that when unraveling the operations of knowledge production on Muslims in Germany as rooted in longer-term epistemologies, I do not suggest a stable, abstract, or disembodied notion of epistemology. Rather, I am guided by Foucault's understanding of epistemologies as *practices*, enabled and enacted by particular political, social, and economic circumstances (Foucault 2006 [1979]: 15f.). The question is therefore why and under which conditions certain epistemological practices—that is, practices of knowledge production and their underlying assumptions about what counts as proper and legitimate knowledge—are more prevalent than others.[4] Because epistemologies are neither stable nor abstract, their grammar necessarily changes over time and in relation to political conditions. I am, of course, not able to tackle systematically the relationship between knowledge production and social-political contexts. Nor is it possible to draw any linear causality between knowledge and governmental interventions. A closer look at the epistemological practices, however, provides a tentative path to think genealogically through the power/knowledge nexus inscribed into ways in which Muslims are studied and governed as subjects of integration. In this sense I take knowledge production itself as a governmental practice: It reflects and enacts epistemological aspirations which are tied to normative and political ones.

Through the lens of epistemological practices, I direct attention to the *conditions* of research on Muslim integration in Germany which have enabled specific methodologies and a specific set of questions. If for that purpose I inquire into exemplary cases, it is not to single out and denounce specific scholars. Rather, I interpret these examples as symptomatic of broader discursive formations in which these studies are embedded and which they convey.

Measuring Integration

Let us have a closer look at the studies commissioned by the DIK in cooperation with related state institutions of migration, such as the "Office for Migration and Refugees" (*Bundesamt für Migration und Flüchtinge*, BAMF), and the *Ministry of Family Affairs*. One of the central rationales of these studies in their claim to gather "representative data" on the Muslim population living in Germany is the parallel assumption that this population can be studied as a distinctive unit of analysis with clear boundaries. Because of its commitment to accurate representation and objectivity, this research is dominated by quantitative methodologies. Its logics can be summarized in a threefold manner. First, the object of research, "Muslims," is deduced from the category of a "migration background" (*Migrationshintergrund*)[5] or "ethnic background" (cf. Johansen and Spielhaus 2012). Second, in their purpose to measure integration the studies relate measured degrees of the religiosity of Muslims to their attitudes (*Einstellungen*) toward "German culture" or, more neutrally, toward "constitutional principles." If Muslims in Germany have recurrently been called on not to place religion above constitutional principles, the studies are designed to test the relationship between religiosity of Muslims and constitutional loyalty. Finally and relatedly, the studies operate with correlations that derive from an implicit and sometimes outspoken hypothesis: strong religiosity constitutes a problem for integration.

Let me exemplify these characteristics by recalling the frequently quoted study, *Muslims in Germany: Integration, barriers to integration, religion and attitudes towards democracy, the rule of law, and politically-religiously motivated violence*, conducted by the criminologists Katrin Brettfeld and Peter Wetzels (2007).[6] With its survey of the attitudes of 1725 respondents from four German cities,[7] the 509-page report has often been praised and quoted for its soundness and pioneering character in compiling the first comprehensive and representative survey on Muslims in Germany. The study was revised and updated first in 2009 (Haug, Müssig, and Stichs 2009) and in 2021 (Pfündel, Stichs, and Tanis 2021) with minor changes regarding the methodology and the questionnaire. The overall aim to measure Muslims in their entirety and in their degrees of integration into German society, however, characterizes all three versions.

A large number of the interviewees were picked randomly from telephone books by identifying names that sound Islamic.[8] Sixty were approached in mosques and interviewed qualitatively through a snowball sampling. The sample choice of this study thus translates the trinity "ethnic background = Muslim = non-German," which runs through public discourses in Germany (Spielhaus 2013), into a scientific fact. The disentanglement of Muslimness and Germanness is further replicated through an elaborate questionnaire with two sections that measure integration into German society and correlate it with religion. In the section "practiced integration," the respondents were asked, for example, about the frequency of contacts and the number of personal relationships they had, with the "German population" (Brettfeld and Wetzels 2007: 93 and 98), implying that Muslims do not belong to that entity. Their degree of integration, furthermore, was evaluated through questions about their level of proficiency of the German language. In the section "degrees of adaptation to German society," the interviewees were asked to tick boxes in scales ranging from 1 (the weakest agreement) to 6 (the strongest agreement) on whether they agreed with statements like "foreigners should protect their culture," or "different ethnic groups should be separated from each other in order to prevent problems" (ibid.: 99). In the sections on the level of religiosity and attitudes toward the state under the rule of law, they were asked to agree or disagree with statements such as: "I think that the Qur'an is the only true revelation of God" (ibid.: 116), "people who modernize Islam destroy the true doctrine," or "I believe that every good Muslim is obliged to convert non-believers to Islam" (ibid.: 118), or "The adherence to the doctrines of my religion is more important for me than democracy" (ibid.: 141) or "the sexual morality in Western societies is corrupt" (ibid.: 121 and 380).

The authors use the answers to these sets of questions to order degrees of religiosity into "not religious," "a bit religious," "religious," and "very religious," and to then categorize these degrees as "marginally religious," "orthodox," "traditional," or "fundamentalist." These categories are briefly introduced in a separate section of the study (ibid.: 53–60). However, indicating their central interest in criminology, the authors focus most intensively on the category of "fundamentalism." "Orthodox" implied a more or less strict observance of religious rituals. "Fundamentalist," in turn, implied strict observance within and outside the religious community and in addition a "clear-cut reference to the dogmas and practices which are considered pure" (ibid.: 57) and hence a scriptural approach to the religious sources: "Aberrations of the pure dogma within one's community are considered dangerous, wrong and as veiling the true message" (ibid.: 57).

On the basis of this data, the study concludes that 40 percent of Muslims in Germany fall under the category "fundamentalist," 21.7 percent are categorized as "orthodox," and 19 percent as "traditional-conservative" (ibid.: 195f.). These categories are correlated with scales of integration into German society. After having surveyed and presented these correlations in detailed graphs, figures, and pie charts, in their summary the authors conclude that "only 43 percent" of the Muslims interrogated "prove to be linguistically-socially [*sprachlich-sozial*] well or very well integrated" (Brettfeld and Wetzels 2007: 7).

Deficits of integration, according to the scientifically certificated deduced conclusion of this study, are centrally based on the right or wrong understandings of religious orientations. They primarily reside in mentalities (*Einstellungen*). The authors repeatedly stress that what they understand as "deficient integration" needs to be correlated with socioeconomic status and levels of education. Accordingly, they also measure social status as well as experiences of discrimination. Ultimately, however, they attribute greater weight to the individual's attitudes and the "religious orientations" that are measured along vague notions such as "German culture" or "democratic values."

The criminological view of individual religious orientations and attitudes as the main source for the lack of integration thus conceals questions about the social, economic, and political conditions under which individuals form their "religious attitudes," including structural social inequalities and forms of institutional racism. Even if repeatedly conceptualized as an enhancement of equal opportunities, the quantitative measurement of integration remains strongly implicated in the assumption that cultural and religious assimilation into German majority society – however vaguely defined – is the prerequisite for a socially cohesive society.[9] This slippery slope from structurally defined integration, which potentially captures structural inequalities, to assimilation, has indeed been upheld in all three versions of the study. The individual's embeddedness in societal contexts and in complex social relations necessarily remains outside of the scope, even if the questionnaire is extensive and differentiated, and if the correlations drawn between different clusters of answers are sophisticated.

It is precisely the reduction of complexities and social dynamics of these formats that renders them highly attractive to political authorities and decision-makers. Summarizing the most relevant findings in the foreword to the study, Schäuble, accordingly highlights that the study proves a worrisome potential for Muslims in Germany to radicalize. This, he goes on, needs to be taken seriously by politicians, security forces, and society at large. More importantly for my concern, Schäuble concludes: "We need to clarify: deficient linguistic and social integration, distance from education [*Bildungsferne*], the one-sided focus on non-German media, and the retreat into ethnic-religiously closed milieus have negative consequences for integration. There is a clear connection between deficient societal integration and fundamental religious orientations" (Schäuble in Brettfeld and Wetzels 2007: 8, translation mine).

Before moving to my analysis of such studies that monitor Muslim's integration into Germany's social fabric, I want to emphasize that similar methodologies and research designs are by no means to be found only in state-commissioned studies. A case in point is the survey conducted by the Berlin Social Science Center (*Wissenzschaftszentrum Berlin*), which was generously funded by the European Commission. The study compares degrees of "religious fundamentalism" among Muslims and Christians in six European countries. It is noteworthy that also here the researchers chose their "Muslim" and "Christian" respondents primarily through telephone books: people whose names sounded German, Dutch, English, French, etc. were interviewed as Christians; people with names that sounded Turkish, Arabic, etc. were grouped as Muslims. The study's coordinator, Ruud Koopmans, regularly appears in the media both in newspapers and in TV talk shows. He has not been reluctant in stressing publicly that his study found out that "46 percent of Muslims across Europe are fundamentalists."[10] Such conclusions are drawn from findings that the interviewees agreed with preformulated statements such as, "Muslims should return to the roots of Islam," "The West as an enemy is out to destroy Islam," or "I don't want homosexual friends" (Koopmans 2015). Having acted as one of the advisors in the latest version of the DIK commissioned survey *Muslimisches Leben in Deutschland* (Pfündel, Stichs, and Tanis 2021), Koopmans is a strong proponent of assimilation. Announcing the findings of his book "Multiculturalism or assimilation? Conditions for a successful integration" (*Multikulturalismus oder Assimilation. Bedingungen gelungener Integration*, 2017), Koopmans affirmatively asserts: "Those who are assimilated are less likely to be unemployed."[11] Interestingly, despite or maybe precisely because of the claim to distance and objectivity, the boundaries between academic knowledge production and political intervention are blurred in such cases.

Surveying and Surveilling—Governing by Numbers

In their pioneering study on quantitative surveys on Muslims in Europe, Birgitte Scheperlen Johansen and Riem Spielhaus (2012) make a similar observation that the formats, methodologies, and sets of questions in commissioned studies converge with those of state-independent academic studies. Furthermore, they denote a significant growth of quantitative studies on Muslims throughout Europe since 2000. Johansen and Spielhaus draw a number of important conclusions, which are relevant for my discussion of the scientific measurement of Muslims in Germany: First, they observe a strong connection between integration discourses and the academic knowledge production that has gained salience across Europe. Furthermore, they diagnose the recurrent conflation of ethnic or migration background with a supposed Muslimness. Finally, the framework in which Muslims are interrogated in these surveys is almost unanimously that of the nation-state, narrowly defined—an observation which is salient, for example, when Muslims are addressed as "foreigners" (*Ausländer*), or when they are asked if they have or would like to have close relationships with "Germans" (Johansen and Spielhaus 2012: 106).[12] Johansen and Spielhaus thus show that Muslims are measured against the backdrop of a putative national entity that, by its vagueness, can be filled with empty signifiers, ranging from "culture," and "customs," to "values," or principles like "democracy" or the "constitution." The authors also allude to the productive force of numbers (data and statistics) that constitute the figure of the Muslim as an object of research and of political intervention. Toward the end of their analysis, Johansen and Spielhaus call for a refinement of research categories "by deploying a clear consciousness for the differences between (im)migration, former nationality, ethnicity, and religious affiliation" (2012: 112).

To understand the mutual relationship between what is conventionally considered "proper knowledge" and the study of particular minorities as units of analysis, I want to push and at the same time redirect Johansen's and Spielhaus's analysis. Pertaining to my analytical lens of governmentality, I propose to focus our attention on the functions as well as the "regimes of truth" that guide such studies on Muslims in Germany. I am inspired here by Foucault's notion of "regime of truth," as, for example, spelled out in one of his lectures on biopolitics:

> ... in other words, to have political significance, analysis does not have to focus on the genesis of truths or the memory of errors. What does it matter when a science began to tell the truth? Recalling all the erroneous things that doctors have been able to say about sex or madness does us a fat lot of good ... I think that what is currently politically important is to determine the regime of veridiction established at a given moment that is precisely the one on the basis of which you can now recognize, for example, that doctors in the nineteenth century said so many stupid things about sex. What is important is the determination of the regime of veridiction that enabled them to say and assert a number of things as truths that it turns out we now know were perhaps not true at all. This is the point, in fact, where historical

analysis may have a political significance. It is not so much the history of the true or the history of the false as the history of veridiction which has a political significance.

(Foucault 2008 [1979]: 36/37)

Many of the studies, indeed, strive toward differentiation. They acknowledge a variety of types of religiosity among Muslims. Often, they confirm that the majority of Muslims share liberal values and are hence integrated (e.g. Becher and El-Menouar 2014). Or they state that degrees of religiosity do ultimately not matter as much as often expected for processes of integration (Pfündel, Stichs, and Tanis 2021). In short, many of the quantitative surveys tend to diagnose compatibility between liberal values and Islam (Johansen and Spielhaus 2012). These efforts of distinction complicate the assumption that Muslims were addressed by academic studies and political authorities as a preformatted "calculable entity" (Dornhof 2009: 387) or comprehensively as a "population" (Tezcan 2012). The attempt to provide differentiated knowledge about Muslims needs to be taken seriously in its logics, that is, as part of cartographic, classificatory, and ordering ambitions of the regime of truth at stake.

For political interventions that are drafted on, and inspired by representative data, it matters, of course, if the numbers in the studies confirm or contest the compatibility or incompatibility of Muslims with "German culture," "liberal norms," or "secularized religiosity." In light of a Foucauldian analytics of power, what matters analytically more, and in the longer run also politically, are the regimes of truth, which enable and structure these very forms of measurement. What therefore has to be unraveled are the epistemological structures of the framework of questions that produce an unmarked, liberal, non-Muslim majority society against which Muslims are investigated as varied and yet distinctive people that are ordered in the very moment in which they are differentiated internally and from "German society" writ large. Attempts at empirical differentiation and refinement rather contribute to homogenize the unseen and unmarked whole against which the other is measured.

In accordance with Foucault's argument, we should ask, for example, why knowledge through numbers—"the strongest language of all" (Asad 1994: 78)—is conventionally considered reliable, real, and proper knowledge. And we should ask why the call for objective and distant knowledge is particularly salient in such a highly politicized field, which in fact renders assumptions about objectivity and distance problematic, if not impossible. Instead of asking if the numbers and categories adequately represent the complex social realities of Muslims living in Germany, I therefore ask which system of truth animates the assumption that Muslim's complex social and religious practices can be studied with positivistic methods. And I ask how such interrogations are complicit in reproducing and normalizing majority-minority divisions by relying on scientific claims to truth.

The technologies of knowledge production that are prevalent in these studies are embedded in specific regimes of truth with longer legacies, and partially independent from the concrete field of inquiry into Muslims in contemporary Germany. To begin with, it is important to remember that the epistemic framework of quantitative data gathering derived from the adaptation by the humanities, and later the social sciences, of the methods and vocabularies of the natural sciences. These attempts to emulate methods of the natural sciences especially in their search for realism and objectivity have been widely studied and critiqued from various viewpoints—hermeneutical, poststructuralist, feminist, or postcolonial, to name just a few (Gadamer 1990 [1960]; Espeland and Stevens 2008; Feyerabend 2010 [1975]; Hacking (2006 [1975]; Haraway 1988; Hindess 1977; Lyotard 1978; Mignolo 2009). Central to many of these critiques is the questioning of the truth claims of objectivism and realism as cut off from relations of power. Relations of power and the unavoidable complicity of knowledge production and politics can, in other words, more easily be concealed with reference to "scientific autonomy" or "objectivity." This critique also pertains to the assumptions that the researching subject could be neatly divided from the object that is studied, and that the research questions and the data solicited are independent of concrete historical horizons.

Keeping track on the above-sketched practices of knowledge production on Muslim integration in Germany, in the following I will engage with three aspects of these critiques: first, the function of statistics, and more generally, of positivist epistemologies, for the governance of minorities in a nation-state framework. Second, the relationship between the knowing subject and the object of knowledge. And last, I will return to the co-constitutive nature of race and religion as central categories of knowledge of secular governmentality.

For the first aspect let me recall Ian Hacking's seminal critical inquiries into the rise and function of probability and statistics. Hacking elaborates on the first peak of the use of statistics as an instrument of measuring *and* governing populations in the nineteenth century. He contends that this first recovery cannot be detached from the constitution of nation-states. Statistics were developed as the means to measure the characteristics and inner truths of the emerging category of "populations," which was comprised of the whole of the people residing within a territory, gradually defined and bound by national borders. The collection and constitution of facts about life, death, status, mentalities, and increasingly race and religion, accordingly, turned into a social technology of making people governable through numbers. Most importantly, the act of counting, measuring, and quantifying individuals and populations has never been one of distant, objective, and real representation but has always been intimately bound by specific policy aims which shifted over time. Hacking writes: " ... social change creates new categories of people, but the counting is no mere report of developments. It elaborately, often philanthropically, *creates* new ways for people to be" (2002: 100). Statistics, according to Hacking, constitute a form of targeting, representing, and governing people's most intimate spheres by measuring them through numbers. The quantitative measurement of populations increasingly aimed at capturing each smallest part of people's social life.

If Hacking assesses the first wave of statistics about populations throughout Europe in the course of the eighteenth and especially nineteenth centuries, he simultaneously emphasizes that the quantification of society as an imagined entity and the inspection of the most intimate parts of people's lives and habits have not lost, but rather, have gained salience since the nineteenth century. In his related works on the history of probability, he points out how statistics gradually turned into a routinized practice of state bureaucracies, measuring, ordering, and governing society to the extent that its necessity and usefulness have become unchallenged and naturalized:

> Probability and statistics crowd in upon us. The statistics of our pleasures and our vices are relentlessly tabulated. Sports, sex, drink, drugs, travel, sleep, friends—nothing escapes. There are more explicit statements of probabilities presented on American prime time television than explicit acts of violence (I'm counting the ads). Our public fears are endlessly debated in terms

of probabilities: chances of meltdowns, cancers, muggings, earthquakes, nuclear winters, AIDS, global greenhouses, what next? There is nothing to fear (it may seem) but the probabilities themselves. This obsession with the chances of danger, and with treatments for changing the odds, descends directly from the forgotten annals of nineteenth-century information and control.

(Hacking 1990: 4–5)

Understanding the functions of statistics as "making people," Hacking analyzes how the representation of people through statistics shrinks the complexities of sociological phenomena, no matter how strong the efforts to capture each and every detail through refinement and differentiation. Surveying, categorizing, and thereby producing populations have thus never been a neutral nor a generic act. It has fulfilled specific functions both in the framework of Western-European nation-state formation and in its colonial expansions. Representing populations and subpopulations has intrinsically been related to governing, transforming, and creating these very populations.

In her seminal work on racism and statistics, Linda Supik (2014) elaborates on the intimate ties between the simultaneous flourishing of statistics and theories about racial differences, and later eugenics, which stood in the service of imperial, colonial, and nationalist projects (see also Kwaschik 2018: 90). The hierarchization into subordinate and dominant races was hence prominently justified and partly also confuted with taxonomic methodologies. The inception and institutionalization of positivistic epistemologies are thus closely related to theories about human races (ibid.: 55–60).

The case of statistics on Jewish populations in the late nineteenth, beginning of the twentieth century in Germany is compelling in this regard. This case also shows that the belief in the truth of numbers and objective data was widespread and promoted by many Jewish scholars themselves, who strongly believed in the possibility of arriving at objective judgments about their own social lives and compatibility with "German culture." For example, in 1914, Arthur Cohen, one of the founding fathers of the "Association for Jewish Statistics" (*Verein für Jüdische Statistik*), praised statistical methods and stated with enthusiasm: "Statistics brings rhythm, measure, and order into the confusing multiplicity of social appearances: they stand in well-ordered ranges and merely turn into a number of the social group to which they belong"

(Quoted in Diner 2014: 584, translation mine). Statistical measurement also transformed the ways in which Jewish people interrogated their own social lives and religious practices. Dan Diner observes in this vein that statistically driven interpretations were increasingly dominated by social factors, anatomy, and biological criteria of race:

> Both adherents of the Zionist movement and their Jewish opponents willing to assimilate attributed strong relevance to statistics. The central question in the turn of the century for both was the hypothesis of degeneration; in this debate all kinds of data about birth- and death-rates, the spread of certain diseases and the number of suicides were consulted.
>
> (Diner 2014: 583)

By trying to counter the negative findings about their incapacity to assimilate into "German culture" with "objective facts," Jewish intellectuals and academics were thus trapped in the game of counting and measuring culture and religion, normality and deviance, with the same methodological tools as those provided by racist theories. This example pertinently illustrates the relationship between modern institutions, techniques of knowledge production, and national projects. The regulative instruments of the nation-state framework are thus structurally bound with instruments for scientifically measuring, regulating, and hence producing minorities as dividable units of analysis who are either identified as conforming or deviating from an unmarked norm.

Recalling these antecedents is crucial as they mark the beginning of the paradox of the assimilatory force of nation-states, which I described with reference to Bauman in the first chapter, and which has been reconfigured in today's integration projects. The scientific measurement of degrees of cultural assimilation of human beings into an alleged homogeneous social body that is determined by national borders is thus a case in point for the human and social sciences to adopt epistemologies from natural sciences. In addition, it reveals the predicaments which expose those who are under suspicion and scrutiny of not having fully adapted to this imagined social whole.

The excesses of biopolitical techniques in which the life of populations and individuals are measured, governed, enhanced, and eventually exterminated had thus gained decisive racial components far longer before its excesses were manifested in the Nazi regime. And they have persisted in new ways in the aftermath of Nazi atrocities. Even if the taxonomic inspection of physical racial differences has been discarded, the scientific inspection of minorities reappeared in new categories. Supik shows, for example, how the legacy of the intimate ties between race theories and taxonomy has been reconfigured in census data-gathering on "ethnic" minorities across Europe (2014: Chapter 4).[13] Looking at the UK she stresses that also attempts to empower ethnic minorities often come at a price. When statistics, for example, aim at proving discrimination, or the relationship between ethnicity and social injustice, the risk of pushing people into boxes persists; ethnicity might then function as a naturalized category not dissimilar from race.

We can conclude from such analyses that "Muslims," even in their variations, are constituted as a distinct subpopulation at the very moment in which researchers turn them into an objectively researchable category. If statistics, literally the "science of the state," render the governance of populations scientific, the statistical measurement of Muslims in Germany has provided a solid basis for bolstering governmental interventions which do not leave people's lives untouched. In the scientific measurement of Muslims, the constituting power of numbers in their attempt to distantly *represent* empirical realities consists in turning Muslims into a distinctive, even if internally differentiated, population. At the same time, it consists in the production of an unmarked and invisible whole that constitutes the measure of the research on Muslims. That whole is squeezed into notions like "German culture," "German society," or more abstract signifiers like "democracy," "liberal values," "secularized," or "moderate" religiosity, against which Muslims are asked to position themselves in scales and degrees. That integration presupposes an entity into which one has to integrate, this very entity—whether conceived of as "nation," "society," "culture," or more abstractly by "constitutional principles"—continuously conceals fragmentation and normative conflicts within that very imagined whole.

There is, of course, no secure way to analyze the dynamics between how (sub-) populations are constructed through knowledge production and the effects on their "real" nature. Also the relationship between data-gathering and governing is neither definitely direct nor necessarily causal. However, precisely because the results of such ways of measuring integration are fed into political programs, they eventually travel as bare facts, and hence gain scientific credibility. That is why we have to understand knowledge production itself as a governmental intervention: it "represents" and hence constructs a milieu into which the state, and increasingly also civil society, is entitled to intervene, on the basis of scientifically proven facts and figures that are constituted by empiricist practices of knowledge production. In this regard, state-managed and -commissioned statistics also symptomatically reveal the mechanisms of knowledge production as a performative practice: knowledge gets authorized through its very circulation by way of experts, civil society actors, and political authorities in the wider public sphere. Precisely because the liberal state is entitled to justice and modes of justifications, statistical knowledge on minoritized populations fulfills the function to evaluate and proof the state's own effectiveness in literally accounting for vulnerable minoritized populations.

Objectifying and Governing—the Geo- and Body-Politics of Antiseptic Research

To better understand the structural connections between powers of objectivism as an analytical virtue, praised in the production of knowledge about Muslim integration, it is important to locate this kind of knowledge production in its positivistic legacy, reminiscent of the subject-object division. This is even more important as the positivistic knowledge production that is prevalent in integration measures has intruded independent research institutions and universities, both in Germany and more broadly across Europe (see Johansen and Spielhaus 2012; Schinkel 2017: 94). The authority of ontological divisions between the knowing subject and an object of research conceived of as a "thing" to be approached independently of the viewer has, of course, a long history in Enlightenment philosophy. The assumption in itself that Muslims could be studied, approached, and eventually integrated as passive objects reactualizes Donna Haraway's (1988) seminal critique of the "view from nowhere." This view from nowhere is predicated on epistemologies and politics of visibility and transparency. Inscribed into these is a correlation between seeing and not-being-seen, which provides authority to the knowing and seeing subject, whose own subjectivity lies outside of the scope of scientific investigation because it is merged into objectified and standardized methods.

The examination of certain populations in their most intimate spheres of life, indeed, reveals what Haraway calls the "leap out of the marked body into the conquering gaze from nowhere. A gaze which inscribes all marked bodies, that makes the unmarked category claim the power to see and not to be seen, to represent, while escaping representation" (Haraway 1988: 581). The abstract researcher, entitled to distantly gaze and measure particular populations, is thus turned invisible precisely through exposing and marking the other as different and particular. Haraway's elaborations on the relationship between the marked body and the unmarked gaze from nowhere provide an interesting vantage point to think through the body-political implications of knowledge production on the integration of Muslims in Germany. It also allows us to reveal the subtle corporeal inflections of integration discourses and their related technologies of knowledge production. It is no longer "culture," or an organically or ethnically construed "national entity" against which integration of minoritized populations is measured. Rather, it is the supposedly disembodied abstract liberal-secular order that structures the grammar of integration minoritoring. The excessive gaze on and the examination of Muslim corporeal practices—veiling, praying, fasting in Ramadan, or handshaking or not—however, have reinscribed dividing schemes with somatic implications[14]: The very fact that certain corporeal practices are so strongly put under scrutiny and considered worthy of public discussion, political and legal regulation, and academic inspection divides and governs forms of life and religious practices into normal, unmarked and marked, exceptional ones.

The attempts to capture and categorize these corporeal practices scientifically both reflect and reproduce the exceptionalizing gaze on the body of the other. Muslim corporeal practices such as veiling, for example, are not simply at the center of debates because they unexpectedly rendered Muslims more visible in European public spheres (Göle and Amman 2004), or because they transgress inscribed and largely embodied ideals of privatized, invisible religiosity. The excessive interest in the Muslim body is based on an inscribed epistemic scheme which *requires* the other's body to be exceptional in order to sustain or reconfigure a specific regime of truth (cf. Amir-Moazami 2016). The abstract viewer from nowhere, in our case state authorities who gather data on Muslims in cooperation with research institutes, necessitates a Cartesian body-mind split. The mind as the seeing and unseen gaze is detached from the sensorial realm, from the body, and from concrete experience to assert disembodied universality. It is through this one-sided focus on the other's body that the allegedly disembodied contours of the liberal-secular nation-state gains currency, while its own corporeal incentives are hidden by the language of abstract universal principles.

As postcolonial theorists have extensively shown, since its inception the scopic view from nowhere, or the "hegemony of the eye" (Comolli 185, quoted in Schaffer 2007: 13), has been coupled with a geopolitical division of the world into what Walter M. Mignolo (2009) called the *humanitas* and the *anthropos*. These metaphors refer to the distinction between the putatively disembodied and universal mind, and the particular, tribal, exotic, or endangering body. *Humanitas* is the unmarked knowing mind that determines the conditions and categories of how to see and know properly from a particular privileged geographical location (Europe, North America, or currently the Global North) that is itself outside of the scope. *Anthropos*, in turn, represents the to-be-inspected and to-be-told body (the Orient, Asia, Africa, South America, or currently the Global South). *Humanitas* and *anthropos* are thus intimately bound by the relationship between geo- and body-politics of knowledge which have been institutionalized through the colonial matrix of power, or as Mignolo puts it, through: "A racial system of social classification that invented Occidentalism [...] that created the conditions for Orientalism; distinguished the South of Europe from its center [...] and, on the long history, remapped the world as first, second, and third during the Cold War" (2009: 161).

Mignolo stresses that the framework dividing the geo- and body-political divisions of the world into *humanitas* and *anthropos* gradually moved from a Christian theological to a secular episteme (Mignolo 2009: 176). The central question that arises from Mignolo's observation is how and under which conditions Eurocentric epistemologies succeeded in concealing their own geo-historical and biographical locations, by creating the idea of universal knowledge predicated on the assumption of the universal knowing subject. Along the grain of this question, I suggest that Islamic (corporeal) practices have appeared so extensively on the political, legal, public, and academic scene of Germany (as in many other European settings) because this very body-mind split is predicated on a specific conception of body-mind distinction with a Christian and later secularized Christian legacy.[15] The other's body is thus paradoxically inspected and rendered legible through the claim to disembodied abstract and universal principles, while these very principles are fed by embodied social conventions, sensibilities, and affects, along which bodies are turned into disproportionate suspect objects of study and regulation.

It would yet be shortsighted to simply assert that the epistemic framework described by Haraway or Mignolo has univocally and coherently persisted from its colonial emergence until today. The contemporary production of knowledge about Muslims in Germany and their levels of religiosity and integration revolves around different and additional dynamics of entanglements between *humanitas* and *anthropos*. The power relations between minorities and established majorities, moreover, have become more dispersed and subtler with the consolidation of liberal freedoms than at the inception of an expanding nation-state framework. The nexus of power and knowledge is thus not merely animated by the will to domination, degradation, paternalism, or hierarchy. The contemporary situation is different too because the scientific justification of Western hegemony has been substantially contested from various vantage points. As Mignolo stresses, the *anthropos* has started to resist being merely the passive object of study and confined within an epistemic framework molded by someone else, and hence is refusing to be ranked in relation to the ideals of *humanitas* (cf. Mignolo 2009: 161).

Considering the practices of knowledge production on Muslim integration in Germany today, one assumption has, however, persisted in new forms: that the scientific investigation of subjects deemed external to the nation in their difference or similarity is necessary and unproblematic, and that the normative and epistemological locations of those who examine do not matter for the outcome of data-gathering. The epistemic silences and the related naturalization of the "view from nowhere" regarding knowledge production on Muslims consist especially in normative assumptions about what proper religion is or should be. To be sure, this epistemic framework expands particular methodologies such as statistical data-gathering on Muslims in Germany. Qualitative methodologies are not immune from positivist assumptions, even if they differ from standardized methods because they are based on personal encounters, and even if their relevance for political authorities is comparatively marginal.[16]

Secular Governmentality and the Problematization of "Religion"

In light of my central argument in this book to take the liberal-secular matrix seriously as a structuring feature of interrogating and integrating Muslims as a *religious* minority, I want to return to Johansen's and Spielhaus's concern about the classification of Muslims along ethnic lines, and put more explicitly to the fore the epistemic framework that animates such equations. To understand the deeper ingrained mechanisms of the scientific measurement of people with Islamic backgrounds as "naturally" Muslims, it is important to move beyond interrogating "race" and to also foreground "religion" as a concept that classifies and orders people not just by their "ethnic descent" but also by their beliefs, practices, and theological traditions.[17] I therefore want to complement the critical analyses of taxonomic methods, which reproduce racialized distinctions on the basis of cultural or ethnic categories, by problematizing methodologies whose target is "religion" as a distinct object of study. This concern requires to problematize the epistemologies of the liberal-secular matrix itself as powerfully structuring ways in which "other" religions are governed through scientific interrogations.

Interestingly, the disciplines that dominate commissioned academic knowledge production on Muslims in Germany—criminology, migration studies, or simply social science—are characterized by an absence of expertise on Islamic or religious traditions more generally. The idea that religion can be unproblematically studied as a measurable object has been normalized to the extent that many studies on Muslims in Germany even surpass the problematic act of defining religion (cf. Asad 2014). That said, they still operate with implicit and largely hegemonic assumptions about what religion is and/or should be, hence with what Michael Bergunder has called "everyday understandings of religion" (Bergunder 2012: 43). Everyday understandings of religion can constitute a starting point for approaching genealogically why and how they have become routinized and hegemonic (2012: 43).

To be sure, I am less concerned about whether the routinized understandings of religion prevalent in the studies on Muslim religiosity and integration adequately capture the complexities of Islam as a dynamic and heterogeneous discursive tradition (see Asad 1986, 2014). In compliance with my genealogical reading of *Islampolitik* in the first chapter, I locate the practice of categorizing religion itself within a specific genealogy of understanding religion as a denotable subfield with specific functions in society. This understanding, while having turned into normalized, conventionalized, and rarely challenged knowledge practices, brings me to one of my central concerns in this book, that is, the relationship between secularism and the politics of the integration of Muslims. If the racial state governs people along skin color, descent, or even more loosely, culture, the secular state governs religion by empirically and prescriptively performing which kind of religion is acceptable and which exceeds the expectations of secular norms. As shown in the first chapter, "religion" as a concept and a unit of scientific analysis has been co-constitutive of race as a structuring feature of nation-states and their instruments of measuring and governing populations and subpopulations.[18]

The production of knowledge on religion not only as a scientific discipline but also as a field of governmental regulation emerged simultaneously with the Enlightenment-Protestant assumption that religion is and should be something subjective, internal to the person's intimate feeling (Scheer 2012), and hence opposed to the natural and empirically observable and testable (Johansen 2013: 10). Paradoxically, the study of religion as an independent field of research was thus born at the same moment as postulates about distinctions between science and belief, immanence and transcendence, theology and politics, church and state, body and mind, etc., took a particular shape during the Enlightenment. While the view of belief as a feeling based on personal experience, and hence internal to the believing subject, potentially escapes the scientific view, a new science was created which studied religion's remnants, its distinct characteristics as well as its (irrational) excesses.

As indicated in the first chapter, moreover, the practice of comparing different world religions partly functioned as a means to universalize a particular Christian-based notion of religion by circumscribing specific experiences as common to all religions (Asad 2014).[19] What Vial calls a "prototypical," and Bergunder a "hegemonic," understanding of religion is thus both shaped by a particular theological tradition (Protestantism) and at the same time conceptualized as a generalizing blueprint for measuring any kind of religion. As Vial suggests religious prototypes have also functioned as "manufacturing" acts in producing (good) religion by pronouncing its ingredients (Vial 2016: 123).[20]

It is therefore important to take the normative and normalizing forces of "religion" as a category of knowledge seriously as structuring the governance of religious plurality in liberal-secular contexts. It is necessary to ask what is at stake when a religious minority is turned into a distinct *religious* population that is measured and researched with analytical tools whose legacy resides within distinct Christian theological repertoires (cf. Daniel 2016; Vial 2016). This question is relevant both if this legacy is concealed by the claim to the universality of secularism as detached from its Christian antecedents as well as if Christianity is explicitly used as a successful model of measurement.

If we agree with Vial's assumption that the very scientific study of religion has contributed to "manufacturing" religion into a factual object of study, then the underlying matrix in the commissioned studies on Muslim religiosity is predicated on exactly this inscribed and largely unmarked point of reference: good religion is the spiritual, internalized, and truly authentic prototypical religious norm, that is, "not believing," "mildly religious," or "moderate," to take up the wording of the commissioned studies mentioned above; bad religion is its "strongly religious," "fundamentalist," "traditionalist," or "radical" deviation which impedes integration.

The common practice for survey data to shrink scales and degrees of religiosity into handy categories is thus predicated on an inherited legacy of scientifically measuring religion from an allegedly distant vantage point—"a view from nowhere"—which under closer scrutiny emerges from epistemological specificities and geographical locations. The question to raise is, therefore, not so much whether the categorizations are able to capture the complex and dynamic social realities of Muslims living in a given society, but which epistemic regime enables and sustains these very categories and acts of classification.

In light of my central focus on the liberal-secular matrix of integration, a critical inquiry of knowledge production should then not only be cautious if Muslims are disproportionately classified as fundamentalist, excessively pious, or as otherwise deviating from what is considered an acceptable religion in Germany. One should also be attentive to the more benign moves through which Muslims are incorporated epistemologically into a liberal-secular order.

We should be vigilant, for example, when researchers compare Christians and Muslims in their respective degrees of liberal attitudes, and attest that the younger generation of Muslims in Germany are gradually adopting liberal gender norms (Becher and El-Menouar 2014: 179). Islamic practice then is considered mere belief, internalized and privatized; Islamic bodily rituals turn into "signs" or "symbols" which Muslims externalize in their search for identity (see Asad 2006).

Even if such findings might be appropriate (even if slightly banal) and probably politically urgent at first glance, they are not unproblematic when scrutinized more closely. For they ultimately tend to leave unaddressed the subtle technologies of power through which subjects are turned into liberal citizens. If we take the complex mechanisms of subjectification seriously, in research as well as in other settings of knowledge production on Muslims in Germany, it is not enough to conjure happy hybrids with multiple, fragmented identities or secularized, individualized Muslims that are compatible with liberal norms and secular ideals. More concretely, if we account for the legacies of knowledge production in *Islampolitik* as well in assimilation projects, Muslims as to-be-integrated minorities are already marked and constituted as subjects before they can freely choose or dispose of their identifications. Their religious practices, moreover, cannot always be grasped with a vocabulary deriving from liberal projects or ideals of secularized religion (Mahmood 2005).

It is, therefore, necessary to be attentive to both overtly exclusivist tones which frame Muslims as the incompatible margins of the nation and those which epistemologically integrate them into an allegedly universal *humanitas*— provided that their religiosity is legible within a secular vocabulary[21]: Islam is then turning into a religion proper, once it is immunized from problematic forms of communitarianism or excessive piety. It becomes compatible with a scientific understanding of religion and therefore also with liberal sensibilities. By squeezing Islam into a corset of a putatively universal category of "religion," such approaches are also complicit with the "secular episteme" (Mavelli 2012). In other words, even if Muslims' path to integration is proven affirmatively, Islamic practices (such as veiling, praying, fasting, etc.) are ultimately reduced to their legibility within emancipatory, liberal, or secular projects. Such diagnoses are thus complicit with normative dimensions of liberal-secular sensibilities. They unavoidably reproduce a conceptual repertoire whose own normative and epistemological location remains occluded and unchallenged. In this field of study, this incapacity to engage in substantial discussions about the difficulties of translation of an implicit or outspoken Christian legacy into "other religions" is compensated by sophisticated demonstrations about data gathering, correlation factors, and the methods employed.[22]

The powers of secular governmentality in the scientific measurement of Muslims' integration into German society, thus understood, consist in the capacity of setting the framework of questions within which Muslims have to position themselves and whose own normative presumptions remain untouched: Are Muslim forms of social life and religious practices compatible with secular lifestyles and sensibilities? Can Islam be reformed and tamed like Christianity? Can it contribute to foster democracy? Are your notions of gender norms and understandings of sexuality compatible with liberal freedoms?[23] To what extent are you in agreement or disagreement with the secular order? What kind of a Muslim are you? This set of questions comes together to form the leading question implicitly or explicitly driving knowledge production on Islam and Muslims in Germany: can Muslims be integrated into Germany's liberal-secular order, molded by Christianity? This very framework constantly gets reenacted *through* the interrogation and inspection of Muslims as differing from or conforming to it. I therefore understand the scientific efforts to structure and divide Muslim religiosity into comprehensive types and categorizations themselves as secular practices. These replicate a repertoire that guide many related dividing practices—body-mind, belief-practice, pious-secular, majority-minority and so on.

To conclude, the problems inherent to knowledge production on Muslim integration in Germany can, therefore, not be captured without also interrogating the secular as its operative matrix, which pervades the will to knowledge, truth, and power. Secularism as a governmental technique of measuring Muslims is more than tied to a specific understanding of reason and science as having gradually been detached from and superseded transcendence, and as having given rise to a specific understanding of the autonomous, self-contained subject detached from the transcendent (God) (see Mavelli 2012).[24] Secularism in this domain of knowledge production, first and foremost, implies the defining authority to denote what falls under the rubric of legitimate religion and what does not, and what therefore counts or does not count as part of the social fabric of the nation. In other words, governmental ambitions to turn religion into a matter of scientific and political inquiry are themselves enabled by secular orders, which are dependent on denoting religion in order to demarcate the boundaries between legitimate and illegitimate transgressions. The liberally defined state, in turn, is dependent on modes of justifications which have to be based on scientific reasoning to render its practices of governing religion justifiable.

The secular governmentality of state-measured integration, furthermore, consists in the scientific practice of replicating an unmarked norm of religion. State-led integration measures, which either externally fund or conduct research, and which are premised on distance and objectivity, are the most visible symptom of broader phenomena of knowledge production on (religious) minorities. Their genealogy is predicated on an imperial structure and, more specifically, on a secular epistemic framework, which interrogates certain religious practices in specific ways while leaving the very framework of interrogation unaddressed.

4

Dialogues with Muslims: Governing through Recognition

In the previous chapter, I showed how the enterprise of integration has turned into a field of social scientific investigation in which Muslims' religiosity has been interrogated as a measure for their degrees of integration into society. In this chapter, I move to a component of integration that is closely related to its measurement, that is an integration practice in which the cognition of the to-be-integrated subject is connected to her *re*cognition. Recognition of Muslim minorities across Europe is conventionally connoted positively and contrasted with measures of securitization or Islamophobia. Because of the long absence of state-structured approaches to actively deal with plurality emerging from immigration, especially in Germany, recognition of "minorities" is touted or tacitly accepted as an overdue measure of multicultural politics.

Pertaining to my analytics of power, in this chapter I challenge such assumptions by examining the intimate relationship between politics of recognition and the regulation of religious plurality under liberal-secular conditions. I argue that integration as recognition of Muslims must take account of secularism as state management of religion and its entanglement with embodied attachments, sensibilities, and social conventions. I thereby read politics of recognition as interwoven with forms of power which remain unaddressed in conventional distinctions between racialized exclusion vs. liberal recognition. In so doing, I return to the DIK, which figures as a prime example of state-recognition politics vis-à-vis Muslims. Instead of offering an encompassing and detailed analysis of the DIK,[1] I analyze this integration measure through a political-theoretical lens on the problematics of the recognition of minorities in nation-state contexts.[2]

My analysis builds upon Patchen Markell's (2003) critique of recognition. Markell's objections to Hegelian-inspired recognition policies contain two key elements which guide my analysis: first, recognition requires a clearly defined subject to be recognized, one that often gains contours through the act of recognition.[3] Second, this subject of recognition requires an authority that articulates and administers recognition. Since Hegel, this recognizing authority has materialized in the more or less centralized (nation-) state, which at the same time experiences an increase in sovereignty through acts of recognition.

If I "apply" Markell's critique in these two areas with respect to Muslims' struggles for recognition in Germany, it is not so much because I am following his core concern. That is to read Hegel against the grain and to deduce an alternative theory of "acknowledgement" from his theory of recognition. I rather want to give a more specific twist to Markell's discussion. By taking Germany as a prototype of a liberal-secular nation-state, I ask how the recognition of Muslims as *religious* minorities operates as a governmental practice that effects the sovereignty of the secular state by turning them into legible and governable subjects.

Markell takes as his starting point political-theoretical discussions that have, since the 1990s, increasingly turned away from policies focused on redistributing material goods, favoring instead policies that recognize cultural identities.[4] On a basic level, he contends that notions of recognition start from the idealized standpoint that injustices could be remedied by a more just distribution of recognition of identities. By focusing on the subject of recognition instead of the structures that (re)produce inequalities, Markell argues, minoritized positions would be replicated instead of being dismantled as a product of unequal power relations:

> Thus, even those exchanges of recognition that express a spirit of inclusion—such as Jewish emancipation or contemporary multiculturalism—deal, at best, with the symptoms and effects of subordination, while simultaneously working to reproduce the problematic aspiration to sovereign agency in which those effects are rooted. At times, this may mean that existing relations of injustice will be preserved or even reinforced, albeit cloaked in a superficial layer of reform."
>
> (Markell 2003: 31)

Against this idea, Markell questions whether identities can ever be recognized as bound and finished entities, and hence raises a critique of the shortcomings of identity politics. By operating with the notion of subjects as sovereign agents, these politics entail a problematic temporality in which identities searching to be recognized are considered as a *fait accompli*. Read against these concerns, the ambition to address Muslims as interlocutors of state-led integration programs qua their Muslimness has contributed to render this very identity into being. This calling into being of a recognizable Muslim subject has, in other words, turned this very subject intelligible and governable for the state.

Most importantly, Markell critically investigates the connections between the formation of identifiable subjects of recognition and the enhancement of state sovereignty through its act of recognizing vulnerable identities.[5] In other words, the subject of recognition requires an authority that is in charge of the distribution of the good of recognition, which materializes in the more or less centralized (national) state. Regardless of whether the state is conceptualized as a neutral set of institutions, distant from "society," or whether it is considered as an active agent in charge of recognition, Markell reminds us that theorists of recognition barely question the centrality of the state. Instead of conceiving of the state as an independent and distant arbiter of recognition, he cautions that the state is closely interconnected with society, and hence always involved in the choices of how and to whom recognition is distributed. In Markell's understanding, the state is "both a participant in and an artifact of the politics of recognition" (Markell 2003: 28). Consequently, it is through the process of recognition that state sovereignty can be effected or secured. Moreover, through the act of recognition the state turns into the identity-forming body for the vulnerable minorities struggling for recognition (ibid.: 125ff). Markell speaks about the displacement through identification with the state (ibid.).

In this reading, state sovereignty is not merely understood as a product of discipline, sanction, nor even of the law or its suspension, but can very well be effected by para- or extralegal governmental techniques like recognition. These intertwinements were already prevalent in the previous chapter, in which I showed how the state enacts sovereignty by governing Muslims through a specific regime of truth and by legitimizing itself through its reliance on robust data. The relationship between sovereignty and governmental practices is also prevalent in the numerous efforts to create and institutionalize a dialogue with Muslims as a way of remedying past misrecognition, indifference toward vulnerable minorities, and because of the liberal promise to secure equal opportunities.

Now, as I indicated in Chapter 2, we have to bear in mind that German migration policies have never come close to any ideals of recognition or multiculturalism that theorists like Will Kymlicka or Charles Taylor had in mind (Amir-Moazami 2005). The absence of institutionalized multiculturalism in Germany notwithstanding, the DIK has been rationalized as a measure of recognition of Muslims. Also, political theorists have interpreted it as a step toward de facto recognition of Muslims by the state, and hence also as a variation of multiculturalist politics (e.g. Laurence 2011; Modood 2012).[6] As a measure of de facto multicultural integration, the DIK, indeed, amply shows how state recognition of Muslims in Germany has functioned as a paralegal governmental technique which potentially enhances the sovereign agency of the secular state. The DIK is also a case in point for the conjunction of integration programs and *Islampolitik*.

Turning "Muslims in Germany" into "German Muslims"

As part of the compiled national integration project Wolfgang Schäuble advocated the DIK as a measure "to make Muslims feel at home in Germany with their faith, so that Muslims in Germany are transformed into 'German Muslims.'"[7] To do so, the DIK had in the course of its existence gradually expanded the scope of the issues that it addresses. These ranged from the compatibility of Islamic and liberal-democratic norms, from anti-Islamic sentiments to Islamic bodily practices and Islamic holidays, to the more recently debated Islamic welfare work in Germany. Thus, almost any aspect potentially of relevance for Muslims' integration into German society has been covered in this dialogical encounter with Muslim interlocutors.

For sociologist Levent Tezcan, this totalizing structure results from the overlap of two parallel and partly competing rationalities: on the one hand, legal concerns that stem from the institutionalization of Islam in Germany, which would turn Muslims into a legally recognized religious community. On the other hand, the DIK has also focused on conduct of life, religious practice, and sensibilities, and often addressed Muslims as problematic subjects with potentially "incommensurable values" (Tezcan 2012: 63) to liberal–democratic ones. Tezcan qualifies these two modes as a coupling of a "politics of religion" (*Religionspolitik*) with a "politics of population" (*Bevölkerungspolitik*), dwelling on Foucault's analysis of the birth of a "population" as the main target of modern forms of governance. He criticizes the politics of population for its effects to subsume diverse actors into *Muslims* and eventually into a "*homo-Islamicus*" (Tezcan 2007) that is distinctive from the rest of society.

What Tezcan is less preoccupied with, however, is how the interrogation of Muslims as subjects of recognition has also functioned as a means to rearticulate a normative notion of religion modeled by a specific understanding of Christianity as secularized and endowing the liberal and democratic spirit of German society. What Tezcan qualifies as the "politics of religion" in fact permeate domains of life conduct, sensibilities, and religious practice. "Politics of religion" are therefore more intimately bound with the "politics of population" than Tezcan's distinction suggests. This connection necessitates a problematization of the ways in which secular politics operate in the particular context of this integration measure which is rationalized as recognition.

Nowhere is the linkage between "politics of religion" and "politics of population" more prevalent than in Schäuble's public speeches.[8] Schäuble's discourse is generally characterized by the deceptively benign desire of incorporating Muslims into the nation. Contrary to what some of his followers had professed, Schäuble emphasized over and over again that Islam and Muslims now belonged to Germany. This welcoming gesture, however, never stood alone. In all his speeches, Schäuble laid bare the conditions under which he thought that Islam could be recognized on equal terms with Christianity. For example, at a workshop at the *Theologisches Forum* in 2009 he emphasized that:

> The churches clarified for themselves: the principle of the *liberal-democratic order* has its *roots in the Christian notion of humanity*. With this they went beyond the mere acceptance of democratic rules and *theologically incorporated* the values of this order. It is therefore correct to say that the political and social order of our country is closely bound to our Christian-based culture. This is a fact which has to be accepted. To say this is not to discriminate against Islam."
>
> (Schäuble 2009, translation mine, emphasis added)[9]

In the same talk, Schäuble specified that:

> The separation of church and state is based on the understanding of the mutual limitation of religious and state authority. We Europeans have learned throughout the wars of religion that there is not much space for religious tolerance if religious truth-claims are coupled with political ones. That is why our state respects the spiritual authority of religion, but simultaneously claims authority to regulate its coexistence. The constitution guarantees the freedom of belief and at the same time limits it. In this way religious freedom does not release anyone from loyalty to the constitution.
>
> (ibid.)

What are the expectations of the candidates for recognition if the conversation starts with the assumption that "we Europeans" have learned lessons that others still have to learn? Which prototype of "good religion" is necessary, or rather how is it reenacted in the very call for Muslims to adjust to this normative division between religion and politics, and what does this tell us about the operations of political secularism and secularity in this specific integration measure? And finally, which kind of state is effected by such ways in which Muslims are called to be loyal to the constitution?

Schäuble re-narrates a well-known success story of Europe's secularization. The story conventionally starts with the Investiture Controversy in the eleventh century, then moves on to the Reformation paving the theological ground for the Enlightenment, and giving birth to a tamed and secularized version of Christianity and Europe's "liberal-democratic" spirit. As we have learned from numerous scholars critical of historicism or of the concept of "history" altogether (Chakrabarty 2000; Seth 2008), the secularization paradigm, which Schäuble invokes as the yardstick for his Muslim interlocutors, functions itself as a historical narrative, that is to say, a story about history. This storytelling about secularization narrates Europe's gradual success to emancipate itself from the all-encompassing domination of the Catholic Church. At the same time, it discards all complexities and all less friendly aspects of that very history, such as imperialism, colonialism, and totalitarianism, which are all, to put not too fine a point on it, inseparable from Christian components.

My aim here, however, is not to counter Schäuble's historicism by questioning such linear narratives that are characteristic of the secularization paradigm itself (Casanova 1994). Rather, I want to take seriously the manner in which such narratives bring to the fore some ingrained tensions on which the recognition of Muslims in Germany sit. One such assumption concerns the intimate relationship between Christianity and the liberal-democratic state, and the simultaneous assertion that "religious truth claims" need to be decoupled from political ones. Another one has to do with the supposed separation of religious from stately authority, and the simultaneous institutionalized cooperation between Christian churches and the state, for which the very inception of state-led dialogue with Muslim groups provides a telling example. And finally, there is the simultaneous embracing of religious liberty and the coupling of this and other institutionalized liberties with the conditionality of loyalty to the constitution.

Conditionality of Recognition

Schäuble does not stop at foreclosing some of the legal and political tensions of Germany's arrangement of church, state, and the nation. In another speech, he more explicitly points out how much he counts on allies within Christian milieus to foster Muslims' integration into German society: "Christian-Muslim dialogue can provide important motivations for an *inner-Islamic* theological debate in Germany over topics such as secularism, human dignity, and gender equality. Such discussions are also unavoidable for Islam to 'feel homelike' [*das Heimischwerden*] in this country" (ibid.: translation mine, emphasis added).

The direction of Schäuble's understanding of dialogue is thus clearly determined. Similar to the prescriptions found in the guidelines published by the Protestant Church, *Klarheit und Gute Nachbarschaft* (see Chapter 2), Christian theologians should instruct Muslim interlocutors to reform Islam internally. At work in Schäuble's proposal is thus a distinctive liberal idea of a civilizing mission guided by the pedagogical aim to convince Muslims of the Christian model of secularized religion and, by that notion, to guide them in their deliberate transformation into secularized citizens. Schäuble navigates between the virtue of state neutrality in religious matters, and the presumption of an intimate and almost natural bond between the secular state and Christianity. While contending that the state plays a different, less direct, and more distanced role on religious matters than theologians do, Schäuble thus symptomatically presumes that Christian political theology should play a genuine role in shaping social cohesion.

Thinking carefully about the power relations and techniques that are prevalent in such integration measures, it is important to recall the cooperative relationship between state and church in Germany, on which Schäuble's delegating of state authority to Christian theologians relies. Some of the ambivalences that Schäuble spells out reside in the ambivalent legal status of religion in Germany which I referred to in Chapter 2. Schäuble's discourse spells out how the DIK's goal of transforming Muslims in Germany into German Muslims is deeply entangled with the aim of shaping their religious sensibilities along Germany's specific status of the Christian religion. At the same time, he takes it upon himself to pronounce the built-in limitations with which Muslims are necessarily confronted in this very endeavor. If liberal democracy is molded by Christianity, as Schäuble tells us, and if the state needs to work hand in hand with Christian theologians to instruct Muslims about "secularism, human dignity, and gender equality," the adaptation of Islam to this determined model of institutionalized religion is both required and impeded. More importantly, legal recognition can only be petitioned for at the level of federal states (*Bundesländer*) and not the central state. The DIK, with its location in the Ministry of the Interior, is thus not even the legitimate institution for Islamic communities to apply for legal status on an equal footing with the established religious communities.

It has often been objected that Islam would lack the legal preconditions for being organized in one centralized religious authoritative institution similar to that of the Christian churches in Germany. However, as Schäuble indicates himself, this is only one part of the truth. The given arrangement of state, religion, and the nation has both furthered but also impeded what has been called the process of the "churchification" (*Verkirchlichung*) of Islam in Germany (Reuter 2014). The ambivalent manifestation of the DIK as a platform for the integration of Muslims that has no legal mandate to legally recognize Islamic organizations as churches is echoed in Schäuble's repeatedly articulated offer that the "state wants Muslims to feel at home here," and his simultaneous reminder that "they will have to make stronger efforts and adapt to a certain degree to their new homeland."[10]

Schäuble's linear historicism on the gradual secularization of Christianity and inherent compliance with liberal democracy is obviously not specific to his discourse but rather runs through much of public discourse in general, especially when the role and place of Islam and Muslims in Germany are at stake (Amir-Moazami 2007a; Mittmann 2011; Rommelspacher 2017). The DIK is unique, however, for having uplifted this narrative at the level of the state, and thereby having translated its premises into an encompassing integration program. This semantic shift in the self-understanding of the German state as the centralized caretaker of a particular religious minority (Muslims) indeed opens a space for a whole set of governmental interventions which are productive of a specific conception of the formally "ideologically neutral" state itself.

If the subject of recognition needs to be legible for the state, as Markell argues (Markell 2003), Muslims in Germany become so under the condition that they fashion themselves along a prototypical ideal of (Christian) religion. The state, in turn, bolsters its authority to govern a population that is considered not yet adequately secularized. But how has this imperative of a Christian model unfolded in this specific integration measure, vaguely sketched by Schäuble as a liberal-democratic order? And how are the politics of religion and the politics of population interconnected?

The Secular Embodiments of Conditional Recognition

> Political or legal institutions are not sufficient for successful integration. The constitution alone will also not be sufficient. In order for it to be given life by the citizens [of Germany], the constitution itself requires different fundamentals. If we all want to feel part of a common order, we need something which unites us on a deeper human level, at exactly the level on which religion and culture, values, and identity are located.
>
> (Schäuble 2006b)[11]

If Schäuble has recurrently foregrounded a specific understanding of the deep attachment of Christianity and German nationhood, many of the state-led integration programs consist in interrogating Muslims about their capacity to transform religious sensibilities and forms of life to make them fit for this imagined secular "common order," as Schäuble put it. This linkage between minority recognition and minority transformation through prescription of norms becomes more pronounced when we move closer to how Schäuble's promise to transform "Muslims in Germany into German Muslims" has been spelled out in the DIK.

One of the central themes that have been discussed in DIK especially in the first phase (2006 to 2009) has been the relationship between religious conduct and liberal norms and sensibilities. The domains of gender norms and sexuality are pivotal here. It is in these domains that the shift from an empirical to a prescriptive norm in state-managed recognition of Muslims has become most salient. In order to illustrate this observation empirically, I want to probe into the case of coeducational sports and swimming classes in state schools, and then return to my conceptual discussion about the political-theoretical implications of governmental integration measures that navigate from recognition to prescription.

The topic of sports and swimming classes in state schools has been regularly brought up in the legal and wider public sphere in controversies on Muslim bodily practices and its limits. This example shows how, through the dialogical encounter, Muslims have been dragged into normative notions of gender equality conform to specific norms of corporeal conduct. The DIK brought up this topic as one of the themes discussed within the framework of "norms and values" in one of the working groups.[12] It was advocated in particular by one of the participants, Necla Kelek, who was invited as one of the "Muslim critics of Islam" (*Islamkritiker*), later reframed as the initiative "Secular Islam" (*Säkularer Islam*).[13] By then, Kelek had already published a highly influential and largely populist book on arranged and forced marriages in Germany (2005). She also acted as an expert in citizenship regulations, as I will show in the next chapter. Prior to the DIK, Kelek had produced a report on mixed sports and swimming classes in state schools, commissioned by the Office for Migration and Refugees (Kelek 2006). There would be a lot to say about Kelek and her fellow secular Muslims, especially with regard to the power of classificatory systems within which Muslims are not passive objects but often complicit.[14] Suffice it to say for my concern that in that report, Kelek called for a more proactive and interventionist stance on rules of conduct and laid emphasis on the religious dimension of integration to censure forms of religiosity that might contribute to the pull into "parallel societies" among young Muslims in Germany (Kelek 2006: 74).[15]

Contrary to such clear-cut voices, the approved and published document of the DIK reveals the attempt to balance concerns about religious freedom and the mandatory participation of students in all classes in state schools. Moreover, the text advises teachers and school directors to accommodate demands for gender-segregated sports and swimming classes principally after the fifth grade.[16] Within the DIK, however as well as in the measures that it generated, coeducational sports and swimming classes were univocally coupled with norms of gender equality, abstaining from these classes was considered a problematic deviation from these very norms. Ute Erdsiek-Rave (of the Social Democratic Party), then Minister for Education and Women in Schleswig-Holstein, stressed that the DIK should "send a signal" to Muslim parents to ensure that their children "naturally participate in classes and swimming lessons."[17] The main goal here was to gently but authoritatively convince Muslims through dialogue that it was better for their own sake to participate in all classes, and to reshape their bodily practices and inner dispositions so that they could become compatible with social conventions that were considered healthy and normal.

A more disciplining incentive occurred, however, when the former head of the Muslim Council (*Koordinierungsrat der Muslime in Deutschland*), Axel Ayyub Köhler, emphasized that, for reasons of modesty, mixed sports classes should be a matter of negotiation. More controversially, in an interview in *Die Zeit*, Köhler argued that Islamic federations would provide legal support for Muslim parents and students if they preferred gender-segregated sports classes, stating and advocating what he called "pragmatic solutions."[18] Köhler's statement provoked a public outcry (Cantzen 2007: 273). More importantly, it led Maria Böhmer, then national Commissioner for Integration and member of the DIK, to react fiercely:

> Cultural diversity is something very nice and enriching. But I want to clarify one thing: it ends at the point where our basic values and rights are questioned. Gender equality is one of these non-negotiable basic rights. It is expressed, among other things, in gender-mixed sports and swimming classes of boys and girls or in school trips. We will not allow a small minority of backward-oriented people to introduce the rules of their grandfathers.
>
> (Böhmer in *Deutschlandfunk*, May 3, 2007)

Repercussions of the notion of the subject as being integrated only if she reveals her bodily conformity to the nation's ideals arose more recently. In a press conference at the integration summit (*Integrationsgipfel*) of 2018 the then federal delegate for integration, Annette Widmann-Mauz, repeated that participation in sports and swimming classes was central feature of integration.[19] But let us move to Böhmer's statement: On a general point, Böhmer's discourse reveals the dominant understanding of cultural and religious plurality in Germany to which I alluded in Chapter 1. The coupling of *values* and *rights*, and the demarcation of how Muslims should embody gender equality, shows the extent to which the acceptance of cultural and religious plurality functions conditionally and is intrinsically tied to relations of power. Böhmer's emphasis on cultural diversity as "something very nice and enriching," indeed, echoes Slavoj Zizek's characterization of liberal multicultural politics as, more generally, based on and enabled by a division between the "antiseptic Other" and the "concrete Other" (1998). The "antiseptic Other" easily merges into folkloristic conceptions of "culture." Cultural plurality is celebrated as an enrichment as long as it is void of normative conflicts, and as long as "cultural richness" does not question consensual and mainly unmarked understandings of dominant social conventions. The concrete Other, in turn, is more difficult to "accommodate" because she reveals concreteness by raising uncomfortable claims to liberal pluralism. In her embodied concreteness the concrete Other thus brings to the fore imbalanced power structures entailed in the very decision of when culture is considered enriching or conflictual, and thus denies the quest to be absorbable into a dominant and hegemonic framework of plurality. Both Böhmer's statement and the more civic pedagogical tones that have accompanied the dialogical encounter in the DIK, hence, symptomatically mirror the prescriptive political rationalities of state-organized integration programs.

Before moving closer to the implications of Böhmer's coupling of rights and values, I find it useful to remind in this context that until the mid-nineteenth century, physical education was part of state education programs that were exclusively reserved for men. They were closely related to the military, and national projects of physical fitness and body disciplining. Throughout the early twentieth century, Germany's national project was buttressed by new doctrines of state-building through education. These asserted that education was the state's "chief industry" of which sports lessons were part of the cultivation of healthy, disciplined, and docile bodies. Sports in its institutionalized and educational components had thus served as both the physical subjection of children and young adults to common corporeal norms, and as ideals for the individual development of the child-citizen's physical abilities (e.g. Kirk 1994; Kirk and Spiller 1994).

In the late nineteenth century, women were incorporated into these nationalizing projects and civilizing body techniques, yet not without initial contestations (Pfister 1998). Both proponents of female physical education and those who warned against it as a transgression of ideals of femininity contributed to the incitement of a discourse about the role of the female body in national and civilizing projects. These discussions demonstrate that both the aim to liberate the female body and the attempt to prevent her from participating in sports activities entailed modes of discipline, even if located on different registers (Pfister 1998).

Moreover, as a matter of fact, sports classes in public schools in Germany remained gender-segregated until the early 1970s, when feminist pedagogues started to advocate against gender-segregated classes and argued that these would reinforce gender hierarchies. A decade later, however, some of the same feminists voiced the critique that mixed classes reproduced gender stereotypes and reinforced sexist behavior among male students during classes (Kugelmann, Pfister, and Zipprig 2004; Scheffel 1996). These pedagogues argued that the structural inequalities between female and male students prevalent in educational institutions were mirrored and even partly reinforced in mixed sports classes (Kugelmann 1999). There are ongoing discussions in gender-sensitive psychology and pedagogy about whether segregated classes might be more beneficial for the success of girls in schools and whether coeducation might reproduce gender hierarchies (e.g. Kugelmann 1986; Kugelmann, Pfister, and Zipprich 2004; Schmolze 2007). These controversies themselves are instructive because they reveal how much the different perspectives on the (dis)advantages of gendered mixed sports classes entail complex grammars about notions of bodily conduct, notions of sexuality, and questions related to the effects of gender segregation or mixing more generally.

Whatever pedagogues have concluded on that matter, my point here is that sports in state schools (whether mixed or divided) have never been immune from gendered perspectives and body politics but rather mirror these very orders and debates, sometimes even in contradictory ways. The decision about when physical interactions are considered normal and when exceptional or deviant, in other words, depends on social, political, economic, and cultural conditions and conventions within which they are discussed and negotiated. The results are neither stable nor neutral, nor even ever uncontroversial. Interestingly, state schools in the federal states of Bavaria and Baden-Württemberg practice segregated sports lessons from the fifth grade onward. Although definitely influenced by Catholic traditions in these federal states, these regulations have not triggered any wider public controversy about gender equality or inequality put forward by a "minority of backward oriented people," as Böhmer had put it in her response to Köhler. The fact that gender equality is addressed in one case and not in the other touches, of course, upon assumptions about Muslims' sexuality and sensibilities. More precisely, it is premised on the view that Muslims' sexuality and related gender conceptions potentially contradict liberal norms and foster their gradual segregation from society at large.

Moreover, the question of when public authorities should intervene into the intimate sphere of the family, protected under the rule of law as "private," is a sensitive and troubling issue. Children are not just any category within the population. They are understood as vulnerable and susceptible to manipulation. This also explains the "sensitivity" surrounding the questions of corporality in public, and in state educational institutions more specifically. Children are at the center of the family, which in liberal thought is ideally protected as private, intimate, and hence outside of state interference. Yet, as numerous scholars have shown in different ways (Mahmood 2015; Scott Wallach 2019; Yuval-Davis 1997), even if imagined as prior to the nation and outside of state interference, the intimate life of the family, sexuality, and gender have never escaped state regulations and normative control but have been at the heart of nation-building. Considered as both attached to the private sphere of the family and the nation's next generation, children are in between parental authority and state governance. As issues as diverse as home schooling, mandatory vaccination, or child custody have shown, this tension engenders a set of essential questions, which have, in turn, provoked ongoing controversies within liberal thought and practice: Where does parental authority start and where should it end in order to protect the children's bodily integrity, or flourishing and push ideals of gender equality to be nurtured? Where should the state monopoly on children's education supplement or even supply parental authority for the child's well-being? To what extent should the state be entitled to prescribe bodily conventions of gender equality, and with which legitimacy and reasoning?

Given these controversial issues, the very public staging of an allegedly consistent moral order on the basis of which specific, that is, Islamic, justifications for modesty are politically delegitimized, works performatively: The coupling of gender equality with the adjustment to a particular understanding of bodily conduct is based on a notion of interaction and bodily display in public life, which gets contoured and normalized at the very moment in which bodily religious sensibilities of Muslims are turned into a political problem. This one-sided focus on potential gender inequalities resulting from an inadequate recourse to Islamic traditions thus contributes to the sharpening of the idea that gender equality necessitates the distinction from specific religious practices and that this has been univocally achieved in German society. Contestations can only emerge from "backward oriented Muslims" who justify their refusal to share majoritarian conventions of gender mixing on the basis of traditions that are external to the social imaginaries of Germany. The exceptionalizing gaze on *certain* religious sensibilities and practices is a discursive practice, which constructs "real" difference by naturalizing a putative consensus over basic constitutional principles, in our case, social conventions of bodily conduct and gender interactions in public.[20]

The call for the sexes to mix naturally and thereby adjust to acceptable social conventions symptomatically unloads the tensions entailed in constructing bodily norms by interrogating one-sidedly its delineated exceptions, in this case those justified with reference to modesty or Islamic piety. What is troubling for Böhmer about Köhler's articulated reservations against coeducational sports and swimming classes is that these concerns are justified with reference to traditions that are marked as *religious* in specific ways and that stand in competition with the state's ambitions to shape the corporeality and aspirations of minors. The objection to participating in mixed gender sports and swimming classes based on modes of justifications in Islamic normativity is thus not just any exception that could be accommodated on a similar level as others. It is, instead, considered a transgression of normative educational ideals in their embodied components, because these marked exceptions are attached to a whole set of sensibilities, which political authorities feel entitled to transform and eventually to discipline.

This example is therefore a landmark for the intimate relationship between political secularism as an organizing principle of state-religion relations and secularity as a contingent set of practices, sensibilities, and affects which are fed into state practices of governing religion. When deciding about the limits of legitimate religious expressions in public, state authorities not just rely on any abstract or formal separation of religion and politics. They also refer to a set of social conventions about what they consider the appropriate use of religion, including bodily practices in public. According to William E. Connolly it is precisely through such ongoing acts of articulating and defending secular political claims that the affective attachments are upheld that passionately bind people to a secular life (Connolly 2000). The recurrent discursive reiteration that Muslims can only be properly integrated, if they properly secularize indeed materializes Connolly's assumption about the performative nature of secular speech acts in liberal public spheres. For it is namely only through religious practices which are discursively constituted as some kind of abnormality that the secular national body (or more neutrally, the "constitutional state") can be contoured and stabilized. The marking of particular religious formations as illegitimate transgressions of conventional understandings of religion, or at least as practices that need to be justified in a secular vocabulary in this sense is a secular practice.

The denouncement of bodily practices as incompatible with these liberal democratic principles, indeed, reveals embodied components of liberal-secular orders and brings us back the subtle corporeal inflections of integration discourses. It is no longer "culture," or an organically or ethnically construed "national entity," into which minoritized populations are asked to "integrate." Rather, it is the supposedly disembodied abstract liberal-secular order that structures the grammar of integration discourses. The specific focus on Muslim corporeal practices and, more generally, the recurrent coupling of sexuality, gender, and religion in integration discourses is not accidental. These spheres, rendered intimate and private in liberal thought, are the quintessential domains in which loyalty to the national body is both shaped and revealed corporeally. Similar to the technologies of knowledge production on the successes or failures of Muslim integration, discursive demarcations such as Böhmer's are therefore governmental techniques symptomatic of the ways in which certain populations are exceptionalized by literally being incorporated into the liberal body.

Finally, Böhmer's paternalistic and alarming tone symptomatically reveals the political authority's uncertainty regarding domains in which Muslims have started to challenge univocal and majoritarian interpretations of basic rights and norms using constitutional principles, most prominently that of religious freedom. In this sense, the DIK's entitlement to admonish Muslims who articulate uncomfortable demands reflects a more central semantic shift in the political state's assessment of Muslims in Germany. As observable in the lawsuits advocating for Muslims' right to ritual slaughter (Lavi 2009), or the right of teachers to wear a headscarf in state schools (Wiese 2008), political authorities started to emphasize their responsibility to regulate religious plurality precisely at the moment when Muslims began to demand spaces for Islamic practice through relying on basic constitutional principles. The head of the Islamic Council, Köhler, thus articulated loudly what had become a common, even if not always successful, practice in Germany, namely Muslim's adoption of basic legal principles (see Schiffauer 2010: 267).[21] Ironically, the often-repeated demand that Muslims should declare loyalty to the German constitutional order became insufficient precisely when they started to use these rights for "their own" purposes, that is, for those not immediately legible in hegemonic connotations of constitutional principles (see also Henkel 2008).[22]

In this regard the DIK is characteristic for the widely held assumption that Muslims' identification with Germany's constitutional principles is not sufficient for their "real" integration as sincerely engaged German citizens. Böhmer thus spells out what has become a conventional discursive practice, both in public discourse and in integration programs: the demand on Muslims to affirm loyalty beyond the realm of the law, and to share normative assumptions about the "good," which, according to liberal thought, are ideally detached from the domain of "rights." The appeal made to Muslims not merely to observe basic laws but also to share their ethical groundings reveals a governmental technique in which the state regulates ethical behavior, the conduct of life, and affective spheres of society—spheres which, according to basic liberal ideals, do not fall under the competence of the liberal state. Integration rationalized as recognition here functions as a source of responding to the liberal-secular state's legitimacy deficit, and as a response to the wide scope of interpretations provided by abstract liberal principles.

Grundgesetz Plus

Independently from public interpellations of Muslims, such as Böhmer's, the appeal for embodied loyalty became explicit in the preparatory meetings of the third plenary session of the DIK in 2008. During this, representatives of Muslim federations were asked to agree to a convention setting out a common basis of values, subsumed under the label of a "Community of German Values" (*deutsche Wertegemeinschaft*), beyond mere legal principles. This agreement was meant to build upon Muslim's simple profession of adherence to the German constitution, and comprised quite detailed requirements about social and religious conduct and codes of behavior. It required, for example, the renouncing of girls wearing headscarves in state primary schools, or, again, the participation of Muslim pupils in mixed swimming classes.[23] Throughout the DIK in working group sessions Muslims were thus asked to affirm this "something which unites us on a deeper human level," as Schäuble had put it when he "welcomed Muslims into the nation" (Peter 2010). The ethical substance of the communal order to which Muslims were asked to express their emotional attachment was also concretized in conversations behind the official scenes and documents published by the DIK. In a conversation with the former spokesperson of the *Islamic organization Milli Görüş* (IGMG) I was told, for example, that representatives of Islamic federations were asked to delete passages in the Qur'an which might encourage gender inequality.[24] These calls for shared values and embodied allegiance to the German constitution have been labeled "constitution plus" (*Grundgesetz Plus*).[25] Because some representatives of Islamic federations had refused to sign the first draft (see Hermani 2010: 114), the published version of the document on the Community of German Values, however, does not do much more than repeat constitutional principles in an accessible language.[26]

Therefore, I do not read Böhmer's indignation as an accidental departure from an otherwise inclusive and universally available set of individual liberties. Rather, it is a case in point for revealing the built-in embodied structures of liberal principles in a given polity on which measures of integration rest more generally. Böhmer materializes Schäuble's call for emotional attachments to the national community beyond formal constitutional principles, while at the same time praising the liberal-democratic order as the backbone for Muslim integration into German society. Such ambivalence is inscribed into liberal democratic orders, and into the politics of integration more broadly.

As the DIK shows, the promise of equal rights, political participation, and legal recognition of Muslims thus comes at a price: it puts those struggling for recognition under the auspices of the state's administration, and urges them to make their religious practice intelligible and governable according to conditions set elsewhere. The discussions around *Grundgesetz Plus* evince that these conditions are contingent, and the invitation to Muslims to turn into "German Muslims" can be postponed along loose and dynamic criteria. The liberal-secular matrix of integration discloses its prescriptive and embodied components especially when it comes to uncomfortable demands raised by minoritized groups whose speech acts or religious practices cannot necessarily be understood through the lens of normative ideals of internalized and privatized religiosity. It is precisely because these moral attachments of liberal-secular orders are not in the first place of a legal or formal kind that it is difficult to dismantle their discursive evocation as an enhancement of state sovereignty.

The DIK's substantiation of constitutional principles with norms of conduct and social conventions can therefore be read in two ways: either as illegitimately overstretching constitutional principles, or as discursively bringing to the fore the ethical and embodied contours of these principles themselves. In this latter reading, the move to fill abstract principles with a moral substance of (German) values does not so much betray liberal principles. Rather, it foregrounds the tensions of liberal assertions to state neutrality and the abstractedness of constitutional principles within a given national political order. According to this reading, the "ethical impregnation" (Habermas 1993: 181) of constitutional principles is then not merely revealed in the DIK because it is the state—and not civil society—that has been in charge of organizing and managing recognition. Rather, the tension between abstract formal liberal rights and their affective attachments is symptomatic of the powers involved in regulating these liberal freedoms.[27] In this regard, integration rationalized as state-managed recognition masks the role of the state in securing dominance over the interpretation of basic principles.

Unlike deliberative theorists, I would thus not argue that reiterations of the ethical impregnation of the German constitution put forward in the discussions on "Constitution Plus" circumvent the otherwise pure and all-inclusive nature of constitutional principles that are transformable according to societal dynamics and discursive exchange (e.g. Habermas 1993). Nor would I conclude that the DIK is actually not engaged in a "real" dialogue, in the terms of consensus-oriented deliberative theorists from Habermas to Benhabib. Rather, I assert that the framework of the liberal-secular constitutional order itself needs to be understood in its built-in and often subtle power structures and techniques. These become apparent only if we do not fall short of reading normative political theory as detached from concrete political practices.

Traps of Integration as Recognition

State-led measures like the DIK, that circumscribe Muslims into subjects of integration via their conditional recognition, pose a more general question which pertains to my analytical framework of governmentality in its relation to state sovereignty: what kind of relationship between Muslims as subjects of recognition and the state as its distributer is enacted in such political measures? There are several striking elements in this regard, which I would like to dwell on in the final section of this chapter. One is a paternalistic state that takes custody of those very subjects it deems, and constructs, as being in need to learn lessons on how to become truly "German Muslims." Another is a state that demonstrates the national body's inclusiveness by swearing "the people" into a consensus over the values they should share, the corporeal practices they should endorse, and the affective attachments to the liberal-democratic order they should cultivate. Most importantly, it is a state that rationalizes integration projects with recourse to dialogue, recognition, and the liberal-secular order as a basis of this endeavor.

The discussions around *Grundgesetz Plus* and Böhmer's concretization of it are indicative of a broader tension entailed in integration discourses, one that paradoxically sets apart the populations considered in need of integration while simultaneously absorbing them into a national body. This tension between recognition and absorption also alerts us to be cautious about the binary often drawn between the politics of assimilation and the politics of recognition—a sharp distinction that is also evoked rhetorically by liberal theorists of multicultural recognition (Markell 2003: Chapter 6). Especially because measures of minority recognition are linked to conditions that have an impact on the conduct of life, sensibilities, and religious practice, which they contribute to shape, they are ultimately not as dissimilar from assimilation as they appear at first glance. Markell writes in this vein:

> If the nationalist version of the project of sovereignty creates incentives toward assimilation, the multicultural version [...] creates incentives for people to frame claims about justice as claims for recognition on behalf of identifiable groups. That mode of address, after all, furthers the state's project of rendering the social world "legible" and governable: to appeal to the state for the recognition of one's own identity—to present oneself as knowledge—is already to offer the state the reciprocal recognition of its sovereignty that it demands.
>
> (2003: 31)

By focusing on the concerns of vulnerable minorities, the politics of recognition paradoxically reproduce the dichotomy between majority and minority, even if these politics are developed to compensate for the injustices that exist within liberal orders and their commitment to equality.[28]

> Multicultural exchanges of recognition [...] demand neither the overcoming of difference, nor its confinement to the private sphere; but they do require that it be observable and manageable: in short, recognizable. They aim to secure the sort of sovereignty James Scott associates with the administrative state, which does not sweep away difference but instead measures it, maps it, categorizes it, renders it "legible" and, sometimes, enforces certain limits on the acceptable expressions of cultural differences.
>
> (2003: 170)

Markell thus brings to the fore something that is central for understanding state-led recognition of minorities in its multifaceted techniques of power. The recognizing authority does not only asymmetrically interpellate the particularized minority in demand of recognition—in our case, political authorities inviting Muslims to state dialogue. At the same time the minority in demand of recognition needs to be rendered knowable within a specific political and moral order which remains untouched through the one-sided interrogation of the Other. The very process of recognition is thus predicated, and even dependent, on the construction and repetition of a moral norm, whose contours appear through the marking of the minority as exceptional and needing recognition.

The move from abstract norms to the moral attachments of these norms ("our values") reprises the strategy at work in the *Fördern und Fordern* paradigm, which runs through integration discourses since its inception. The burden is thereby placed on Muslims. They are called on to first reveal their affective endorsement of the fundamental norms and values of German society before they can even be considered as legitimate candidates in the struggle for recognition. It is *through* such acts of knowledge production and recognition that the state attempts to render intelligible and manageable the field of potentially deviating social differences, and not only through coercion, discipline, or misrecognition.

As interlocutors of state recognition, Muslims are thus subjected to the conditions which the state determines and deems necessary for their recognition. They are welcomed if they reveal their recognizability as Muslims in conformity with a contingent set of expectations of the German secular nation-state. They are disciplined if they question the terms of the conversation and raise demands or reveal embodied religious practices that political authorities consider an inadequate expansion of constitutional norms. The traps of integration as recognition also consist in the fact that the goal of recognition by the state is tempting because it promises emancipation from a subordinate position. Precisely because it is framed as the opposite of discrimination, discipline, or control, integration as recognition is an offer that Muslims almost unavoidably must accept. For any refusal to participate in the dialogue would be interpreted as yet another sign of their refusal to transparency and their segregation into "parallel societies" (cf. Schiffauer

2008b). Integration, even if conceptualized as recognition, therefore necessarily navigates between marking and dissolution, assimilation and segregation, and exceptionalization and normalization.

Because the struggle of recognition is always at the same time a struggle for recourses programs of integration as recognition tend to generate another trap: The call to speak in the name of a recognizable voice as an interlocutor of the state merges heterogeneous, horizontal and dynamic groups, movements, or actors into a vertical structure. In the struggle over the resources of recognition, this necessarily creates frictions among these very groups that are interpellated to represent themselves univocally. In her seminal genealogical reading of "minority management" in Western Europe, Anya Topolski (2018) brings to the fore the traps which this verticalization of state-minority relationships has provoked for Jewish minorities and, more recently for Muslims. Starting from current state attempts to create representative Islamic councils in different European contexts, Topolski traces these efforts back to the politico-theological structure of "intercession" or "mediation" (*shtadlanut*). She shows how Jewish communities tried to use this institution to gain favor with the ruling elites in order to achieve the desired inclusion. Since this mediation process required an intercessor in each case, Jews were split—especially in the course of the emergence of the nation-state in the nineteenth and twentieth centuries—into "good" (submissive and compliant) and "bad" (closed-minded and bound to religious traditions) ones. For Topolski these provoked frictions as part and parcel of a power structure which finds repercussions in today's minority management of Muslims (ibid.: 2189).

Indeed, the state's search for Muslim interlocutors for state-organized dialogue in the DIK, for example, has by no means contributed to the anticipated goal of creating a representative Muslim spokesperson (not a corporative body!), while maintaining Muslim's internal diversity. On the contrary, it has reinforced frictions among Muslims who were classified in advance as representatives of specific Muslim branches (liberal, secular, critical of Islam, conservative, orthodox). These frictions also became apparent in the course of the DIK when the "critics of Islam" ("*Islamkritiker*"), more recently "secular Muslims," denounced Muslims organized in mosque movements for their backwardness.[29] Representatives of Islamic federations, in turn, complained that they would not get the same access to the German public sphere as these secular Muslims (Tezcan 2012). The state's offer to foster integration thus potentially contributes to the displacement of identification of marginalized groups with state authority, as different fractions claim to speak for the entire "Muslim community" and discredit each other of not adequately representing Islam. If classificatory systems of knowledge production divide Muslim religiosity into manageable ideal types, integration measures, framed as recognition potentially contribute to stabilize the self-labeling as real types.

To conclude, we can put aside the overt assimilationist moves prevalent in such measures, and acknowledge that they have contributed to institutionalizing a structured conversation between the state and Muslims. However, even these inclusive components of integration put to the fore the ambivalence between state neutrality *and* the state regulation of religion in public and private life, which is characteristic of the secular state more generally. Through the exclusive focus on Islam as the epicenter of integration politics, the DIK has publicly staged this ambivalence while not tiring of constantly reiterating its outstanding achievements.

5

Blood, Race, Religion: Governing through Discipline

With the focus on knowledge production and political recognition, I have so far investigated two political rationalities of integration politics in which the promise to include Muslims into the nation operates on the premise of preformatted, and yet contingent ideals of proper religion. In both cases, the liberal-secular matrix of integration functions with paralegal, at times quasi-pedagogical incentives, in one case through inspection and classification of religious minorities, in the other through the promise of their conditional recognition. As critical migration studies scholarship throughout Europe has shown, however, measures of integration have simultaneously revealed more overt disciplinary incentives. Scholars have termed these disciplinary components of integration as a "civic turn" (Meer, Mortisen, Faas, and Witte 2015) or a "neo-nationalization" (Schinkel 2017: 232) in the politics of dealing with the growing plurality caused by global migration. Willem Schinkel, for example, contends that integration discourses fostered a shift from a "relative focus on formal citizenship to an emphasis on moral citizenship" (Schinkel 2017: 197). Moral citizenship, Schinkel clarifies, entails an "extra-legal normative concept of the good citizen" (ibid.: 198). For that matter he speaks about an equalization between "integration" and "citizenship," or rather the definition of "integration" as "citizenship." The introduction of citizenship or integration tests across Europe figures as prominent examples for this trend. Because they also operate as legal instruments, these tests, moreover, provide a salient case for the convergence of Schinkel's distinction between "formal" and "moral citizenship."

In academic discussions, scholars have often distinguished between those variants of citizenship tests that transmit knowledge and those that target the inner attitudes of applicants toward the constitutional order. In their study of naturalization practices, Christian Joppke and Rainer Bauböck (2010) distinguish, for example, between legitimate, that is to say "liberal," forms of interrogations, and what they call "illiberal" practices, that is citizenship tests that target the candidate's inner loyalty to the normative foundations of the political orders within which they seek to be naturalized. Similarly, Liav Orgad differentiates "thick," that is, culture-oriented, from liberal-democratic versions of citizenship tests. He argues that many European countries throughout the early 2000s moved illegitimately toward cultural assimilation as a prerequisite for admission (Orgad 2010: 98f.). In turn, the requirement to subscribe to constitutional principles in order to obtain citizenship in a specific country, Orgad argues, is a legitimate form of "national constitutionalism." Investigating Germany, more specifically, political theorist Tine Stein (2008: 48) goes a step further and defends the introduction of integration classes for candidates for German citizenship as a constructive tool. Inspired by Habermas's idea of "constitutional patriotism," Stein stresses that such classes could provide a suitable forum for a discursive exchange on constitutional principles. In the spirit of cultivating the virtues of citizenry, she argues, this process could eventually contribute to the immigrant's "inner affirmation" of these principles.[1]

All scholars share the view that interrogating future citizens about their *knowledge* of universal liberal principles and their implementation into national constitutions conforms to the standards of liberal democracies. Testing mindsets and inner attitudes or requiring the cultural identification according to these liberal theorists instead transgresses the state's guarantee to neutrality, especially when the liberal state is conceptualized as necessarily abstaining from issues of the good of its citizens. In this view, it is thus liberally justifiable in a citizenship regime predominantly based on birthright to interrogate immigrants and candidates for naturalization both about their knowledge of political rights and duties and about society's cultural conventions. The "illiberal" move comes with those tests that prescribe and target "attitudes."

My aim in this chapter is not to join these normative discussions on the dualities between civic inclusion versus ethnic exclusion and liberal versus blood-based notions of citizenship. I have recalled these conventional distinctions because I understand them as articulations of an inherent tension that liberal theorists often tend to discard. The distinctions between political and ethnic conceptions of nationhood, as well as liberal and illiberal forms of testing future citizens, rest on some deeper shortcomings of liberal theory. In their attempt to rescue the purity of liberal principles, liberal theorists often overlook the discursive productions of these very principles as dividing practices *within* a framework bound by the nation-state, and its specific legacies of dealing with membership and belonging, especially for those populations that are discursively and sometimes even formally constituted as not fully belonging to the nation. Moreover, such shortcomings are similar to the conventional distinction between ancestral and territorial routes to membership of a nation.[2] Divisions between liberally justifiable and non-justifiable practices of testing future citizens thus fail to address the deep-seated predicaments of nationality and citizenship in immigrant societies. Importantly, they conceal instead the exclusionary workings of citizenship itself, which a closer reading of the political rationalities of such tests would allow us to dismantle.

A critical perspective of the productive force of political liberalism and secularism, therefore, cannot distinguish between pure and impure forms of liberal values. Rather, it has to investigate how liberal principles are concretely articulated within and beyond the regulation of formal membership in a given political order. The testing of knowledge about the nation or the promotion of *constitutional* rather than *national* patriotism, does not, in other words, remedy some of the integral problems of political liberalism in a nation-state framework.

In this chapter, I am thus neither concerned with the question of whether or not the tests transgress liberal principles, nor with whether or not they are constitutionally dubious. Instead, I use them as sites to unpack their *functionalities* within the paradigm of integration organized by a liberal-secular matrix. I inquire into two examples of citizenship tests, one that examines constitutional loyalty and one that tests knowledge. My analysis is guided by two main arguments. On the one hand, I claim that these governmental practices of integration are productive of a specific notion of Germanness as liberal, progressive, and secular *through* the inspection of would-be citizens who are conceptualized as potentially unruly and deviating from liberal-secular norms. Thereby the legacy of race and blood both reappears and is occluded by the adoption of a liberal vocabulary that distinguishes the liberal (German) core from its illiberal (Muslim) margin. Turning to one of my central threads in this book, on the other hand, I read these tests as a resurgence of discipline and state sovereignty within the field of governmentality. I therefore investigate the very fabric of such tests, their political constructions of the national body, and the visceral components of how they enact constitutional loyalty of future citizens. Before dwelling into the two examples of citizenship test, it is important to recall the racial legacy of German nationality laws.

Blood-Based Nationhood

Nationhood and citizenship regulations in Germany had been based on ethnicity and were entrenched with ideologies of blood, race, and descent. The very term "kinship of the state" (*Staatsangehörigkeit*) instead of "citizenship of the state" (*Staatsbürgerschaft*) suggests a specific notion of nationhood that approximates that of kinship. This understanding has also deeply molded the legal rulings and principles of citizenship and naturalization since the unification of German territories into the Reichsgesetz of 1913.[3] From that moment onward nationality was almost exclusively defined by the principle of right of blood (*jus sanguinis*). It is important to remind that the few federal states which had adopted elements of *jus soli* prior to the unified Nationality Code of 1913 severely controlled processes of naturalization. Belonging to the Catholic Church or abstaining from military service, for example, could have been reasons for the refusal of naturalization (Gosewinkel 2001: Chapters 4.6 and 4.7). Historian of citizenship Dieter Gosewinkel also mentions a distinctive anti-Polish and anti-Jewish naturalization policy characterizing the German *Kaiserreich* (ibid.: 279) and remarks: "The nation predominantly constitutes itself through the definition and rejection of common enemies" (ibid.: 247). The selective control of naturalization is thus not entirely unprecedented in German history. Structural and legal divisions between friends and enemies have functioned cyclically to restate blood or moral purity of the German nation.

Jus sanguinis was, of course, not invented through during the nation-state formation but inherited from Roman law. In the formation of the German nation-state, German politicians and legal authorities, however, extended the principle of blood to turn it into a racial and exclusionary category of membership (Brubaker 1992; El-Tayeb 2001; Gosewinkel 2001) to the extent that elements of birthright were abolished entirely in 1913, and was only marginally reintroduced after 1945.

Historians of citizenship and nationhood often evoke the lateness of the creation of the German nation-state as one central reason for its ethnically driven conception of nationhood that was close to the understanding of the nation as bound by blood and destiny (Brubaker 1992; Gosewinkel 2001; Plessner 1974). Germany's lack of territorial unity, accordingly, created a mystical bond, justified either by the Herderian idea of a *Kulturnation* (nation by culture) or by openly racist justifications of Germanic superiority. The legal exclusivity of citizenship that was extracted from both justifications was directed at Polish immigrants outside of Germany and at Jews within German territories. Gosewinkel (2001) contends that the harshness of the 1913 law can only be understood if we account for imperialism and the threats to "racial purity" that it brought about. The expansiveness of the German *Kaiserreich* and its African colonies elicited pertinent debates about access to German nationality. The idea of the strengthening of blood was thus central to the protection of the purity of German nationhood from infiltration by indigenous people in the colonies (*Eingeborene*) or of people of "mixed blood" (*Mischlinge*) (Gosewinkel 2001: 121; see also El-Tayeb 2001: Chapter 3).

Remarkably, despite numerous efforts to ban race from the German political and public landscape after 1945, as shown in Chapter 2, the legal institution of a racially justified distinction between native Germans and foreigners remained untouched and largely unchallenged until very recently. Moreover, apart from minor introductions of elements of *jus soli*, the law from 1913 was readopted after 1945. This law also continued a tradition that protected the German nationality of "native Germans" and their ancestors who had emigrated or who were displaced after the Second World War. Analyzing the history of the relationship between the emergence of the German nation-state and its ethno-cultural, differential understandings of nationhood, Rogers Brubaker summarizes that Germany's definition of citizenship has been "remarkably open to ethnic German immigrants from Eastern Europe and the Soviet Union, but remarkably closed to non-German immigrants" (Brubaker

1992: 3; emphasis added, see also Gosewinkel 2001: 259). Uli Linke more explicitly reads the legal tradition of German citizenship as codifications of an understanding of nationhood obsessed with race, whiteness, and blood: "Deeply embedded in Germany's imperial history, the blood-principle of citizenship is defined by racial premises, which were established at the turn of the century to deny colonial subjects inheritance and voting rights" (Linke 1999: 122; see also El-Tayeb 2001: Chapter 3).

It was only in 2000 that the nationality code was reformed and that elements of *jus soli* (birthright) were strengthened.[4] This reform was largely celebrated as a turn in the right direction toward a politically defined national community that is open to immigration. Sociologists of immigration, therefore, interpreted the reform as a central adjustment of Germany to the liberal standards of immigration policies or as the right move toward integration (Bade and Bommes 2004; Heckmann 2014). Strangely enough, the inception of citizenship tests as a measure of reintroducing barriers to equal membership and discursively demarcating the borders of the nation has not become a central topic for scholars of migration in Germany.

Investigating Suspicious Muslims

The federal state of Baden-Württemberg adopted its own citizenship test (in the following: BW-test) in 2006. Its legal basis was Article 10.1 of the 2000 Nationality Code which states that the applicant has to "affirm the liberal-democratic order and to claim that s/he does not follow or support or has not followed or supported tendencies that are oriented against the democratic basic order, the existence or the security of the state or a federal state (*Bundesland*)."[5] This test is unprecedented in that with it the practice of marking populations as suspicious and eventually testing their loyalty to the nation-state became formalized for the first time, and at the same time translated into a vocabulary that conforms to the liberal-democratic order as its backbone. The test, cryptically entitled "An Interview Guide for the Naturalization Authorities. Commitment to the liberal-democratic basic order according to the Nationality Code,"[6] targeted one group of immigrants, defined as applicants from the fifty-seven member states of the Islamic Conference.

The measure was harshly criticized by public opinion and legal scholars as potentially violating the very liberal principles of the German constitution that were supposed to be protected.[7] Much of the criticism also focused on the inefficiency of the measure, especially because of the largely suggestive character of the questionnaire, and because the candidates could access the questions prior to the test and therefore prepare for it. In addition, legal scholars criticized the test because it was addressed only to immigrants from Islamic countries, and because the testing of inner attitudes was considered unconstitutional.[8] Interestingly enough, what was much less questioned was the very idea that the state should and could lay claim to the constitutional loyalty of immigrants. Hence it was not so much the goal of the testing itself but rather its methods that were up for debate. It is, therefore, not accidental that the BW-test, in use from 2006 to 2011, laid the groundwork for similar tests in other federal states (Björk 2011), as well as for the nationwide test adopted in 2008 to which I will turn later in this chapter.

A Civil Servant's Confession

Rainer Grell (2006), the main public official responsible for the BW-test, provided one of the most intriguing documents that revealed its backstory and underlying reasoning.[9] Grell is a retired lawyer who worked as the senior legal secretary of Baden-Württemberg's department for nationality law (Referat Staatsangehörigkeitsrecht). His 233-page online text, *Imagination and Truth. The Story of the "Muslim Test" in Baden-Württemberg* tells us a lot about the authority of senior civil servants (*Beamte*) to draft and legally endorse measures with far-reaching consequences. The text thus provides a useful indication of the social life of this particular measure. Moreover, the report demonstrates on a microscopic level how a specific kind of expert knowledge on Islam and Muslims, that I analyzed in Chapter 3, has found its way to state officials who insinuate the intervention into the lives of people regarded as suspect.

The rhetoric of the document is also compelling in its navigation between the technocratic language characteristic of official state documents, and a distinctively personal and subjective narrative. This navigation, indeed, reflects the whole initiative of the BW-test as marked by an inherent tension between the allegedly distant and neutral "view from nowhere" and the constant shift to a largely subjective assessment by officially neutral and objective civil servants. Grell's report, moreover, shows that the test was not introduced to mobilize voters primarily, as various commentators argued.[10] Rather, it stemmed from the personal concern of this civil servant who gained influence through his political function.[11] Despite his status as a former state bureaucrat, Grell, indeed, discards all professional confidentiality by openly putting on the table what had been discussed behind the official curtains of the Ministry of the Interior. While admitting that his text was a personal account, he concretizes, and sometimes also contradicts, what is found in the official documents. For example, he does not maintain confidentiality about why the test was initially designed for people addressed as Muslims only, bluntly stating: "Muslims are our main problem group," (2006: 150) and repeatedly emphasizing how alarmed he felt by the growing Islamization of Germany: "May we, can we, should we, allow Germany to be gradually, but not at all imperceptibly, turned into an Islamic society, into an Islamic state?" (2006: 23).

One of the driving forces for Grell's identification of Muslims as the main problem for the liberal constitutional order of Germany is rooted in his individual inquiries into popular scientific readings about Islam's potential opposition to liberal democracy. Grell's list of references is made up of best sellers ranging from journalistic accounts like those of Oriana Fallaci to the social-scientific assessments of Bassam Tibi to Islamic Studies scholars such as Tilman Nagel. In one way or another, all of Grell's quoted studies repeat the recurrent juxtaposition of Islam and liberal democracy as two opposed holistic containers. The diagnoses vary from the attestation of an unbridgeable difference (Nagel) to the call for the reactivation of Islam's rationalistic tradition (Tibi). The variety notwithstanding, the selection of expert scientific knowledge reinforces Grell's suspicion about the potential incompatibility between Islamic norms and the German constitution.

What is more interesting for my concern is Grell's main explanation for initiating the citizenship test. His impulse to develop the test, Grell tells us, was triggered by an article in 2003 by Michael Bertrams, then President of the administrative court in Münster. In that article, Bertrams raises doubt about a veiled teacher's loyalty to "our constitution and its values" (Bertrams 2003).[12] Animated by Bertrams's reasoning, Grell notes that if the affirmation of the German constitution at the local level of a state school was questioned by constitutional lawyers, this skepticism should hold more generally for "the related affirmation of a candidate applying for German citizenship" (Grell 2006: 63).[13]

Unsurprisingly, Grell acclaims his test not as a measure that should facilitate legal integration via the acquisition of citizenship rights. Instead, he understands integration as some kind of prize to be gained at the end of the applicant's successful display of her "sincerity of the affirmation to the liberal-democratic order, as stated in the nationality code (§ 10 Abs. 1 Satz 1 Nr. 1 StAG)" (ibid.: 115). As an inherently porous, ambivalent, and strongly emotional category, loyalty to what is recurrently qualified as the liberal-democratic order becomes a variably shifting enterprise. What kinds of affective ties to the abstract universal constitution are necessary so as to not fall under the radar of state examination? What kinds of emotions are set into motion in that mode of inspection? While Grell does not concretize how loyalty to the constitution can be properly disclosed, or why it should be a measurable attribute at all, we learn at least that the lack of loyalty is potentially expressed through an individual's adherence to Islam. Yet, Grell adds: "Since nobody can see if a Muslim applicant ascribes to a traditional understanding of the Qur'an, or to the enlightened so-called Euro-Islam, because of this difficulty, there is general doubt. I said a general doubt, note well, not more than a doubt. And this [doubt] should be dispelled in the interview [between the applicant and officers]" (2006: 122, translation mine). Grell fills the vagueness of the notion of loyalty to the constitution with similarly vague attributes such as "traditional," "enlightened," and "European." The term "traditional" is occasionally replaced with "orthodox," "conservative," and "fundamentalist," while "enlightened" is equated with "secular" (ibid.: 71).

Recapitulating how race and religion operate as interwoven categories of classification and examination in this integration measure, the act of determining everybody with migration backgrounds from Islamic countries as naturally "Muslim," and as potentially suspect, is an obvious case for the racial inflictions of citizenship regulations: While Grell asks Muslims to adopt the norms and values of liberal freedoms instead of referring to an ethnically bound notion of Germanness, it is their "descent" that determines them as Muslims and hence subjects of suspicion. At the same time Grell's argumentation reveals the close interplay of race and religion in that his racializing endeavor entails a system of internal classification, which categorizes and hierarchically ranks Muslims by the degree of their commitment to Islam. With a strong commitment to Islam, one's sincere affirmation to the liberal-democratic order is unlikely. Underneath this classificatory scheme in which "traditional," "conservative," "orthodox," or "fundamentalist" is used as a code for "bad religion" (Vial 2016: 216) lurks the prototype of "good religion," enlightened, European, and by definition, in accordance with liberal-democratic principles, and therefore immune to closer examination. The nineteenth-century calls directed at Jews to privatize their religious markers, and to become publicly invisible, as Jews, in order to be termed "assimilated," is here reconfigured in the call to be identifiable as a "Euro-Muslim."[14] The test thereby translates the scheme of distant knowledge-gathering according to which Muslims' strong commitment to Islam is correlated with their lack of integration into political action. The loose and sweeping ingredients of good and bad religion have thus moved from the domain of academic knowledge production into the domain of arbitrary state power.

Ironically, Grell himself recalls Germany's violent history of forced assimilation and extinction by devoting one part of his introduction to Michael Wieck. Wieck—a musician and writer—was invited to write the "Foreword by a Jew," which, incidentally, was followed by the "Foreword by a Christian." Wieck praises Grell's courage for taking action against the "threatening menace of terror by Islamic fundamentalists everywhere" (Wieck in Grell 2006: 13). Particularly worth noting here is Wieck's paternalistic tone toward Muslims in light of his own sufferings under the Nazi regime:

> The many non-problematic and peace-loving Muslims in the Federal Republic of Germany are conflicted in loyalty, and should not be left alone. How should they decide, given that on many issues their dogmas are not compatible with our constitution? Shouldn't *we help them*, and shouldn't we delimit more straightforwardly and more clearly for all, but especially for those who are willing to *assimilate* [*assimilationswillig*], what religious freedom is in all domains in which religious prescriptions about lifestyle contradict the constitution? For Jews and Christians this would not be a major problem.
>
> (Wieck in Grell 2006: 13, emphasis added, translation mine)

Alongside the abovementioned interlocutors, Necla Kelek, former member of the DIK and a founding figure of the initiative "Secular Islam," stands out as a central advisor on the BW-test as she drafted the questionnaire. Grell mentions that he was particularly inspired by Kelek's (2005) bestselling book *The Foreign Bride* (*Die fremde Braut* (Grell 2006: 68). Addressing the issue of forced and arranged marriages in the context of Germany and Turkey this inquiry navigates between a sociological study of women's experiences and an outward accusation of Islam as being the central motor for backward and oppressive regimes of kinship and marriage.

There would be a lot more to say about such bestsellers and their potency to inform the masses about the problems and failures of Islam. My point here is, however, a different one. What I find worth emphasizing is that the inclusion of such "voices from within" into the state apparatus of integration measures is symptomatic of how expert knowledge is selectively distributed and fed into political measures. Moreover, it also reveals the close interconnections between state and civil society actors, and further confirms my point that the state is not an a-priori given but is effected and legitimized by such interconnections—in this case, Muslims providing expertise about how to examine and control fellow Muslims. It is in this vein that Grell emphasizes that "without books like 'The Foreign Bride' or 'The Lost Sons' [*Die verlorenen Söhne*] I would not have dared to think, not even to mention to spell out certain of my thoughts" (ibid.: 5). Grell proudly adds that Kelek was "spontaneously ready to support us, without even mentioning a word about an honorarium (her entire participation as an advisor to the citizenship test was free)" (ibid.: 68).[15]

Membership Speech Acts

Despite the peculiarity of the arrangement of his arguments and the mixture of his technocratic and colloquial style, Grell's personal inquiry into what he identifies as "our Muslim problem," his "doubts" gradually entered into the official statements that justified the BW-test. Given the web of experts, advisors, and personal interlocutors on whom Grell relies, it is important to bear in mind that this former civil servant is merely the carrier but not the perpetrator of the virulent discourse about Muslim's sincere loyalties to the liberal constitution or lack thereof. It is useful in this regard to recall some of Judith Butler's observations on the performativity of speech acts, especially in her analysis of hate speech (Butler 1997). Relying on Austin's speech act theory, Butler distinguishes between "perlocutionary" and "illocutionary" kinds of doing things with words. While perlocutionary acts recall a discursive repertoire prior to the articulation, illocutionary acts imply the transitive act of speaking, in which social reality is put into effect through speech (including its unintended effects) (see Butler 1997: 51).

If we analyze the inception of the Baden-Württemberg citizenship test in terms of performative speech acts that not only name a social subject ("Muslim") but also partly constitute this very subject as potentially deviant, unruly, and disloyal through disciplining forms of interpellation, it would be misleading to single out Grell as the only perpetrator of this discourse. Of course, the architects of the test partly act as sovereign speakers, especially because they speak in and through the name of the state. Their speech acts are, however, situated in a broader discursive arena, and they are reiterated and performed at an official level. The discourse on what constitutes the nation and how "Euro-Muslims" are to be manufactured is thus not mere speech. As a speech *act* this discourse performatively orders and divides society into an unmarked population of native Germans, based on an invisible Christianity inscribed into the secular social and political order, and a religiously marked subpopulation that is turned into a problem that needs to be addressed.

We therefore have to be attentive both to the discursive transitivity *and* the historicity of speech acts that name, classify, and interrogate certain kinds of populations. The interpellation to speak and act as a Muslim, and to justify oneself in that very subject position along a classificatory scheme of good and bad religion, reenacts a discursive order that has already been in place for decades, as I showed in the previous chapters. The discursive harm enacted by speakers like Grell reiterates discursive formations, which are institutionally anchored, and which reference deeper stocks of knowledge. Grell relies on a classifying scheme, which divides and hierarchizes people into sub-groups belonging to "good religion" ("Euro-Muslims") and "bad religion" ("traditional Muslims"), and so evokes and performs the interconnection between a racial and secular structure of the German nation-state. Let us recall from the first chapter C. H. Becker's deliberations on how Islam could be made compatible with European standards of secularized religiosity during the peak of German imperialism. The notion of "Euro-Islam" had indeed already been coined before sizable numbers of Muslims settled into Europe, and before contemporary scholars of Islam in conversation with political authorities molded their visions for a Euro-Islamic fusion (cf. Mavelli 2012; Tezcan 2012: Chapter 1). What makes Grell's interpellation particularly compelling in this case is that it is articulated in the voice of a state representative. It thereby performatively enhances the authority of the state to mark, inspect, transform, and eventually eliminate certain forms of life and belonging that are deemed lacking constitutional loyalty.

The speech act that turns Muslims into potentially problematic and testable objects simultaneously constitutes a community of civilized and loyal citizens, who are paradoxically both abstract (liberal democratic) and concrete (native Germans). The interpellation of the marked Muslim body (configured in the veiled teacher whose constitutional loyalty is found wanting) unmarks the body politic and unites all those who question the loyalty of the bodied other. Alluding to a similar relationship in incidents of hate speech, Butler contends: "The speaker who utters the racial slur is thus citing that slur, making linguistic community with a history of speakers" (1997: 52). Grell is, in other words, merely the bearer of a discourse which translates the vague category of constitutional loyalty of a minoritized population into a tangible and measurable feature. Most importantly, the speech act by which the loyalty of Muslims is questioned simultaneously enlarges the scope of governmental interventions.

Testing Loyalty

The dividing scheme between a liberal-secular order and a marked Muslim body (personified in the covered teacher) further materializes in the questionnaire. The architects of the citizenship test translated Grell's unspecified suspicion into questions, which translate the common basis of the constitution into social conventions and in specific kinds of life conduct. After a long passage on Germany's constitutional order and a set of instructions about the necessity of declaring one's loyalty to that order, the applicant is confronted with a total of thirty questions.[16] These are clustered under different themes, and range from the applicant's sympathy for, or membership of, Islamic movements that are currently under secret service surveillance to their potential ambition to subvert the political system, or their potential anti-Semitic attitudes.[17] In the following I will zoom a bit closer into those questions that focus on the applicant's conduct of life and religious sensibilities, which dominate the questionnaire. It is in this domain, and especially in regard to gender and sexuality, that the dividing line between liberal-secular and Islamic norms of conduct is most pertinently spelled out. Here are some salient examples which provide a taste of the intrusive character of the questionnaire:

- What do you think about the statement that a woman has to obey her husband and that he can beat her if she disobeys? (Question 6)
- Do you think that it is appropriate to keep one's daughter from leaving the house, in order to prevent her from breaking "honor rules"? (Question 7)
- Do you consider it progressive for men and women to be equal in Germany under the law? What should the state do, in your opinion, if men do not accept this? (Question 9)
- We often hear that parents do not allow their fully grown up daughters to work in certain professions. How do you relate personally to this behavior? What would you do if your daughter married a man of a different faith or if she wanted to be trained in a profession that you did not like? (Question 13)
- What do you think about the fact that some parents force their children into marriage? Do you think that such marriages are compatible with human dignity? (Question 14)
- In Germany, sports and swimming lessons are part of the normal school curriculum. Would you let your daughter participate in these? If not, why? (Question 15)
- *In the case of female applicants*: Your daughter wants to be dressed like other German girls and women but your husband is against it. What do you do? (Question 18)

The strongly suggestive and stereotyped character of such questions has often been emphasized (e.g. Bahners 2011; Michalowski 2011). It is also obvious that in their ambiguity and broadness the questions provoke counterquestions, instead of leading to the expected clear-cut answers. In light of my analytical framework, however, my primary concern is not whether what these questions presuppose about the sexuality and gender norms of Muslims, or non-Muslims, is correct or not. I am more concerned with the fact that these presumptions have penetrated the walls of state bureaucracy and have turned into instruments for the inspection and control of membership. While such questions tell us nothing about the complex social realities of gender norms and conceptions of sexuality by Muslims or non-Muslims in Germany, they have much to tell us about the efficiency of the production, circulation, and discursive stabilization of the knowledge about these norms.

As we saw in the previous chapters, commissioned studies about Muslim integration take the discursive circulation of Islam as the main cause of integration deficits as a starting point for scientific investigation. Meanwhile, state-organized recognition measures request loyalty to a thickened ideal of the liberal constitution as a prerequisite for Muslim integration. The BW-citizenship test, in turn, dramatizes such discourses by translating them into empirical evidence that forms the basis of a legal rationality of state intervention. What is similarly revealing is how this knowledge is coupled with presuppositions about how constitutional principles trickle down to conventionalized forms of life conduct that are considered to be shared unanimously by all native non-Muslim Germans.

It is thus through the moral judgments and assumptions about the *deviance* of Muslims from liberal norms that a community of liberal citizens is discursively constituted. The testable loyalty to the constitution "and its values" (remember "Constitution Plus") is here concretized by social conventions like mixed swimming classes in school, dress norms for "German girls and women," or marriage conventions. Muslims are compelled to situate themselves within the underlying story of progressive liberal norms and values. The divisive practice of juxtaposing liberal forms of sexuality and gender conceptions and those deviating from this liberal prescriptive norm, are thus intimately bound to a specific temporality, which Ruth Mas has framed as "secular time" (2011). The casting of problematic gender norms for Muslims functions as part of a developmental narrative that portrays and produces a coherent image of the normal German citizen. If we pose the speech act question, what do such questions want, the answer would be that they want Muslims to become like we imagine ourselves to be: ripped away from "bad religion" and transformed into liberally minded subjects of freedom.

More importantly, the urgency with which the state feels entitled to supervise and control the social conventions of particular populations tells us much about the intrusive character of liberal state power, and its assumptions about how properly free subjects should potentially behave and look like. This scheme of contrasting Muslim gender norms as illiberal with liberal achievements of gender equality is well known from public controversies, especially about Muslim corporeal practices and the efforts to regulate them legally (Amir-Moazami 2007a, 2016; Lavi 2009). What the questionnaire shows is how these discourses have nurtured state-led integration measures, and have turned into a solid basis of interrogation.

This state-managed inspection of Muslims acquires an interesting twist when read against the background of the principle of ethnic belonging to the nation that has characterized the German citizenship regime since the formation of the nation-state. The central criterion for becoming a German citizen is no longer simply based on descent, even if *jus sanguinis* is still the central category that determines citizenship. Because of the strengthening of *jus soli*, in principal it is enough, however, to agree to the politically (and not ethnically) defined community to be eligible for German nationality. Constitutional principles on which this political community is formally based are, however, ambiguous, abstract, and essentially contested. This initiative can therefore be read as an attempt to rescue the moral substance of constitutional norms in light of their principled openness to a plurality of interpretations. The door to enter into the political community is, thus, only partly opened. Its opening depends on the agreement with, and display of, embodied affects, social conventions of bodily visibility and transparency, freedom of sexuality, and a normative understanding of gender relationships. The test thus symptomatically epitomizes a political rationality that is geared to the regulation of values, conduct of life, and emotions in public life and also in the private sphere.

With reference to the abovementioned liberal theorists, one could argue that this mechanism precisely exceeds the liberal consensus, which ideally disentangles the domains of the good life from domains of individual rights. Similar to the politics of recognition, I suggest that the test elicits the moral, emotional, and habituated components of abstract norms: it both reveals and prescribes how shared constitutional principles should be embodied.

In this sense, integration as the required affirmation of the constitution in its abstractions gains a corporal dimension, which the employed liberal vocabulary simultaneously denies.

Instead of considering this as an illegitimate encroachment of otherwise neutral state institutions, we could also argue that the test flattens an available discursive repertoire into a very simple scheme: The questionnaire translates a cyclically reiterated request that the agreement to the constitution should be manifested in incorporated codes of behavior amongst citizens. Again, contrary to the concerns raised by several of the abovementioned liberal theorists that in such measures constitutional principles would be illegitimately translated into issues of the good, I do not assert that the constitution is a neutral institution detached from normative claims that are thicker than bare universal rights. Addressing such state interpellations merely within the framework of rights eclipses the long legacy of the exclusion of particular ways of life from conceptions of the right-bearing individual. The problem is rather that ethical conduct, social behavior, sensibilities, and ways in which social relationships should be understood have turned into an issue of the state-managed examination of exceptional populations. This renders one model of the good into a matter of fixation and prescription of constitutional norms. More importantly, the way in which constitutional principles are filled with assumptions about the adequate conduct of life rests on a selective ideal of the compliant liberal German citizen, and thereby manufactures all native Germans (naturally considered non-Muslims) as sharing and embodying the ethical substance of liberal-democratic principles. The distinction between allegedly disembodied insiders and embodied others is of course a central characteristic of modern nation-states, and not exceptional at all. What I find worth interrogating in the repercussion of this distinction in the BW-test is the division of disembodied bureaucratic inspection and the bodied other.

The Sensorial Guise of the Unmarked State Official

One and a half years after the implementation of the test, and the first waves of criticism, then Minister of the Interior of Baden-Württemberg, Heribert Rech, publicly repeated his defense of the measure as being an "efficient" and "flexibly applicable tool" to test the mindset of individual applicants for German citizenship (Press notice, Ministry of the Interior, July 18, 2007). Flexibility refers to those cases in which the officials had doubts about the candidate's "inner convictions" with regard to the liberal-democratic order of German society. Rech adds that in 79 percent of the cases, the officials did not feel encouraged to even apply the test. In the cases in which they did, which indeed meant questioning applicants "according to necessity" and by "combining and completing" the questions (as Rech reminds us), the majority of the applicants successfully passed the test, only twenty-eight persons failed. According to Rech, these numbers indicate that the officials "lead the interviews openly and with a sense of proportionality [Verhältnismäßigkeit]" (ibid.).[18]

Let us recall that Grell articulated "doubts" about Muslim's sincere identification with constitutional principles. His story about "doubts, note well not more" is here handed over to state officials—the "administration" (Behörde), as Grell called it (2006: 66)—who are asked to "feel" or "not feel encouraged to apply the test" and to eventually decide whether a candidate would be naturalized or not. These state officials become examiners without being examined themselves. This echoes a longer tradition in the state regulations of foreigners in post-1945 Germany, as alluded to in Chapter 2. More importantly, it showcases the ambivalent status attributed to these officials, whose decisive authority is based on the assumption that they have incorporated and embodied the normative principles of the German constitution, which they should now evaluate in others. We therefore need to pay particular attention to the status attributed to civil servants as the executive arm of state bureaucracy.[19]

Civil servants are here considered to represent the state, and literally to serve it, and at the same time they are assumed to retain personal views, emotions, and sensibilities. Yet, these very personal viewpoints, emotions, and sensibilities form the ground on which they should "sense" the sincerity of an applicant's affirmation of the constitutional order. The civil servant appears here simultaneously as the personalized and depersonalized ambassador of liberal sensibilities thickened by the affective ties of social conventions attributed to them. All attributes that render the official's body invisible are paradoxically those that shall enable them to sense the candidate's embodied attachments to the constitution. The duality of the rational constitutional state representing the mind and the irrational passionate Muslim representing the body had already been blurred in Grell's passionate pamphlet. The questionnaire and its application even more sharply disclose the visceral architecture of the allegedly rational state bureaucracy. Both in the questionnaire itself and in the call for the need to sense the applicant's sincerity, the abstract and distant bureaucracy of the state in charge of detecting disloyal future citizens acquires its face through the figure of the civil servant who is asked to sense and inspect a candidate's true identification with the liberal sensibilities of the constitutional order.

This specific encounter between an interrogator and the interrogated requires a sensorial intimacy between the state and the citizen subject, and therefore provides a concrete incident of how Uli Linke has conceptualized the notion of "contact zones" (2006). Linke's understanding of contact zones, I suggest, helps us to better grasp the various ways in which the state can be understood as an effect of power techniques constituted also through *interactions* between the state and its citizens (or prospective citizens). More concretely, Linke calls for an understanding of the state as not only a site of meaning production, emotional investment, or fantasy, but also in its embodied and corporal dimensions: "My analytic gaze is centered on those sensually concrete spaces of power, where the machinations of the state and the embodied subject collide: in these zones of contact, the political field assumes a somatosensory gestalt" (2006: 206).

In this understanding the social life of state power exceeds the performative textuality of signs, as I have suggested above with regard to Grell's speech acts. Instead, it guides us to take the notion of embodiment seriously for the state as a bodied, somatic, and not just imaginary sphere, which is performed through cultural signification: "Under the state's optical apparatus of violence, there is a merging of bodies, of seeing and being seen, in concrete contact zones, whereby the political enters subjective experience" (2006: 112). In this sense the state official is the corporeal site of the state through whom the emotional attachments of the liberal-secular nation gain material shape and are mobilized. In this sense, the unseen, uninspected, and largely unmarked inspector repeats in different ways the pattern of the "view from nowhere" (Haraway 1988) that is characteristic of scientific knowledge production on Muslims. Similar to the unseen, distant, and objective researcher who conducts scientific inquiries into Muslim attitudes and ways of life, the civil servant's subjectivities and embodiments are rendered opaque. More precisely, they have to remain invisible and below the radar, as they represent the executive arm of the objectified and neutralized state bureaucracy in the contact zone of testing future citizens. The abstract viewer, entitled to gaze on the other, is rendered invisible precisely through the exposure and marking of the other as strange and exceptional.

Speaking and acting from the position and in the name of the law, Grell and his fellow state bureaucrats who are entitled to test suspect applicants symptomatically bring to the fore an inherent tension between the formalized state bureaucracy that claims neutrality and rationality, and its inbuilt visceral scope. Moreover, the act of marking others in their sensibilities, habits, and bodily practices works through the process of morally loading liberal norms, which paradoxically become the unmarked lens of its scrutinizing gaze on the other. The paradox lies in the image of the state as a neutral and emotion-free zone that governs the rule of law on the one hand, and on the other, the necessity it has for a sensorial repertoire, whose criteria remain outside of the scope of inspection. It is through the delegation to the invisible, interchangeable, and depersonalized official, entitled to inspect suspect subjects, that the implicit consensus about the shared and embodied norms and values of the nation gains flesh. The hegemonic norm that usurps the state's political and social imaginary becomes the invisible background against which a particular kind of difference is mounted as the nation's main problem. It is, thus, neither the ontological difference of liberal orders and Muslim forms of social life and religious practices that is at stake here nor an abstract universalism that is available to each and everybody. The contours of both are performed in their entanglement with each other, which, in this case, is located in the contact zone between the state official and the applicant. The allegedly unmarked carrier of universal ideals, whose disembodiment is dependent on the body of the other, provides another compelling example for the interdependency of state sovereignty and governmentality. Before moving to the national citizenship test, I want to use this example to further reflect on this interdependence.

Different from recognition in dialogue measures, state sovereignty is here delegated to bureaucrats entitled and enabled to manage suspect populations. Very similar to other measures of securitization, the decision whether a candidate is morally worthy of equal treatment as a member of the nation, depends on the judgment of the civil servant. This comes very close to what Judith Butler in her chapter on the "indefinite detention" of Guantanamo prisoners has called the "discretionary judgments that function within a manufactured law or that manufacture law as they are performed" (2006: 58). The performative act of suspending or manufacturing can thus work, as Carl Schmitt suggested, through recourse to the exception, or in the sense that new rules are created on the basis of personal presuppositions of civil servants who are entitled to make decisions about the lives and deaths of imprisoned individuals: "[…] precisely because our historical situation is marked by governmentality, and this implies, to a certain degree, a loss of sovereignty, that loss is compensated through the resurgence of sovereignty within the field of governmentality" (2006: 56). The suspension of the law and of the separation of powers, Butler goes on, in the case of Guantanamo creates the basis for what she calls a reconfigured version of sovereign power, enacted in the moment of the very suspension: "we have to consider the act of suspending the law as a *performative* one which brings a contemporary configuration of sovereignty into being or, more precisely, reanimates a spectral sovereignty within the field of governmentality" (ibid.: 61, emphasis mine). Butler concludes: "The new war prison literally manages populations, and thus functions as an operation of governmentality. At the same time, however, it exploits the extra-legal dimension of governmentality to assert a lawless sovereign power over life and death" (ibid.: 94/95). State sovereignty in Butler's example is thus strengthened and legitimized through governmental techniques of power.

Of course, in cases of integration measures with an overt disciplinary rationality like in the BW-test the civil servant's judgment does not determine the candidate's life or death, at least not immediately. However, I find Butler's argument useful to think more carefully through the implications of the enhancement of civil servants as the executers of an extralegal practice and its relationship to sovereign power. Governmental power in this case operates primarily as a technique of surveilling and x-raying suspect populations that are constituted as problematic in the moment of being named and investigated: "descendants of countries of the Islamic Conference," "Muslims as our main problem group," and so on. The means of surveillance are coupled with disciplinary techniques, in which each individual applicant can be potentially investigated. The potential threat of sanction thus performs a disciplinary function. It admonishes Muslims or people marked as such to either remain outside of the radar of state inspection, or to make sure that their constitutional loyalty appears "sincere" when performed in front of state authorities.

In the case of the bureaucratic entitlement to decide about the candidate's status as members or nonmembers of the social fabric of the nation, the law has as of yet, not been suspended. However, since the interpretation of how the law should be applied ultimately lies in the hands of individual officers, the scope of inspection, and hence intervention, has been definitely expanded. Because the questionnaire targets people's inner lives and sensibilities, which are difficult to capture with the abstraction of the law, sovereignty is not constituted by the possibility of deciding whether to enact an exception or to suspend the law. Sovereign power is created by the delegation to state bureaucracy and their multiple advisors who are entitled to detect insincere loyalty by interpreting an extralegal moral substance attributed to the law as the social bond of the nation-state. The extralegal dimension of governmentality consists in the bureaucratic arm of the state to interpret the law, and to assert a form of sovereign power over insiders and outsiders.

Thus understood, Böhmer's interpellation of Muslim communities to submit to what is called "Constitution Plus" gains a juridical and hence openly coercive dimension in the BW-test. The immunity and untouchability of the embodied contours of the sovereign nation-state in this case are not performed by individual politicians who welcome Muslims under certain conditions. They are performed in the abstract-present civil servant as the depersonalized figure of the state administration. What matters in this juridical rationality is both that state officials are authorized to sanction and the very threat of sanction. This performatively enacted sovereignty, personified in the official, is at once bound by the law at the same time as it tacitly suspends it. It is the act of displaying the possibility and right to sanction without any accountability—remember Rech's "sense of proportion"—in the name of the state, which reenacts state sovereignty. At the same time the BW citizenship test has legalized, institutionalized, and routinized a prevalent suspicion against Muslims as potentially lacking loyalty to the liberal-secular order. These mechanisms are, indeed, not substantially dissimilar in Germany's national citizenship test, whose legitimacy has been endorsed by liberal theorists because of its conformity with the rule of law. In this case state sovereignty appears in the governmental practice of instructing and interrogating future citizens in their *knowledge* of the liberal German order.

Learning the Nation

The approach to testing immigrants' knowledge about state and society, the ideal of constitutional loyalty, and, especially, the conviction that citizenship should be "earned" has been widely adopted across Europe (Schinkel 2017: 82). In Germany, this logic is paramount in knowledge-based citizenship tests. These tests were praised as reasonable instruments in conformity with "objective scientific standards"[20] or as means to create "politically mature subjects," as Maria Böhmer put it in defense of the measure.[21] These ambitions are most saliently manifest in the national citizenship test that has been in use since 2008. While the Federal Office of Migration and Refugees provided the infrastructure for conducting the test, an institute usually in charge of measuring educational standards in state schools was commissioned to develop the questionnaire.[22] The test comprises a pool of 310 questions, from which thirty-three are picked randomly in each test.[23] The candidate has to answer a minimum of nineteen questions correctly within one hour to pass the test. Unlike in the BW-version, the questions are addressed anonymously to the candidate, and the questionnaire does not contain any open-ended questions but only a multiple-choice sample.[24]

Recalling the suggestion by liberal theorists about the liberal legitimacy of knowledge-based tests, the national citizenship test, indeed, differs from the previously analyzed one. Each and every applicant has to undergo it. The selection of questions is not dependent on what a civil servant thinks the applicant does or does not represent. It is instead standardized by algorithms. *Knowledge* about Germany's liberal-democratic order, moreover, does not require the applicant to embrace but merely accept its attached values. Indeed, to frame it in a liberal vocabulary, the national citizenship test translated questions of the "good" into questions of rights. Attitudes about democracy, social norms, gender relations, or sexuality are not raised in terms of convictions but as questions of (un)lawful behavior. If assessed against the abovementioned scheme, by thus asking about the *legality* of a certain integration practice, the questions have indeed been turned into a neutralized integration measure that conforms to liberal standards. Analyzing the test as a governmental practice of integration, the central question that interests me, however, is not *that* but *how* these liberal standards are conveyed, and what this tells us about the productive forces of the liberal state in fostering ideals of the good citizen. It is therefore important to capture the different layers of the shift from an inspective mode to objectification and standardization, and the underlying political rationalities that are revealed by the conception of integration as based on knowledge of rights and duties.

Many of the questions have, indeed, kept a specific orientation. In those that couple nation and religion, for example, applicants have to answer questions such as, "which religion has molded European and German culture—Hinduism, Christianity, Buddhism or Islam?" (The only correct answer is Christianity.) All questions regarding German holidays focus exclusively on Christian holidays. Moreover, while attitude tests operate with the explicit assumption that an embodied and externalized commitment to Islam potentially entails a set of illiberal practices, the knowledge-based test more innocently clarifies a number of basic issues about morally correct behavior. It does not address the anticipated candidate as tied to a specific religious group nor does it identify the threats to the liberal-democratic order as a problem of Muslims. The questions tackle social conventions and spheres of life conduct that are located outside of the legal domain, and retranslate these questions into issues of legality and illegality. Instead of being asked what they personally think about homosexuality, candidates are asked questions such as:

Who is allowed to cohabit in Germany?
    ☐ Hans (twenty years old) and Marie (nineteen years)
    ☐ Tom (twenty years) and Klaus (forty-five years)
    ☐ Sofie (thirty-five years) and Lisa (forty years)
    ☐ Anne (thirteen years) und Tim (twenty-five years)

Instead of being interrogated about marriage practices, education, or family structures, the candidates have to select answers from samples such as:

In Germany ...
    A: one is allowed to be married only with one partner.
    B: one is allowed to have several spouses simultaneously.

C: one is not allowed to remarry after a divorce.
D: a woman is not allowed to remarry if her husband died.

Or:

A young woman in Germany, twenty-two years old, lives together with her boyfriend. Her parents do not like this because they do not like the boyfriend. What can they do?
A: They have to respect the decision of the adult daughter.
B: They have the right to bring the daughter back into their home.
C: They can report her to the police station.
D: They can look for another boyfriend for their daughter.

Which form of living arrangement is not allowed in Germany?
A: Man and woman are divorced and live together with new partners.
B: Two women live together.
C: A single father lives with his two children.
D: A man is married to two women at the same time.

Regarding the questions about the democratic order, candidates have to answer questions such as:

If a party in Germany tries to establish a dictatorship, is this party
A: tolerant.
B: oriented toward the rule of law.
C: law-abiding.
D: unconstitutional.

In this version of the test, candidates do not have to adopt a particular stance regarding homosexuality, forced or arranged marriages, kinship, or gender norms more generally. They merely have to demonstrate *knowledge* that in Germany forced or arranged marriages are forbidden or that homosexual relationships are allowed. Although the questions are thus addressed to all immigrants who seek to be naturalized, many of them have kept their specific angle and direction. More importantly, the questions condense a discursive repertoire which is conventionally associated with the presence of Muslims in Germany: homophobia, polygamy, unequal gender norms, or marriage of minors.

The fact that a candidate has to assert knowledge that homosexual couples are legally allowed to live together reveals a whole set of unexpressed assumptions about the moral horizon of the applicants. The most obvious is that because in many Islamic countries homosexuality is legally banned, it causes a problem for people with migration backgrounds outside of the EU. Similarly, the question if Anne (thirteen years) and Tim (twenty-five years) are allowed to cohabit implies that immigrants potentially arrange marriage of underage girls. I don't aim to counter such assumptions by asserting that they are principally wrong, for partly they are not. My concern is that these assumptions have constituted the basis for a test that is designed for all non-EU migrants, while constructing a moral community of native Germans and Europeans for that matter. In its assumption that only immigrants would potentially carry patriarchal norms and attitudes, the test simultaneously represents German society as consensually sharing norms of gender equality and liberal principles. This move not only culturalizes complex social relations. It also represents the notion that the liberal state would not actively intervene into the private lives of citizens by abstaining from governing sexuality, family, and kinship. As the feminist scholarship on liberal conceptions of citizenship has amply shown, the institutionalization of citizenship itself has since its inception been based on an inherent tension: on the one hand, the liberal state declares sexuality and gender relations as belonging to the private domain; on the other hand, it has actively and sometimes arbitrarily reordered human life and behavior into what Carole Pateman (1988) has called the "sexual contract."[25]

More importantly, the questionnaire operates with a notion of citizenship as tied to standardized and shared rules of conduct, social relationships, kinship, and family, which could be learned by heart and gradually embodied. Reducing complex and dynamic social relations to multiple-choice knowledge that can be assessed by standardized questions constitutes and stabilizes the very framework against which the citizen-in-the-making is imagined and measured. In this one-sided direction, knowledge-based tests do not operate dissimilarly from those tests that inspect attitudes: they enact majority norms against the marking of not-yet-nationals as deviant subjects; however, they do so by signaling transparency, rationality, and accountability.

In their analysis of citizenship tests across Europe, Löwenheim and Gazit (2009) claim that the power of these tests consists in their examining rationality. The candidate is targeted, investigated, and, through this examining encounter, simultaneously disciplined, sometimes directly, sometimes more impersonally, as in the standardized versions of the test. The authors, moreover, hold that citizenship tests enact a specific relationship between the state and the immigrant subject in strongly hierarchical terms. Agency is attributed to the listener, in this case to an objectified questionnaire distributed by a depersonalized state office and invisible inspector. I agree with Löwenheim and Gazit that we should be attentive to the relationship enacted between the disembodied view from nowhere and the modes of surveillance which are legitimized, formalized, and even normalized in such measures. I would, however, not read knowledge-based tests merely as part of a regime of surveillance, nor even as indicative of a rationality of examination alone.

In the German case, the inception of the test itself, for example, did not result from an unprecedented rush for naturalization which the state attempted to better control. Quite the contrary. The National Office of Statistics (*Bundesamt für Statistik*) indicates, after a sudden sharp increase immediately after the reform in 2000, a constant decline in naturalizations in Germany.[26] The test was thus not primarily developed because of a perceived need to better control the rising numbers of new Germans, for this rise simply did not happen.

One of the most intriguing aspects of knowledge-based tests, therefore, resides in their productive and largely performative rather than examining posture. The test stage-manages a notion of the rightful, good, and educated German citizen, respectful of gender equality and homosexuality, and embracing a tamed and secularized version of religion. Such measures therefore complement the civilizing features of integration projects, more generally. They performatively produce the idea of a preexistent society that only risks fragmentation because of the presence of immigrants with diverging lifestyles and religious practices.

Indeed, the state offices in charge of matters of migration provide a variety of possibilities to learn and memorize the correct answers to the questionnaire: Integration classes prepare for the test, the National Office for Migration and Refugees (BAMF) created an online test center, where applicants can access all questions and answers and simulate taking the test as often as they want.[27]

In addition, numerous online materials and brochures are made available for the applicants to get acquainted with the questionnaire. It is, therefore, unsurprising that after the first year, 98.9 percent of the applicants passed the test.[28]

These forums of knowledge-based citizenship operate through didactics and with a pedagogical rationality. They resemble school classes and textbooks. Many of the questions are also repetitive, especially those that pertain to Germany's constitutional principles, such as freedom of speech, religious liberty, human dignity, and gender equality. Applicants for citizenship are thus treated like immature subjects in need of acquiring democratic knowledge. Knowledge is not reflected upon; rather, it is ordered and ordained. This test therefore provides a prime example for what Schinkel called the "virtualization of citizenship," in which "citizens" are distinguished from "nonintegrated persons that are discursively exorcized from society" (Schinkel 2017: 216).

In other words, we should understand such measures not only as tools of testing, examining, and integrating future citizens into the nation, but also as instruments which demarcate the moral borders of this nation through its imagined counterparts. It is the conceptualization of test-takers as not yet mature, not yet liberal, not yet secular enough to count as properly integrated citizens which renders the liberal-secular order fully intelligible. The precondition for immigrants to become incorporated into this national community is their willingness to get acquainted with and prove ordained knowledge through which this very community is conditioned. With their educational impulses, such integration measures are part of a project of civic education.[29] Education is to be understood in the multiple sense of the term as teaching, learning, cultivating, and shaping people to enable them to become part of the imagined community of educated, law-abiding, self-governing, liberal, and secular citizens.

Returning to my concern about the state effected by such integration practices, let me emphasize the specific relationship between the interrogator and the interrogated subject: The state appears as a distant monitoring pedagogue and at times as a therapist, instructing vulnerable subjects on how to turn into good citizens. The standardization and translation of what literally needs to be known about German ways of life into questions about lawful behavior resonate with the methodologies of knowledge production operative in the statistical measurement of Muslim attitudes correlated with their stages of integration, which I analyzed in Chapter 3. Contrary to distant survey questionnaires with guaranteed anonymity and ambivalent effects, knowledge-based citizenship tests ordain knowledge by announcing the threat of sanction and therefore entail a juridical component. The statistical knowledge about good or bad religion and success or failure of integration here turns into imperative knowledge.

The state appears as a pedagogical paternal authority. In both versions of the citizenship test, the liberal-secular state expresses its commitment to guarantee basic rights and principles for all citizens, and it seeks to promote a modality of the lawful citizen who embraces diversity and freedom. The same state, however, that secures equality and rhetorically enjoins the citizenry from exclusion and immaturity, simultaneously engages in exclusionary and infantilizing practices: it addresses immigrants generally and Muslims in particular as potentially immature, illiberal and not yet secularized populations. These apparent Janus-faced characteristics are more than mere hypocrisy or a collateral damage of the liberal-secular state. They are, rather, precisely what the liberal-secular matrix of integration as a regulating and state-legitimizing project renders possible if not to say necessary.

Conclusion

My conclusion that integration does not solve but rather brings to the fore problems of power relations in liberal-secular states might not come as a surprise. In a similar vein, it will not be surprising that a power-sensitive analysis of integration discourses cannot claim to provide a solution to unequally distributed normative conflicts arising from plural ethical conceptions of the good life and their related social practices. I conclude this book by recalling why such critical diagnoses are nonetheless an inevitable starting point, and a continuous corrective for any political program that aims at going beyond re-inscribing majority-minority constellations.

One central lesson to be drawn from my analysis is that in order to understand the diverse interrogations of Muslims in liberal-secular nation-state contexts in their complex techniques of power it is important to move beyond the most obviously racializing or excluding practices. This implies being attentive to the powers prevalent in programs that are geared to include or empower minoritized populations. Integration is such a program. I therefore suggested governmentality as an analytical lens (and less as a compact theory) to critically examine some of the shortcomings of integration as a tool to govern Muslims in Germany.

Governmentality, State Sovereignty, and Intersections of Empirical and Prescriptive Norms

Governmentality, I argued, allows us to see beyond the surface of overtly racist, exclusionary, or restrictive interrogations of Muslims, and to be attentive instead to power operations condoned in a liberal vocabulary and gestured in invitations to minorities to become part of the social fabric of self-declared secular societies. As the different variations of integration explored in this book show, integration of Muslims understood through the lens of governmentality entails mechanisms of distinction and differentiation which go beyond simple juxtapositions between Muslims and the non-Muslim German society. They also work in more complex ways than as a mere construction of a holistic "Muslim population" (Tezcan 2012) or as a conflation between race or ethnicity and Islam. Rather, the interrogation of Muslims as subjects of integration functions with ideal-typical and empirically measured classificatory systems. This became most obvious in the analysis of the state-commissioned studies on Muslim forms of religiosity. Certain kinds of Muslims—abstracted into ideal types but governed as real existing groups—are considered more prone to be investigated than others: "traditional-conservative," "orthodox," or "fundamentalist," "not very religious" vs. "not believing," "mildly religious," or "moderate"—to take up the vocabulary running through the integration measures. Certain Islamic practices and certain justifications of these practices grounded in an Islamic morality are more systematically put into the scope of the state and civil society than others. Integration as a governmental technique thus functions by dynamic logics of organizing society along distinctions between normality and deviation. In our case these are productive of—contingent and shifting—distinctions between good vs. bad religion, and liberal vs. not-yet-liberal subjects.

The project of integration entails various, partly contradictory political rationalities. I identified three such rationalities which I denoted as governing by knowledge, governing by conditional recognition, and governing by discipline. These political rationalities can, of course, only be distinguished analytically. In reality, they are intimately connected. What unites them is that the basis of their intervention is not in the first place the law but the norm. Relevant instruments are the apparatus of knowledge, civic pedagogy, and social or bureaucratic control.

Governing by knowledge through empirical methodologies in our case implied knowing and at the same time constituting the subject of integration as an object of study. Preformatted categories and orders of knowledge—what integration means and how it can be measured as well as prototypes of religion—functioned as the unmarked measure that categorizes and hierarchizes subjects of integration. This unmarked measure that constitutes the norm unfolds in broad notions underpinning the system of classification, such as "liberal," "democratic," "secular," to recapitulate just the most obvious ones. As abstract and yet positively connoted signifiers these norms are immune from critical reflection about internal tensions or contradictions. They become concrete, however, at the moment in which they function as units of analysis against which Muslims are measured. The production and circulation of representative data on Muslims' degrees of integration, especially in their policy orientation, therefore compellingly reveal how a norm of secularized religion and ideals of the integrated Muslim have been constituted through the very act of constructing an empirical norm.

Governing through knowledge is a central component of the liberal state that justifies its political practices by relying on facts and findings—proper and reliable knowledge—and also by rendering transparent its modes of reasoning and justification. In this power-knowledge nexus, knowledge has, however, not only this instrumental function to serve power by legitimizing political action. As I argued, knowledge is productive of power because it sets the epistemological rules and the epistemic framework to which Muslims are incited to respond.

If integration by knowing—cognitively capturing the other's mindset—already hints at an intimate relationship between empirical and prescriptive norms, integration through recognition and discipline exposes this nexus even more saliently. Conceptually, this interrelation complicates assumptions about governmentality as being primarily a mode of power that operates along an empirical, in contrast to a prescriptive, norm or as distinctive from discipline or state sovereignty. The interchange between empirical and prescriptive norms can amount to the appeal to externalize one's inner loyalty to the constitution (as in the discourse on *Grundgesetz Plus*). It can also reveal itself in connections between scientific and bureaucratic investigation (as most saliently in citizenship tests). The norms associated with the liberal democratic order into which Muslims are invited to integrate, thus, have gained its prescriptive contours *through* the empirical interrogations of Muslims—as objects of knowledge, as subjects of conditional recognition, or as individual bodies of inspection and discipline.

As I showed, the production of state sovereignty understood as exercising power through governmental integration techniques is not static but dynamically configured. If we understand the state as not plainly an already-constituted ensemble of institutions and actors but also as an effect of various, partly contradictory techniques of power, the very establishment of centralized integration programs is a governmental technique through which the state enhances its scope of action. By investing in the search for the inner truths of certain people (subjects of integration), and by investigating whether and how these people embody liberal principles, the state increases its scope of knowledge, vision, and control. This scope of knowledge, vision, and control is not merely directed at what an empirically constructed and internally differentiated Muslim "population" *does*. Integration is first and foremost directed at what this population and individual *ought to become*—that is what German society imagines and performs itself to be constituted of: educated, reflexive, constitutionally loyal, and worldly minded citizens. Schinkel has aptly called this the "empty subject of liberalism": "a reflexive and reflective screen whose innermost core is a freedom, a noncausal causality that is recognizable mainly by what it is not (e.g., religious in a particular way)" (Schinkel 2017: 186).

State sovereignty *through* governmental techniques in integration programs can be effected through knowledge production and (conditional) recognition as well as through disciplinary means, as in case of depersonalized state bureaucrats immunized from their corporality and yet operating as the embodiment of constitutional principles. As the example of citizenship tests amply shows, integration comprises juridic rationalities in which state sovereignty is paradoxically enacted in an extralegal grey zone: in the bureaucrat's entitlement to measure constitutional loyalty along gut feelings. In all three instances, integration practices potentially enhance the state's abilities to intervene precisely into domains which lie outside of the state's scope or into which the state should not intervene according to liberal understandings: diagnosing constitutional loyalty and managing conceptions of the good life. Thus understood, the central problematic of state-organized and -regulated religious plurality through governmental techniques of integration resides not so much in the frequently evoked dichotomy between the telos of homogenous vs. pluralistic conceptions of society. Rather, it consists in the production of sovereign agencies that judge the success or failure of this endeavor (cf. Markell 2003: 153).

Conclusion

Recursive Aporias

As I showed notably in Chapter 2, calls for integration paradoxically gained salience in the moment in which immigration had irreversibly pluralized German society and when Muslims had started to become durably (and not temporarily) rooted. Muslims have thus been interrogated as the nation's erosive margins when they became internal to the nation. The call for integration thus entails an elusive tension of including the Other by simultaneously marking her disturbing difference. Recalling *Islampolitik* and assimilation as antecedents of interrogations of religious others as in need of transformation was necessary to detach this mechanism from the contemporary "Muslim Question" and instead understand it as intrinsic to the operations of secular nation-states.

The humanistic ideals that animated colonial and imperial projects of *Islampolitik* as a civilizing aspiration outside of Germany's territories during colonialism recur today in the state's ambitions to structure and monitor the institutionalization of Islam within Germany. Muslim integration through knowledge production, recognition, and citizenship regulation signals a complex reworking of these civilizing ambitions. These civilizing ambitions were also apparent in the traps assimilation which demonize and simultaneously absorb minorities. Reworkings and recursions, to borrow from Stoler's conceptual tools, do, however, not imply linear continuities.

As became clear throughout this book, the politics of integration have traced new paths and transformed in ways which complexified and sometimes also occluded their power-laden dynamics. The commitment to liberal-democratic principles, the justificatory modes of governance as well as the indebtedness to state neutrality as central tenets of liberal rule are paramount to the liberal grammar that animates projects of integration. This stands in contrast to assimilation as a project of absorbing cultural or religious identities into the nation framed as a cultural body. Integration projects conceptualized in a liberal language explicitly recognize the value of "culture" or "religion" (protected as the "good life" of each and every individual). And yet precisely because they scrutinize minorities in their cultural or religious difference, they immunize the malleable set of sensibilities entailed in liberal projects themselves. The "demand and support" programmatic of integration discourses has translated civilizing logics into a liberal vocabulary of rights and duties.

The connection of integration with assimilation therefore consists less in the call to minorities to give up their "culture" or "religion" for that matter, and to merge into the imagined culture of the nation. Its connection rather consists in a set of structural aporias.

One of these aporias is that the scope of integration in nation-state contexts is by definition vague and wide-ranging. Because of this comprehensiveness and vagueness, the transformation of minoritized subjects into integrated citizens remains an indefinite endeavor. The question as to when exactly the process of integration is accomplished, that is, when "Muslims in Germany" have truly transformed into "German Muslims," prevails. That is because the success or failure is dependent on the judgment of the arbiter of integration, on what Bauman has called "the *arbitrating power*, a force entitled to set the exams and mark the performance" (Bauman 1991: 107, emphasis in the original).

Liberal constitutional orders with ambivalent genealogies and anchorages in nation-state constituencies thus by necessity mediate the ways in which universal principles are conventionalized and embodied. The guarantee of freedom operates with incorporated normative understandings of how to be properly free, and these gain contours through the ongoing exceptionalization of people that are marked as not yet adequately free. These aporias are amplified when the paradigm of integration is coupled with politics of religion that impinge on the religious practices of exceptionalized minorities.

The affective and embodied attachments of liberal and secular principles, and the indeterminacy of integration as conditional recognition, add salience to the predicaments of integration: to be recognized on an equal footing it is necessary to articulate one's "religion" in a vocabulary that is legible within liberal rule, and in its translations into the incorporated contours of particular nation-state structures. The different kinds of integration practices, which I investigated in the different chapters, are variations of these predicaments.

Shifting the Gaze to the Liberal-Secular Matrix

If we contend that *We* as the imagined whole offering integration remains abstract, universal, and unmarked, while the individual or group interrogated as needy of integration is particular, bodied, and concrete, one task of this book has been to mark the supposedly universal, abstract, and putative disembodied interrogator in its embodied particularities. To understand this supposedly abstract "view from nowhere" as animated by the liberal-secular matrix has enabled me to interrogate the epistemic framework that nurtures the various interrogations of Muslims. If governmentality generally operates as a technique oriented at instructing and enabling people to govern themselves, the liberal-secular matrix of integration more particularly works as a contingent set of techniques oriented at enabling subjects to transform into secularized citizens, compliant with hegemonic understandings of religion. As I showed in the different chapters, the liberal-secular matrix of integration should not be misunderstood as an ontological constant of liberalism or secularism that has successfully torn itself off from religion. As a matrix it is contingent and nurtured by varied techniques of power which measure, regulate, tame, control, or recognize religion, and which draw boundaries between the religious and political realms in various ways—for example, by addressing minoritized religious communalities unevenly. The matrix's ongoing reiteration as the only adequate means to organize society conceals subtle inscriptions and at the same time secures its potency.

For my analysis it has therefore been crucial to interrogate secularism in integration discourses as productive of "religion" and as ordering people along their beliefs and practices. As I showed these modes of classification are circumscribed by hegemonic and often normalized understandings of how religion should look like. In the case of Germany, they are intrinsically and sometimes overtly modeled by Christian repertoires. Sometimes these Christian inflictions emerge explicitly, when Muslims are asked to orient themselves along a Christian model of organizing religious practice and authority. Sometimes they emerge more opaquely, when Muslims are measured with epistemologies whose hegemonic location is obscured by universalist claims. This privileged status—calls for liberal equality notwithstanding—is discursively reiterated in the very promise of recognition on the condition of adjusting to a progressive understanding of a tamed Christianity. Muslims are thereby not only dragged into a specific social contract but also into a specific historical narrative which Islam is asked to undergo—tearing away belief from politics. And yet there is no consensus about how Islam should look like when turned into an appropriately integrated religion—except a shriveled narrative of Christianity's path to secularization.

The general questions that characterize secular practices about the boundaries between religion and politics, between state and civil society, and between public and private also structure the set of questions that an integrating body poses to the religious minority: Does this minority fulfill the criteria of the existing state-church relationship? Does it bear loyalty to the state, to the liberal constitution or even to the nation? Is it capable of democracy? Does it share liberal principles of freedom and equality? Problematizing instead of accepting and answering this set of questions showed that the repetitive series of such interrogations potentially contributes to stabilize the liberal-secular matrix as the unmarked, disembodied norm that conceals its own affective attachments, internal contradictions, and contestations.

For my analysis it was therefore important to be attentive to the intertwinement between contingent, that is, not determinant, embodied dispositions, and the distinct modes of power which mobilize the liberal-secular matrix as a yardstick for minorities. I therefore read the unidirectional interrogations of Muslim forms of life and religious practices as suspect and in need of secularization via their integration as indications of the performative nature of secular practices in liberal public spheres, and as a blueprint for secular embodiments at work on a microscopic scale. If the secular is to be understood as relational, the secular order is discursively marked and valorized as secular only because it constitutes itself through distinctions from practices that are considered religious in a particular way—for example, by condoning religion as a clearly defined object of analysis (Chapter 3), or by reiterating Christianity's successful path to liberal democracy (Chapter 4), or by coupling the nation's borders to social conventions of everyday behavior (Chapters 4 and 5).

It is precisely the fact that the secular is not a preformatted thing but a contingent and malleable set of dispositions, institutions, and discursive practices that govern and shape religious life and practice in a given polity which adds salience to the vagueness and infinitude of Muslim integration as an open-ended endeavor. It can imply that Muslims be generously invited to adjust to social conventions that supposedly constitute the secular consensus of constitutional norms, as in the case of Böhmer's indignation at Köhler (Chapter 4). It can, however, also include a whole catalogue of norms and codes of behavior which—through inspection and threat of sanction—intrude into the most intimate spheres of the individual, as in the case of citizenship tests (Chapter 5).

The liberal-secular matrix of integration, in other words, functions as the absent-present framework that guards what kind of religious practices are legitimate, where the borders to the political are crossed, and when the state has to intervene into the "private" lives of individuals. This brings me back to my introductory call to give more serious consideration to the intimate relationship of what Mahmood distinguished as "political secularism" as the political and legal regulation of religion, and "secularity" as sensibilities, emotions, social conventions, and embodied practices (2015: 206). The regimes of knowledge and the presumptions that categorize certain populations as inherently deficient on the basis of their racial and/or religious backgrounds and practices infringe the very assumptions about political liberalism imagined as treating each and every one equally, independently of racial, class, gender, or religious backgrounds. Such tensions bring to the fore the affective attachments and in-built exclusions of liberalism and secularism itself.

Interrogations of Muslims as subjects of integration entail corporeal components, and they also work as interventions into bodies understood both as individual bodies and the body of the population. It is nonconformist corporeal practices like veiling or Islamically justified practices of gender segregation that neutralize secularism as allegedly abstract, disembodied principles available to everybody. Such practices both trouble and put to the fore inscribed secular sensibilities that animate integration practices. While not residing outside of what is legally permitted, Muslim corporeal practices have provoked discourses which exit the terrain of all-inclusive individual rights or rather mark these with moral substance.[1]

The secular embodiments about how one should practice and display (or conceal) religion properly in order to adjust to the moral substance of constitutional principles further uncover inherent tensions between a liberal discourse of universally available individual rights and the monitoring functions of national projects. The marking of the other's body as exceptional, illiberal, or not secular enough is an intrinsic component of liberalism's and secularism's self-confessional logic, which contributes to ongoing deflections from its own embodiments.

Interrogating the relations of power that (re)produce minority-majority constellations, should, of course, not succumb to the illusion that social inequalities, normative conflicts, and marginalization in pluralistic societies could thereby be solved or misunderstanding precluded. However, shifting the gaze to the conditions and epistemic structures of interrogations could help to destabilize their unquestioned authority including the state's political agency for organizing plurality. For my context, shifting the attention from the minority to the majority, from the ruled to the rulers would imply interrogating unmarked majorities instead of replicating minority questions. It would further imply asking the "European Question" instead of the "Oriental Question" or the "Refugee question" (De Genova 2016), or to raise the "Christian or secular Question" instead of the "Jewish" or "Muslim" Question (Anidjar 2015), etc. Such a shift of scope could open a horizon to envision a polity not as a division into vertically organized majorities and minorities, or established and outsiders, but rather as complex and dynamic assemblages.

Notes

Introduction

1. See, for example, https://www.bildungsserver.de/onlineressource.html?onlineressourcen_id=31629, or: https://www.oezdemir.de/themen/islam-einbuergern/.
2. https://www.bundesregierung.de/Content/DE/Artikel/2016/08/2016-08-05-integrationsgesetz.html (accessed September 6, 2020).
3. The slogan "Demand and Support" was first introduced in 1979 in the so-called "Kühn" memorandum, which was the first governmental attempt to systematize immigration policy in Germany (see Chapter 1). The Immigration Act of 2005 for the first time codified the slogan with the introduction of state-organized integration classes: https://www.bpb.de/gesellschaft/migration/dossier-migration-ALT/56351/zuwanderungsgesetz-2005?p=all (accessed September 6, 2020).
4. While scholars of migration advocated a structured immigration policy, they mainly equated integration with inclusion in the labor market. Even Klaus Bade, who had studied immigration into Germany historically, neither conceptualized nor questioned integration as a more substantial problem of minority-majority relations in a nation-state framework.
5. The changed view is connected to political economy and a transformed Europe, which after the Westphalian peace was oriented toward a balance of forces between European states. This became a central feature of the *raison d'etat*. The development of the police as the safeguard of internal security was paralleled by a transformed role of the state as the carrier of contingent relations of power.
6. Saba Mahmood's critical engagement with the "subject of freedom," on the other hand, made clear that even these critiques often relied on "liberal assumptions about what constitutes human nature and agency" (2005: 5).
7. Hindess distinguishes between three different methods: the persecution or erasure of non-liberal/non-conformist subjects, compulsion, and a gentle intervention with a patronizing approach of remodeling through education. All versions are based on the assumption of an evolution of behaviors and sensibilities of human beings.

8 Thus understood, even Isaiah Berlin's idea of negative freedom as not interfering with other people's freedom presupposes norms of how to be free.
9 Throughout Europe, many similar initiatives have developed since the late 1990s. In France, the ministry of the interior started to invite Muslims to sit "at the table of the Republic" from the late 1990s with the objective to create a representative Muslim body, which in 2003 lead to the formation of the *Conseil français du culte musulman* (CFCM) (Peter 2008). In the Netherlands, programs that aim at molding the acceptable ways of being a Muslim in the Dutch context have flourished since the assassination of Theo Van Gogh (cf. Van Bijsterveld 2015). In Italy, attempts to structure conversations between the government and Muslim organizations led to the creation of a state-administered dialogue platform (Jasch 2007).

Chapter 1

1 In his overview of the emergence of a "European Islam," Patrick Franke locates the beginning of politics of Islam in Europe in the late fifteenth, early sixteenth century and the expulsion of Muslims from the Iberian Peninsula. The expulsions of Muslims between 1609 and 1614 are probably the peaks of politics of Islam in Europe that was animated by the forced remodeling through conversation or expulsion (Franke 2012).
2 For a thorough analysis of Becker's discourse, see Suzanne Marchand (2010: 361f.); for an analysis of Becker in the context of German Islamic Studies, see Alexander Hariri (2005).
3 Historical studies (e.g. Habermas 2014) emphasize the close relationship between Christian missionary movements and the civilizing ambitions of the Prussian state during German imperial rule (Hoffmann 1982: 37), even if the interpretations of the "Islam problem" sometimes differed substantially. Rebekka Habermas (2014) stresses the important role that missionaries played in collecting knowledge about Muslim forms of social lives and religious practices deriving from their interactions, and not from studies of ancient texts (2014: 241). Catholic missionaries in the African colonies were much less clear-cut and less complacent than, for example Becker, in their assessments of Islam as a threat to colonial order (ibid., 234–5). Paradoxically, the declining power of Catholicism in the German Empire and its role as an "internal Other" (Borutta 2011) seem to have created the crudest of stances, which treated Islam as the most dangerous enemy among some Christian missionaries in the African colonies.

4   In her analysis of the Protestant theologian Ernst Troeltsch, for example, Masuzawa points out that his idea of creating a bastion of all world religions against what he felt was excessive secularism was ultimately guided by the idea that Christianity was its binding core, which consolidated Christian universalism (2005: 29 and Chapter 9).

5   The high quality of these critiques notwithstanding, the scholarship on German Orientalism has mainly focused on the politics of representation and knowledge production without linking this to the broader question of how these epistemologies correlated with political interventions. Even if there is no linear causality between Orientalist knowledge production and material interventions into the social lives of Muslims, and religious practices in the colonies or in the former Ottoman Empire, we need to understand the politics of knowledge production of nineteenth-century Orientalists and sociologists alike as interventions into regimes of knowledge whose effects were long-lasting. There is thus an intimate connection between the history of thought and colonialism or imperialism, even if this linkage is not always immediate, direct, or linear, but rather contingent and complex (Marchand 2010: 380). Marchand accordingly observes: "Specialists who offered their services to the German Empire could indeed be useful; though the services they wished to provide were sometimes also superfluous or undesirable in the eyes of political decision makers. It also shows that even the most dedicated agents of empire sometimes contributed to the diversification of European culture, even though their intentions were openly to spread and strengthen it" (2010: 380).

6   Marchand thoroughly traces these legacies in her careful account of the relationship between German Orientalism and imperialism. She reminds us that even if Becker was an important figure as the founding father of modern Islamic Studies in Germany, his scholarship was connected to a broader web of scholars, both contemporaries and a generation before, who were implicated in an imperial project and order.

7   This biologistic somatic grounding was also inscribed in US migration studies emerging in the late nineteenth and early twentieth centuries (Aumüller 2009: 29).

8   In a similar vein, Hannah Arendt (2004 [1951]) situates the emergence of the "Jewish question" in direct relation to that of the nation-state and the subsequent crises that befell it. Arendt does so by giving an account of the older history of Western Europe toward its Jewry, which explains why Jews—more than any other minority group—figured as the central target of various forms of particular

inspection and violence, which later culminated in Germany's politics of extermination (Arendt 2004 [1951]: 41).

9   In her biography of Rahel Varnhagen, Hannah Arendt (1981) conceptualizes this mechanism with the figure of the parvenu. The parvenu's attempts to assimilate failed, especially in its individualistic aspiration. According to Arendt, it is impossible to select autonomously what one likes to assimilate into and what to discard because assimilation meant inclusion not only into Christianity, but also into the hatred against Jews (Arendt 1981: 207f.) For Arendt, the loss of a consciousness of collectivity among those who individually made it into the bourgeois class by culturally assimilating, simultaneously led to their incapacity to understand the ongoing exclusions of Jews on a structural level.

10 It is important to note that the promise of equal rights to Jews was guaranteed only in the 1869 constitution of the *Norddeutscher Staatenbund*. The concession of citizenship rights was regulated by a growing state bureaucracy, which simultaneously acted arbitrarily and with ambitions to remodel future German citizens (Aumüller 2009: 142).

11 Prominent and vocal figures in this enterprise were Moses Mendelsohn, Abraham Geiger, or Samuel Friedländer. While their argumentation and degrees of engagement in Jewish theology differed, they all promoted the de-ritualization of Jewish practices and an emulation of Protestant theology by prioritizing internalized spirituality over corporeal practices, private belief over public organization (Batnitzky 2011; Aumüller 2009: 149).

12 The Prussian Edict of 1812, for example, addressed Jews as: "Persons of Jewish faith (*jüdische Glaubensgenossen*)" (quoted in Markell 2003: 136). For a detailed analysis of Jewish emancipation across Europe, see Sorkin 2019.

13 In her seminal intellectual historical analysis, Leora Batnitzky (2011) thoroughly investigates the transformations of modern Jewish thought and practice into a modern understanding of "religion" modeled by Christianity, and in particular by Protestant thought.

Chapter 2

1   For thorough analyses of immigration policies after 1945, see Bade and Bommes (2004); Bade (2007); Mandel (2008).

2   In his book *Beyond the Swastika*, Peter O'Brian analyzes how the attempts to reconstruct a new, that is, liberal, nation-state after the Nazi era were strongly guided by the Western Allies who tried to replace excessive nationalism with

the establishment of liberal institutions and values (1996: 18–19). He studies in detail the various measures guiding this project, mainly in the form of intrusive reeducation programs at various levels of political institutions and civil society. As is well known, de-Nazification was not accomplished, especially at the level of state institutions and universities. However, the attempt by Western Allies to restructure the German educational system was driven by the goal of implementing a liberal citizenry (ibid., 21). What emerged from these efforts, according to O'Brian, was a very specific version of liberalism, entrenched with the vestiges of nationalism precisely because it was mainly imposed, and only adopted by some of the German intellectual elite. O'Brian conceptualizes this tension as "technocratic liberalism."

3 This memorandum, drafted by the first delegate for foreigners Karl-Heinz Kühn, was not fully realized at the beginning but formed the backdrop of the "Süssmuth Commission" led by the CDU-politician Rita Süssmuth, in which integration became the master narrative (Meier-Braun 2002: 46–7).

4 Peter O'Brian shows how the technocratic liberal ethos was reoriented toward reunification, and the extent to which East Germans turned into subjects who had to be cured and reeducated, and the belief in their supposed illiberal past was displayed by the attacks made on foreigners and asylum seekers. O'Brian concludes his tour de force through these various forms of imposed liberalism by pointing to the teleological impetus of technocratic liberalism: "However, East Germans and foreigners were not forever condemned. They could shed their letters as soon as they could convince their liberal mentors of their genuine, inner conversion to liberalism" (ibid.: 127).

5 In his analysis of parliamentary debates on Islam in Germany from 1990 to 2009, Sebastian Matthias Schlerka notes that these topics were regularly taken up both in the debates on Islamic countries (especially Iran) and in the discussions on immigration. In the latter case, they were increasingly attached to integration.

6 Angela Merkel at the "Day of Germany" (*Deutschlandtag*), October 16, 2010.

7 Die legal sources that regulate the status of religion in Germany are anchored in the basic right to religious freedom (Art. 4 of the basic law), the "freedom of association for religious communities" (*Freiheit der Vereinigung zu Religionsgemeinschaften*) and the "status of a statutory body under public law" (*Körperschaft des öffentlichen Rechts*). The German constitution simultaneously fixes the separation between church and state in the so-called "clause of limitation" (*Schrankenklausel*) which, ever since the Weimar Constitution, has placed limits on the autonomy and privileges enjoyed by Christian churches and other religious communities (cf. Link 2000: 106; Muckel 2012: 63).

8   So far only the *Ahmadiyya Muslim Jamaat* successfully fought for that status in the federal states of Hessen (2013) and Hamburg (2014).
9   Many public institutions, such as the educational sector, prisons, theological faculties at universities, hospitals, and even the media, are to a large percentage attached to the Protestant or Catholic churches. The number of church-led kindergartens, social and medical services also indicates that Christian churches provide a large amount of employment in Germany. This privileged role is, furthermore, institutionalized through the financial guaranties granted to the churches. Especially the church taxes (Kirchensteuer) that each church member has to pay from the salary mark an exception on the European level.
10 For an intriguing critique of the coupling of the categories of "Judeo" and "Christian" in Protestant writings, and its problematic recoding against the background of the Nazi past, see the work by Anya Topolski (e.g. Nathan and Topolski 2016).

Chapter 3

1   http://www.deutsche-islam-konferenz.de/DIK/DE/Magazin/magazin-node.html; see Tezcan (2012: 131).
2   https://www.deutsche-islam-konferenz.de/DE/DIK/Ziele/ziele_node.html.
3   In his chapter on the inflationary production of survey data on immigrant integration in the Netherlands, Willem Schinkel similarly observes that this ritualistic "moral monitoring of integration" has contributed to conceal and marginalize voices that have been critical of such kind of research in Dutch academic landscape (Schinkel 2017: 105).
4   Reflecting on epistemological practices in the context of Empire, Ann Laura Stoler (2008) alludes to the instability of epistemologies and emphasized that in the colonial context, epistemologies also did not have a pre-constituted architecture but were generated through the practice of categorization, classification, and hierarchization—in Stoler's case of human races. Stoler is interested in particular in the inconsistencies, instability, and contradictions, which occur in the process of knowledge production.
5   The denomination "migration background" functions as a loose marker for denoting people as being ethnically, religiously, and/or culturally somewhat different from native Germans. However, it also has an official implication: it comprises people who have themselves migrated and/or who are born from at

least one parent of non-German nationality (https://www.bamf.de/DE/Service/Left/Glossary/_function/glossar.html?lv3=3198544).

6 This study had been commissioned prior to the inception of the DIK by then Minister of the Interior from the Social Democratic Party (SPD), Otto Schily. In the aftermath of 9/11, Schily established wide-ranging measures for securitization, and he also did not hesitate to hold that "assimilation" was the only solution for social peace in Germany (Hermani 2010; Tezcan 2012: 61). For a detailed critical analysis of this study, see Dornhof (2009) and Johansen and Spielhaus (2012).

7 The interviewees lived in Hamburg, Berlin, Cologne, and Augsburg.

8 See also Becher and El-Manouar (2014), who claim to have copied a name-related "random telephone sample" on the basis of public telephone lists from the second edition of the study *Muslimisches Leben in Deutschland* (2014: 32).

9 For example, in the third edition of the survey *Muslimisches Leben in Deutschland* the authors provide a compact definition of integration as a "process which preferably leads to equal participation of all people with and without migration background in central domains of societal life" (Pfündel, Stichs, and Tanis 2021: 123). In refining their definition of integration, however, they refer to an integration model, developed by Hartmut Esser, who divided integration into four components: cognitive/cultural, social, structural, and identificatory (ibid.: 123). In the course of their study, moreover, the authors constantly evoke "assimilation" or "acculturation" as the components that constitute a measure for the process of integration (ibid.: 23, 84, or 123).

10 Astheimer, Sven (2016). "Migrationsforscher im Gespräch: Die meisten Menschen wollen unbequeme Fakten nicht hören," *Frankfurter Allgemeine Zeitung*, April 29, 2016: http://www.faz.net/aktuell/wirtschaft/migrationsforscher-koopmans-haelt-multikulti-fuer-fatal-14202950.html.

11 *Frankfurter Allgemeine Zeitung*, April 29, 2016.

12 In a similar and yet more general vein, Schinkel shows how the social scientific measurement of "immigrant integration" throughout Europe uses "society" as the measure that is bound by, and equated with, the borders of the nation-state: "Where immigrant integration is measured, 'society' is the measure" (Schinkel 2017: 4). Schinkel therefore argues that the social scientific measurement of "integration" has become a means of rendering "society" imaginable by identifying what potentially resides "outside" of it: "The work of definition of 'society' is shifted toward the 'outside society,' and 'society' becomes preoccupied with fending off outside incursions that threaten its wholeness and integrity. Yet

it is in this problematization that 'society' gains plausibility, boundaries, order, stability, and cohesion" (2017: 72).

13 This holds true especially for the UK, where statistics on minority groups are particularly salient, and where ethnicity tends to be used at face value and as an unproblematic category.

14 The DIK devoted a whole page on the issue of veiling with a set of studies, interviews, and random information about this Islamic practice: http://www.deutsche-islam-konferenz.de/DIK/DE/Magazin/SchwerpunktKopftuch/schwerpunkt-kopftuch-node.html.

15 For a very rich and thorough analysis of the politico-theological grounding of this distinction in its operations to cast Judaism as the carnal, bodied, and non-spiritual, non-rational other of Christianity, see Nirenberg (2013). For an excellent analysis of the Christian theological legacy of the Cartesian body-mind split and its implications for Europe's encounter with Islam as an "empirical other," see Luca Mavelli (2012), most particularly Chapter 2.

16 Asad (1994), for example, addresses fieldwork and ethnography as practices prone to reinscribe in an uncontested way data on the characters and types of people through the "real," "experienced" encounter of the anthropologist with his/her interlocutors.

17 Tellingly, especially in the context of Germany, race is often put in quotation marks while religion is not, and tends to pass unnoticed as an unproblematic category.

18 It is necessary to be aware of the premodern legacy of the race/religion nexus as deriving from a theological structure not only of Christianity but also of Judaism and Islam (Kalmar 2016; Nirenberg 2013; Topolski 2018; Westerduin 2020).

19 In his genealogical analysis of the academic discourses on "political Islam," Armando Salvatore (1999) extends the scope to the neighboring discipline of sociology of religion, molded a decade later. Salvatore points out how comparative sociologists of religion like Max Weber and his interlocutors, well versed in Oriental or Islamic Studies (see also Marchand 2010), gradually fused Islam from a complex ethical tradition into a broad "civilization," that is, a wide-ranging unit defined at once as territorial, cultural, theological, and political. The paradox emerging is that religion turned into a universal category and a concept of scientific comparison, while Islam necessarily failed the litmus test because it was either always more—culture, politics, civilization, law—or not enough, that is, mired into Arab ethnicity (Masuzawa 2005, Chapter 6). Weber's scholarship, Salvatore

shows, molded the leading and at the same time unmarked idea of religion as internalized belief.

20 Vial borrows the idea of "manufacturing religion" from Russel McCutcheon's book *Critics Not Caretakers: Redescribing the Public Study of Religion* (2001) and translates it into his own elaborations on the role that the "two Friedrich's" (2016: 94, Friedrich Schleiermacher and Friedrich Max Müller) played in the formation and evolvement of the discipline of Religious Studies (Vial 2016: chapter 3) (Albany: State University of New York Press, 2001) Manufacturing Religion.

21 The recurrent juxtaposition between "organized" Muslims and "ordinary Muslims" (see Akca 2020) and the juxtaposition between "Islamic piety" and "everyday Islam" are similarly problematic (see Fadil and Fernando 2015).

22 As critical scholarship on the very foundations of religious studies and related disciplines like sociology of religion (Daniel 2016; Masuzawa 2005; Mavelli 2012; Salvatore 1999) taught us, academic representations and conceptualizations of religion have often been complicit in constructions of a teleological understanding of secularization as a gradual adaptation of religion as modeled by Christianity with its successful taming through entanglements between the Reformation and Enlightenment thought.

23 In an illuminating article on the debates on veiling in Belgium, Sarah Bracke and Nadia Fadil (2012) argue that this scheme of interrogation is centrally structured around the question whether the headscarf is emancipatory or oppressive. This framing, the authors go on, leaves covered women in a deadlock: it scrutinizes *their* views on gender roles and relations and *their* agency or lack thereof, while imposing the ways in which the questions, and therefore necessarily also the answers, are framed. Bracke and Fadil impressively show how much they themselves as scholars have become captured by this very framing. They speak revealingly about their own discomfort when constantly being maneuvered into the position of either defending or condemning veiling, while they were inclined to voice a critique of the discursive structures which sustain the very act of exceptionalizing the veil as a problem to be scrutinized politically, culturally, and epistemologically.

24 Luca Mavelli traces the gradual transcendence of the senses from Aquinas via Descartes to Kant and later the founders of sociology of religion, Weber and Durkheim. He notes that Descartes especially inaugurated a new epistemic framework with his call to liberate oneself from the burden of the body and from God as a prerequisite to turn to the real intellect. Recalling Foucault, Mavelli speaks about the "Cartesian moment" which was marked by the withdrawal of

man in the individual space of the cogito. Interestingly, Mavelli connects these modern ideals of a secular subject and its withdrawal from the "transcendental other" (God) to what he calls the "withdrawal from the empirical other." "The moral impoverishment of the secular subject, it was suggested, can be accounted for as the result of the secular separation of knowledge and faith. By postulating a self-sufficient knowledgeable subject who no longer needs to become 'other than herself' in order to access the truth, the possibility is open for a progressive withdrawal of the self from the transcendent Other/God and from the empirical other" (Mavelli 2012: 45.) This withdrawal, Mavelli goes on, was one reason for the contemporary lack of engagement with Islamic norms in Europe in any dialogical manner, which would imply the transformation and not only just the confirmation of oneself: "Europe […] has overall neglected the possibility that its transformation could be a necessary and possibly enriching component of its encounter with Islam" (Mavelli 2012: 63).

Chapter 4

1. There is a growing scholarship that has investigated the DIK's structure, topics, and themes in great detail. For an analysis that is interested in configurations of power, see Tezcan (2012). For an analysis that looks at the DIK through a critical race studies angle, see Aguilar (2018).
2. Here I presuppose the empirical finding that western European countries with high rates of immigration have agreed in different ways with the basic approach of recognizing religious cultural minorities (on this, see Brunn 2012; Peter 2008; Tezcan 2012).
3. Although this is not central to my argument, I should note that Markell formulates this criticism more radically. He transfers the subject of recognition into a genealogy, according to which the modern subject is imagined as self-determined and autonomous. As critics of liberalism from Isaiah Berlin to Wendy Brown have shown, this conception of the autonomous, self-determining subject is as much based on presuppositions as it is normative. It requires the capacity, the will, and the preconditions for independent action and thinking, and it deliberately conceals power relationships.
4. The reasons for this are evident: marginalized groups, especially in the United States, have increasingly challenged standards of justice and demanded political and, to some extent, legal recognition of their specificity.

5   Markell's starting points are conversations in political theory that flourished especially in the late 1990s and which shifted from the politics of the redistribution of material goods to the politics of recognition of cultural identities, most famously put forward by Charles Taylor (1992). Taylor's suggestions were gradually taken up and developed further with a more outspoken liberal, individualist component by multiculturalist theorists, most prominently Will Kymlicka (1995). On a general level, Markell's criticism is that these politics would start from an idealized standpoint that injustices could be remedied by a more just distribution of the good of recognition of preformatted identities. Markell thereby also raises a critique of identity politics and the notion of subjects as sovereign and autonomous.

6   In the context of the DIK as well as the CFCM in France, Tariq Modood makes the paradoxical observation that the implementation of multicultural politics was part of the anti-multicultural discourse (2012: 14).

7   http://www.deutsche-islam-konferenz.de/DIK/DE/Service/Bottom/RedenInterviews/Reden/20060928-regerkl-dik-perspektiven.html?nn=3331014.

8   Schäuble actively participated in various forums organized by church institutions and often related to interreligious dialogue. Most of his speeches on these occasions are documented on the DIK website: http://www.deutsche-islam-konferenz.de/SiteGlobals/Forms/Suche/DIK/DE/Servicesuche_Formular.html?nn=3331014&resourceId=3332096&input_=3331014&pageLocale=de&templateQueryString=sch%C3%A4uble&submit.x=0&submit.y=0.

9   http://www.deutsche-islam-konferenz.de/DIK/DE/Service/Bottom/RedenInterviews/Reden/20090306-theologisches-forum.html?nn=3331014. My analysis is based on a close reading and selection of all public speeches listed on the DIK website.

10 http://www.deutsche-islam-konferenz.de/SharedDocs/Anlagen/DIK/DE/Downloads/LenkungsausschussPlenum/dik-rede-minister-plenum-2012-download.pdf?__blob=publicationFile.

11 For a similar statement, see Schäuble (2008).

12 The topic of mixed sports and swimming classes had already been subject to legal decisions. Back in 1992, the Supreme Administrative Courts in Münster and Lüneburg had decided in support of girl's abstaining from coeducational sports lessons. The case remained relatively remote from the wider public sphere. The topic, however, has started to preoccupy lawyers, public opinion, and increasingly also state agents more intensely in recent years as part of the wider incitement to discourse on Muslim gender norms, sexuality, and bodily practices. The more recent legislation by Hamburg in 2007 and Münster in 2008 indicate,

furthermore, how much the interpretation and application of the law is itself closely related to specific social and political climates, and to local dynamics and traditions. While in the Hamburg decision students are neither allowed to abstain from mixed swimming classes or to wear "Burkinis," in the other decision in Münster, participation in mixed swimming classes is mandatory in school but the wearing of a swimsuit covering the entire body is allowed.

13 The initiative "Secular Islam" (*Säkularer Islam*) was founded in the fall of 2018 shortly before the last plenary session of the DIK in November 2018. It was constituted mainly by members of the DIK who had been labeled "critics of Islam" during the first years of the DIK, joined by some new members, such as the professors Bassam Tibi and Susanne Schröter, as well the Green Party politician Cem Özdemir. This initiative launched a "ten-point program" in which it calls for a reform of Islam, a stricter separation of religion and politics, and also formulates rules of conduct for Muslims, such as a historical critical reading of the sources or the prohibition on minority-age girls to wear the veil. For the founding text and the main goals of this initiative, see: http://saekulare-muslime.org/. For a critical public response, see Amir-Moazami in *Die Zeit Online*, November 27, 2018: https://www.zeit.de/gesellschaft/zeitgeschehen/2018-11/initiative-saekularer-islam-konferenz-muslime-deutschland-integrationsparadox.

14 For a conceptual analysis of the interconnection between secular power and the production of subject positions of secular Muslims in the context of France, see Ruth Mas (2006; 2011). For a critique of the figure of the secular Muslim feminist in the DIK, see Amir-Moazami 2011. For a general critique on secular Muslims as key witnesses for hegemonic discourses on intrinsic alliances between Islam and patriarchal structures, see Shooman (2014: 20, 32, and 100–23). For a more recent critique on intended and unintended alliances between publicly vocal secular Muslims and far right movements, see Göpffarth and Özyurek (2021).

15 The report draws the alarming picture that pious Muslims, and Muslim girls in particular, serially and consistently refuse to participate in co-education sports and swimming lessons, "even if this refusal is not always formally requested" (2006: 44). More importantly, from there Kelek draws a linear causality between Islamic notions of modesty and patriarchal structures symptomatized by girls abstaining from co-education swimming and sports classes.

16 The published resume of the DIK of 2009 states: "If such a solution is not possible for organizational reasons (timetables of sports halls, number of sports teachers, numbers of students or other), Muslim students have the right to

abstain from mixed sports or swimming classes if they can plausibly present an *objectively provable moral conflict*." See: http://www.deutsche-islam-konferenz.de/SharedDocs/Anlagen/DIK/DE/Downloads/LenkungsausschussPlenum/2008-anhang-zwischenresumee-schulpraktische-fragen.pdf?__blob=publicationFile (translation mine, emphasis added). This is of course a cunning formulation since the criteria for the "objective" proof of a moral conflict are not specified. As Winnifred Sullivan (2005) has deduced in her seminal book, *The Impossibility of Religious Freedom*, the demand for religious freedom necessitates the merging of subjective relationships to religious traditions into legally intelligible categories.

17 "Islamkonferenz: Schäuble zufrieden, Muslime kritisch":http://www.focus.de/politik/deutschland/islamkonferenz_aid_55127.html.

18 *Die Zeit*, 2007, No. 17.

19 https://www.bundesregierung.de/breg-de/mediathek/pressekonferenz-nach-dem-integrationsgipfel-1141922.

20 Willem Schinkel pointedly calls such kinds of juxtapositions "neutralization of liberalism": "It is a way of, at the same time, claiming distance from hierarchical evaluations of 'cultures' and of excepting liberalism itself from the realm of culture by elevating it hierarchically above that realm" (Schinkel 2017: 169).

21 In his ethnography of the Turkish Islamic organization *Milli Görüş* (a section of the Islamic movement funded by Erbakan in Turkey in the 1960s), anthropologist Werner Schiffauer devotes one subchapter to the legal department of this organization. In the past decades, lawyers engaged in *Milli Görüş* have advised and supported Muslim families in Germany in lawsuits on abstaining from coeducational sports and swimming classes. They also pushed forward the struggle for the permission for ritual slaughtering, which was legalized in 2000. Schiffauer shows that these lawsuits were monitored by the secret services and interpreted as a proof for the misuse of the constitution for smuggling in "shari'a-oriented legal interpretations" (Schiffauer 2010: 298).

22 Indeed, this concern is echoed by some constitutional lawyers in Germany who have argued that Muslims use constitutional principles as an arena that provides "too much" religious freedom, and pushed forward the well-known argument that the liberal state should not be abused by illiberal purposes. The most polemic voice here was raised by Schachtschneider (2011) who argued that the basic law of religious freedom should be limited due to the rise of Muslims and of what he called the "Islamization" of Europe. A milder version of a similar argument was raised by the constitutional lawyer Christine Langenfeld (2011).

23 This is information that has not been published, but which I gathered in personal interviews with representatives of Muslim organizations. See also Schiffauer, in *Berliner Zeitung* (March 26, 2009).
24 Conversation with Oğuz Üçüncü, conducted in Cologne-Kerpen, April 1, 2008. See also Werner Schiffauer's article in *Berliner Zeitung* (op.cit.).
25 This information is based on several conversations with participants and organizers of the DIK that I conducted during the first phase of the DIK (2006–09).
26 The results are documented on the DIK website at: http://www.deutsche-islam-konferenz.de/SharedDocs/Anlagen/DIK/DE/Downloads/LenkungsausschussPlenum/DIK-viertes-Plenum-Zwischen-Resuemee.pdf?__blob=publicationFile.
27 Of course, in dialogue models, offered by deliberative thinkers like Habermas or Benhabib, the ethical substance of constitutional norms is not demarcated a priori by one of the dialogue partners but is ideally constituted in the course of the encounter and under fair conditions. However, the presupposition of a universally understandable language is also ethically impregnated, and it functions prescriptively (see Amir-Moazami 2011).
28 In his discussion of Will Kymlicka's concept of multiculturalism, Markell elaborates on this tension concisely. Kymlicka's ultimate goal, Markell argues, was to make plural societies fit for liberal sensibilities, by fostering minorities' internal liberalization by granting them special rights or by exempting them from common law (2003: 159 and 60, 69).
29 See, for example, Seyran Ateş, "'Sie verglühen vor Leidenschaft", interview in *Der Spiegel*, October 12, 2009: http://www.spiegel.de/spiegel/print/d-67282871.html; Necla Kelek, "Die gescheiterte Islamkonferenz", in *Frankfurter Al/gemeine Zeitung*, June 25, 2009.

Chapter 5

1 For related arguments, see de Vries (2019) and Hansen (2010).
2 Stevens questions the uncritical acceptance by Brubaker and others of birthright as a "liberal" criterion of membership of a nation: "Territory as the criterion for membership only defers the site of birth invocations from the politically constituted family to the politically constituted territory. The effect of the citizenship criterion of birth in a territory is to sacralize the political borders, not to de-fetishize birth as a membership criterion" (Stevens 1990: 61).

3   This law was drafted after the 1842 "Prussian civil code" (*Preußisches Untertanengesetz*), which was the basis of all the nationality laws that followed, and in which descent was coined as the central element.
4   The nationality law, implemented in 2000, introduced much easier access to German nationality for immigrants who have lived in Germany for eight years (instead of fifteen), and thereby complemented the long-time dominance of *jus sanguinis* requirements with an increase of elements of *jus soli*. Naturalization in Germany is still particularly complicated and takes an exceptionally long time. A detailed account of the citizenship law and the criteria for admission to German nationality can be found under: http://www.verwaltungsvorschriften-im-internet.de/bsvwvbund_13122000_V612400513.htm.
5   https://www.gesetze-im-internet.de/stag/BJNR005830913.html.
    Taking into account Germany's diverse federal traditions, it is not purely accidental that Baden-Württemberg introduced the first naturalization test that focused exclusively on attitudes and social conduct. It was in the federal department of Baden Württemberg too, where the first nationwide debate on a teacher's headscarf was triggered (Amir-Moazami 2007a). And it was the federal government of Baden-Württemberg that first adopted laws banning headscarves for teachers on the basis of the federal constitution's emphasis on Germany's "Christian" heritage. Other federal states adopted different variations of citizenship tests, some of which similarly focused on the attitudes of those aspiring to be naturalized (e.g. in Hessen, see Björk 2011: 10).
6   In German: *Gesprächsleitfaden für die Einbürgerungsbehörden. Bekenntnis zur freiheitlichen demokratischen Grundordnung nach dem Staatsangehörigkeitsgesetz (StAG)*.
7   See, for example, Gössner (2006), Ekardt and Radtke (2007), Pressemitteilung Innenministerium Baden-Württemberg December 14, 2005; *Frankfurter Rundschau*, January 3, 2006; *Süddeutsche Zeitung*, January 3, 2006; *Frankurter Allgemeine Zeitung* January 5, 2006; *die tageszeitung* January 5, 2006; Welt am Sonntag January 8, 2006; *Frankfurter Allgemeine Zeitung*, January 10, 2006; *Süddeutsche Zeitung* January 9. 2006; *die tageszitung* January 11, 2006; *Frankfurter Rundschau* January 11, 2006; Pressemitteilung Stadt Heidelberg January 20, 2006; Pressemitteilung Hessisches Ministerium des Inneren und für Sport January 30, 2006.
8   The various criticisms about the discriminatory nature of the test led to its slight revision, or, more adequately, to the replacement of ten of the most controversial questions with a set of nine reformulated ones that mostly targeted the topic of security and extremism. The most controversial question—"Imagine that your

18-year old son tells you that he is a homosexual and wants to live with another man. How would you react?"—was abandoned entirely (Press note Ministry of the Interior, July 18, 2007: 4).

9   For a detailed account of Grell's rhetoric, and an analysis of his publication, see journalist Patrick Bahners (2011: Chapter 5).

10 See, for example: "Wahlkampftaktik oder einfach nur blanke Ignoranz?" *StZ*, January 14, 2006; *Rhein-Neckar-Zeitung*, January 21, 2006 "Der Fragebogen wird zum Wahlkampfthema" s. auch LT-BW Plenarprotokoll 13/106, S. 7652 l.Sp.

11 Grell was not bound to any political party and depicts himself as oscillating between his own leftist background and the conservative government, which hosted him. Such personal insights largely put into question the widely shared view of the exceptionality of the BW-test as a representation of a strongly conservative government.

12 Bertrams gradually gave up his interrogative tone and became more and more outspoken about what veiling symbolized for him: "A battle instrument for the implementation of an idea of the human that is partly incompatible with the constitution," https://www.welt.de/politik/deutschland/article138611955/Stellt-Karlsruhe-das-Kopftuch-besser-als-das-Kreuz.html.

13 Grell quotes the paragraph in the nationality laws in which nationality is attributed on the basis of the acceptance of the democratic order according to the democratic constitution in accordance with § 85 Abs. 1 Satz 1 Nr. 1 AuslG (today § 10 Abs. 1 Satz 1 Nr. 1 StAG).

14 Grell borrows his understanding of "Euro-Islam" from the political scientist Bassam Tibi (1998, 2000, 2009) who was based at the university of Göttingen. Tibi has elaborated his ideas about Euro-Islam in numerous publications. He evokes the French version of secularism as the remedy for preventing the intrusion of Islam into public life and into state institutions in Germany. Denouncing "immigrant cultures" in Europe for their "backwardness" (1998: 95), Tibi contends that to become truly European, Islam has to undergo the global process of transformation modeled by the Christian Reformation (Tibi 1998: 244). The test's unquestionable racializing impetus is thus coupled with a hierarchical ordering of how a successfully integrated religion should be displayed. A "sincere" affirmation of the liberal-democratic order not only means one's readiness to render one's belonging to Islam invisible by privatizing it. It means one's willingness to transcend one's belonging to the Islamic tradition through an affirmation of a Christian past and its supposed transformation into a secular, that is, universally accessible, presence. The idea of the German nation

as a "community of descent," which Tibi harshly critiques (1998: 92), is here replaced by a universal community of humans ("Weltbürger," in Tibi's terms, ibid.). The message is neither complex nor ambiguous: everybody is welcome into the "politically" defined community if they conform to Tibi's version of "Euro-Islam" (see Amir-Moazami 2007b).

15 He adds that some of her suggestions went too far even for him. He feared especially that questions like "Why do you want to apply for the German citizenship" or questions related to veiling could be in conflict with the German constitution. Grell reminds us, however, that questions addressing participation in sports and swimming classes were initially deleted after advice from church representatives. The questions were reinserted after Ulrich Goll, then Baden-Württemberg Minister of Justice responsible for immigration, and also a law professor, had stated: "For me, it is not acceptable when parents forbid their children from participating in swimming or biology classes. It is similarly unacceptable if children are not allowed to participate in school trips. Such a forced withdrawal by parents [of their children] is neither religiously or culturally justifiable; it harms the integration of children, and leads to their isolation" (Quoted in Grell 2006: 70). Grell admits that for "us subaltern [sic!] civil servants, this was a definite signal to address these issues and to reintroduce them into the questionnaire" (ibid.).

16 The full questionnaire can be found here: https://www.baden-wuerttemberg.datenschutz.de/gesprachsleitfaden-fur-die-einburgerungsbehorden-stand-01-09-2005/ (accessed October 1, 2020).

17 Question 5 asks, for example: "In Germany, political parties and associations can be forbidden due to unconstitutional actions. Would you nonetheless support such parties or associations? Under which conditions?" Question 2 asks: "You learn that people in your neighborhood or from your family or friends have conducted or are planning a terrorist act. How do you act? What do you do?" Question 23 asks: "You have heard about the attacks of September 11 in New York or March 11 in Madrid. Do you consider the perpetrators terrorists or freedom fighters? Explain your statement." Question 27 asks: "Some people make Jews responsible for all evil in the world and even claim that they were behind the attacks of 9/11. What do you think about such statements?"

18 In a manual attached to his report, Grell specifies when and how state officials should conduct the test, namely when they had doubts about whether the candidate had "really understood the content of the affirmation to the liberal-democratic order and if this affirmation corresponded to his or her inner conviction" (Grell 2006: 190).

19 The status of state officials in governmental integration practices oriented toward immigrants has only rarely been chosen as a topic for ethnographic investigation. An interesting exception is, for example, Oskar Verkaaik's article on Dutch civil servants in the context of citizenship ceremonies (2010). Verkaaik explores the tensions experienced by civil servants who, while first disapproving the measure as a neo-nationalist endeavor, were gradually caught within a logic of "cultural intimacy."
20 Jörg-Uwe Hahn, politician of the Liberal Party in Hessen, in PIPro 16/99, March 30, 2006: 6833.
21 "Integrationsdebatte. 'Einbürgerung macht Mündig'" in *Süddeutsche Zeitung*, September 7, 2008: http://www.sueddeutsche.de/politik/boehmer-zur-integrationsdebatte-einbuergerungstest-macht-muendig-1.214427 (accessed October 2, 2020).
22 "Institute for quality development in the domain of Education (Institut für Qualitätsentwicklung im Bildungswesen" (IQB).
23 Full information about the questionnaire and all 310 questions are available at the homepage of the Bundesamt für Migration und Flüchtlinge (BAMF): http://www.bamf.de/DE/Willkommen/Einbuergerung/WasEinbuergerungstest/waseinbuergerungstest-node.html.
24 The questionnaire consists of three sections: "Living in a Democracy," "History and Responsibility," and "Man and Society." These sections are divided into subsections covering Germany's legal and political order, German geography, German history, most particularly the recent past (National Socialism, the postwar era, and the fall of the wall) and, finally, questions related to "intercultural life" in German society.
25 The relegation of marriage from the church to the state has meant that reproduction as well as the collection and distribution of taxes turned into the contested domain of state authority. Pateman centrally argues that the sexual contract encapsulates marriage and the nuclear family as the core and instrument of modern forms of patriarchy. The state-contracted marriage encourages reproductive sex for the constitution of the liberal-political order, while relegating it to the private juridical domain. This partly explains why polygamous marriages are considered a serious threat to the existing legal order. Precisely because marriage is legally confined to private law, polygamous marriage causes a threat for the state to deal with it because it has not been previewed in the "sexual contract." The topic of polygamous marriages therefore appears in citizenship tests and in public debates, and it has also been under legal

investigation. There have even been suggestions by some political authorities to deprive naturalized immigrants with polygamous marriages from German nationality: http://dip21.bundestag.de/dip21/btd/19/105/1910518.pdf.

26 See http://www.integration-in-deutschland.de/SharedDocs/Anlagen/DE/Migration/Publikationen/Forschung/WorkingPapers/wp17-einbuergerung,templateId=raw,property=publicationFile.pdf/wp17-einbuergerung.pdf. See also Van Oers (2010).

27 http://www.bamf.de/DE/Einbuergerung/OnlineTestcenter/online-testcenter-node.html.

28 http://www.bpb.de/gesellschaft/migration/newsletter/57229/deutschland-einbuergerungstest-wirdfast-immer-bestanden.

29 On the intertwinement between power, knowledge, and pedagogy in the domain of recent integration measures in Germany, see also Ha and Schmitz (2006).

Conclusion

1 For a similar argument for the French context, see Fernando (2014: 236).

References

Agrama, H. A. (2012), *Questioning Secularism. Islam, Sovereignty, and the Rule of Law in Modern Egypt*, Chicago: Chicago University Press.

Aguilar, L.H. (2018), *Governing Muslims and Islam in Contemporary Germany. Race, Time and the German Islam Conference*, Leiden: Brill.

Akca, A.A. (2020), *Moscheeleben in Deutschland. Eine Ethnographie zu islamischem Wissen, Tradition und religiöser Autorität*, Bielefeld: transcript.

Amir-Moazami, S. (2005), "Buried Alive: Multiculturalism in Germany", *ISIM Review*, 16: 22–3.

Amir-Moazami, S. (2007a), *Politisierte Religion. Der Kopftuchstreit in Deutschland und Frankreich*, Bielefeld: transcript.

Amir-Moazami, S. (2007b), "Euro-Islam, Islam in Europe, or Europe Revised through Islam? Versions of Muslim Solidarity within European borders", in N. Karagiannis (ed.), *European Solidarity and Solidarity beyond Europe*. 186–213, Liverpool: University Press.

Amir-Moazami, S. (2011), "Dialogue as a Governmental Technique: Managing Gendered Islam in Germany", *Feminist Review*, 98: 9–27.

Amir-Moazami, S. (2013), "The Secular Embodiments of Face-veil Controversies across Europe", in N. Göle (ed.), *Islam and Public Controversy in Europe*, 83–100, Farnham: Ashgate.

Amir-Moazami, S. (2016), "Investigating the Secular Body: The Case of Male Circumcision", *ReOrient*, 1 (2): 25–48.

Anidjar, G. (2008), *Semites. Race, Religion, Literature*, Stanford: Stanford University Press.

Anidjar, G. (2015), "Christianity, Christianities, Christian", *Journal of Religious and Political Practice*, 1 (1): 39–46.

Arendt, H. (1981), *Rahel Varnhagen: Lebensgeschichte einer deutschen Jüdin aus der Romantik*, München: Piper.

Arendt, H. (2004 [1951]), *The Origins of Totalitarianism*, Orlando, Austin, New York, San Diego, and London: Harvest Book/Harcourt.

Asad, T. (1986), "The Idea of an Anthropology of Islam", in Georgetown University (ed.), *Center for Contemporary Arab Studies, Occasional Papers*, 1–14, Washington, DC: Georgetown University.

Asad, T. (1994), "Ethnographic Representation, Statistics, and Modern Power", *Socia Research*, 61 (1): 55–88.

Asad, T. (1993), *Genealogies of Religion. Discipline and Reasons of Power in Christianity and Islam*, Baltimore and London: Johns Hopkins University Press.

Asad, T. (2003), *Formations of the Secular, Christianity, Islam and Modernity*, Baltimore and London: Johns Hopkins University Press.

Asad, T. (2006), "Trying to Understand French Secularism", in H- De Vries and L. E. Sullivan (eds), *Political Theologies: Public Religions in a Post-Secular World*, 494–526, New York: Fordham University Press.

Asad, T. (2014), "Genealogies of Religion. Twenty Year on: An Interview with Talal Asad", *Bulletin for the Study of Religion*, 43 (1): 12–17.

Attia, I. (2009), *Die "westliche Kultur" und ihr Anderes: Zur Dekonstruktion von Orientalismus und antimuslimischem Rassismus*, Bielefeld: transcript.

Aumüller, J. (2009), *Assimilation. Kontroversen um ein migrationspolitisches Konzept*, Bielefeld: transcript.

Bade, K. (2007), "Leviten lesen: Migration und Integration in Deutschland", *Leviten lesen: Migration und Integration in Deutschland*, Göttingen: V&R unipress.

Bade, K. (2017), *Migration – Flucht – Integration: Kritische Politikbegleitung von der „Gastarbeiterfrage" bis zur „Flüchtlingskrise". Erinnerungen und Beiträge*, Karlsruhe: Von Loeper Literaturverlag.

Bade, K. and Bommes, M. (2004), "Migration und politische Kultur im „Nicht Einwanderungsland", in Klaus Bade (ed.) *Sozialhistorische Migrationsforschung*, 437–72, Göttingen: V&R unipress.

Bahners, P. (2011), *Die Panikmacher. Die deutsche Angst vor dem Islam. Eine Streitschrift*, München: C.H. Beck.

Balibar, E. and Wallerstein, W. (1988), *Race, nation, classe: les identités ambiguës*, Paris: La Découverte.

Bauman, Z. (1991), *Modernity and Ambivalence*, Cambridge: Polity Press.

Batnitzky, L. (2011), *How Judaism Become a Religion. An Introduction to Modern Jewish Thought*, Princeton: Princeton University Press.

Bazian, H. (2016), "Muslims Are Studied but Not Known", *Daily Sabah*, March, 30, 2016, available online: http://www.dailysabah.com/columns/hatembazian/2016/03/31/muslims-are-studied-but-not-known

Becher, I. and El-Menouar, Y. (2014), *Geschlechterrollen bei Deutschen und Zuwanderern christlicher und muslimischer Religionszugehörigkeit*, Bundesamt für Migration und Flüchtlinge, available online: http://www.deutsche-islam-konferenz.de/SharedDocs/Anlagen/DIK/DE/Downloads/WissenschaftPublikationen/studie-geschlechterrollen.pdf?__blob=publicationFile

Becker, C.H. (1909), "Christentum und Islam", *Religionsgeschichtliche Volksbücher für die heutige Gegenwart III*, 3 (8): 3–55.

Becker, C. H. (1916), "Islampolitik", *Die Welt des Islams. Zeitschrift der Gesellschaft für Islamkunde*, 3: 101–20.

Bergunder, M. (2012), "Was ist Religion? Kulturwissenschaftliche Überlegungen zum Gegenstand der Religionswissenschaft", *Zeitschrift für Religionswissenschaft*, 19 (1, 2): 3–55.

Berlin, I. (1958), *Two Concepts of Liberty: An Inaugural Lecture Delivered before The University of Oxford on 31 October 1958*, Oxford: Oxford University Press.

Berlin, I. (1969), "Two Concepts of Liberty", in I. Berlin (ed.), *Four Essays on Liberty*, 118–72, Oxford: Oxford University Press.

Bertrams, M. (2003), "Lehrerin mit Kopftuch? Islamismus und Menschenbild des Grundgesetzes", *DVBl, Deutsches Verwaltungsblatt*, 118 (19): 1225–34.

Bigo, D. (2002), "Security and Immigration: Toward a Critique of the Governmentality of Unease", *Alternatives: Global, Local, Political*, 27: 63–92.

Bigo, D. and Tsoukala, A. (2008), *Terror, Insecurity and Liberty: Illiberal Practices of Liberal Regimes after 9/11*, New York: Routledge.

Binswanger, K. and Sipahoglu, F. (1988), *Türkisch-Islamische Vereine als Faktor deutsch türkischer Koexistenz*, Benedictbeuern: Rieß-Druck und Verlag.

Birt, Y. (2006), "Good Imam, Bad Imam: Civic Religion and National Integration in Britain Post 9/11", *The Muslim World*, 96 (4): 687–705.

Björk, A. (2011), *The Politics of Citizenship Tests. Time, Integration and the Contingent Polity*, Dissertation Thesis, Jyväskyla Studies in Education, Psychology and Social Research University of Jyväskyla.

Borutta, M. (2011), *Antikatholizismus: Deutschland und Italien im Zeitalter der europäischen Kulturkämpfe*, Göttingen: Vandenhoeck & Ruprecht.

Bracke, S. (2011), "Subjects of Debate: Secular and Sexual Exceptionalism, and Muslim Women in the Netherlands", *Feminist Review*, 98 (1): 28–46.

Bracke, S. and Fadil, N. (2012), "'Is the Headscarf oppressive or emancipatory?' Fieldnotes from the 'Multicultural Debate'", *Religion and Gender*, 2 (1): 36–56.

Brettfeld, K. and Wetzels, P. (2007), *Muslime in Deutschland – Integration, Integrationsbarrieren, Religion und Einstellungen zu Demokratie, Rechtsstaat und politisch-religiös motivierter Gewalt*, Hamburg: Universität Hamburg, available online: https://www.deutsche-islam-konferenz.de/SharedDocs/Anlagen/DE/Downloads/WissenschaftPublikationen/muslime-in-deutschland-lang-dik.html?nn=598216.

Bröckling, U., Krasmann, S., and Lemke, T. (2012), *Governmentality. Current Issues and Future Challenges*, London and New York: Routledge.

Brown, W. (2006), *Regulating Aversion. Tolerance in the Age of Identity and Empire*, Princeton: Princeton University Press.

Brubaker, R. (1992), *Citizenship and Nationhood in France and Germany*, Cambridge, MA: Harvard Press.

Brunn, C. (2012), *Religion im Fokus der Religionspolitik. Ein Vergleich zwischen Frankreich, Deutschland und dem Vereinigten Königreich*, Wiesbaden: Springer.

Butler, J. (1997), *Excitable Speech. A Politics of the Performative*, London and New York: Routledge.

Butler, J. (2006), "Sexual Politics, Torture, and Secular Time", *British Journal of Sociology*, 59 (1): 1–23.

Butler, J. (2006 [2004]), *Precarious Life. The Powers of Mourning and Violence*, London and New York: Verso.

Caldwell, A. (2007), "Die Regierung der Menschheit. Gouvernementalität und Bio Souveränität", in S. Krasman and M. Volkmer (eds), *Foucaults "Geschichte der Gouvernementalität" in den Sozialwissenschaften*, 107–26, Bielefeld: transcript.

Cantzen, R. (2007), "Der ,deutsche Wertekonsens' und die Religion der Anderen. Kulturalisierung des Islam: Die 2. Islamkonferenz in ausgewälten Printmedien", in I. Attia (ed.), *Orient- und Islambilder*, 267–77, Münster: Unrast,.

Casanova, J. (1994), *Public Religions in the Modern World*, Princeton: Princeton University Press.

Castro Varela, M. (2013), *Ist Integration nötig? Eine Streitschrift*, Ettenheim: Lambertus.

Chakrabarty, D. (2000), *Provincializing Europe. Postcolonial Thought and Historical Difference*, Princeton: Princeton University Press.

Chin, R. (2009) "Guest Worker Migration and the Unexpected Return of Race", in R. Chin, H. Fehrenbach, G. Eley, and H. Grossmann (eds), *After the Nazi Racial State: Difference and Democracy in Germany and Europe*, 80–101, Ann Arbor: Michigan University Press.

Connolly, W. (2000), "Pluralism, Multiculturalism and the Nation-State: Rethinking the Connections", *Journal of Political Ideologies*, 1 (1): 53–73.

Daniel, A. (2016), *Die Grenzen des Religionsbegriffs. Eine postkoloniale Konfrontation des religionssoziologischen Diskurses*, Bielefeld: transcript.

Danzelot, J. (1997 [1977]), *The Policing of the Family*, Baltimore and London: Johns Hopkins University Press.

Davidson, N. (2012), *Only Muslim: Embodying Islam in Twentieth-Century France*, Ithaca: Cornell University Press.

Dean, M. (2001), *Governmentality. Power and Rule in Modern Society*, London, Thousand Oaks, New Dehli, Singapore: Sage.

De Genova, N. (2016), "The 'European' Question: Migration, Race and Post-Coloniality in 'Europe'", in A. Amelina, K. Horvath, and B. Meeus (eds), *An Anthology of Migration and Social Transformation*, 343–56, Cham, Heidelberg, New York, Dordrecht, and London: Springer International.

De Vries, B. (2019), "Are Civic Integration Tests Justifiable? A Three-step Test", in A. Lever and A. Poama (eds), *The Routledge Handbooks of Ethics and Public Policy*, 407–21, London and New York: Routledge.

Diner, D. (2014), "Statistik", in D. Diner (ed.), *Enzyklopädie jüdischer Geschichte und Kultur*, Vol. 5, 180–5, Stuttgart: J. B. Metzler.

Dornhof, S. (2009), "Constructing a Sociology of Islamist Radicalisation", *Race & Class*, 50 (4): 75–82.

EKD (ed.) (2006), *Klarheit und gute Nachbarschaft. Christen und Muslime in Deutschland. Eine Handreichung des Rates der EKD*, EKD Texte 86, Hannover, Kirchenamt der Evangelischen Kirche in Deutschland.

El-Mafalaani, A. (2018), *Das Integrationsparadox: Warum gelungene Integration zu mehr Konflikten führt*, Köln: Kiepenheuer und Witsch.

El-Tayeb, F. (2001), *Schwarze Deutsche: Der Diskurs um »Rasse« und nationale Identität 1890–1933*, Frankfurt am Main: Campus.

Elias, N. (2000 [1939]), *Über den Prozess der Zivilisation. Soziogenetische und psychogenetische Untersuchungen*, Bd. 1: *Wandlungen des Verhaltens in den weltlichen Oberschichtendes Abendlandes*, Frankfurt am Main: Suhrkamp.

Elsas, C. (1983), "Religiöse Faktoren für Identität: Politische Implikationen christlich islamischer Gespräche in Berlin", in C. Elsas (ed.), *Identität, Veränderungen kultureller Eigenarten im Zusammenleben von Türken und Deutschen*, 139–42, Hamburg: Rissen.

Espeland, W. N. and Stevens, M. L. (2008), "A Sociology of Quantification", *European Journal of Sociology (Archives Européennes de Sociologie)*, 49 (3): 401–36.

Fadil, N. (2011), "Not-/Unveiling as an Ethical Practice", *Feminist Review*, 98 (1): 83–109.

Fadil, N., De Koning, M., and Ragazzi, F. (eds) (2019), *Radicalisation in Belgium and the Netherlands. Critical Perspectives on Violence and Security*, London, New York, Oxford, Delhi, and Sydney: I. B. Tauris.

Fadil, N. and Fernando, M. (2015), "Rediscovering the 'Everyday' Muslim. Notes on an Anthropological Divide", *Journal of Ethnographic Theory*, 5 (2): 59–88.

Fernando, M. (2014), *The Republic Unsettled: Muslim French and the Contradictions of Secularism*, Durham and London: Duke University Press.

Feyerabend, P. (2010 [1975]), *Against Method*, London: Verso.

Fincke, G. (2009), *Abgehängt, chancenlos, unwillig? Eine empirische Reorientierung zu Integrationstheorien zu MigrantInnen der zweiten Generation in Deutschland*, Wiesbaden: VS Verlag.

Foroutan, N. (2010), "Mehr Muslime in gesellschaftliche Schlüsselpositionen", *Telepolis*, September 28, 2010.

Foucault, M. (2006 [1977–1979]), *Sicherheit, Territorium, Bevölkerung. Geschichte der Gouvernementalität I*, Frankfurt am Main: Suhrkamp.

Foucault, M. (2006 [1979]), *Die Geburt der Biopolitik. Geschichte der Gouvernementalität II*, Frankfurt a. M.: Suhrkamp.

Foucault, M. (2008 [1979]), *The Birth of Biopolitics. Lectures at the Collège de France 1978–79*, New York: Palgrave Macmillan.

Franke, P. (2012), "Der Islam: Staat und Religion im Europa der Neuzeit", in *Europäische Geschichte Online (EGO), des. Leibniz-Institut für Europäische Geschichte* (IEG), Mainz 2012-12-13, available online: http://www.ieg-ego.eu/frankep-2012-de.

Franz, J. (2018), "Verfremdungen: Muslim_innen als pädagogische Zielgruppe", in S. Amir Moazami (ed.), *Der inspizierte Muslim. Zur Politisierung der Islamforschung in Europa*, 309–34, Bielefeld: transcript.

Fülling, H. (2019), *Religion und Integration in der deutschen Islampolitik: Entwicklungen, Analysen, Ausblicke*, Wiesbaden: Springer V.S.

Gadamer (1990 [1960]), *Wahrheit und Methode. Grundzüge einer philosophischen Hermeneutik*, Frankfurt am Main: Suhrkamp.

Göle, N. and Amman, L. (eds) (2004), *Islam in Sicht. Der Auftritt von Muslimen im öffentlichen Raum*, Bielefeld: transcript.

Göpffarth, J. and Özyurek, E. (2021), "Spiritualconizing Reason, Rationalizing Spirit: Muslim Public Intellectuals in the German Far Right", *Ethnicities*, 21 (3): 1–23.

Gosewinkel, D. (2001), *Einbürgern und Ausschließen: Die Nationalisierung der Staatsangehörigkeit vom Deutschen Bund bis zur Bundesrepublik Deutschland*, Göttingen: V. & R.

Gössner, R. (2006), *Rechtspolitisch-gutachterliche Stellungnahme zum Gesprächsleitfaden für Einbürgerungsbehörden in Baden-Württemberg*, available online:http://www.igmg.org/fileadmin/pdf/muslime_und_sicherheit/gossnerstellgnahmenf2_06o.pdf

Gray, J. (2000), *Two Faces of Liberalism*, London: Polity.

Grell, R. (2006), *Dichtung und Wahrheit. Die Geschichte des ‚Muslim-Tests' in Baden Württemberg*. Unpublished manuscript, available online: http://www.pi-newsnet/wp/uploads/2008/02/muslimtest.pdf.

Ha, K. N. (2007), *Der nationale Integrationsplan auf dem Prüfstand*. Dossier der Heinrich-Böll Stiftung, Berlin: Heinrich-Böll-Stiftung.

Ha, K. N. and Schmitz, M. (2006), "Der nationalpädagogische Impetus der deutschen Integrations(dis)kurse im Spiegel post-/kolonialer Kritik", in P. Mecheril and M. Witsch (eds), *Cultural Studies und Pädagogik*, 226–66, Bielefeld: transcript.

Hacking, I. (1990), *The Taming of Chance*, Cambridge: Cambridge University Press.

Hacking, I. (2002), *Historical Ontology*, Cambridge, MA and London: Harvard University Press.

Hacking, I. (2006 [1975]), *The Emergence of Probability. A Philosophical Study of Early Ideas about Probability, Induction and Statistical Inference*, 2nd ed. Cambridge: Cambridge University Press.

Habermas, J. (1993), "Anerkennungskämpfe in einem demokratischen Rechtsstaat", in C. Taylor (ed.), *Multikuturalismus und die Politik der Anerkennung*, 147–96, Frankfurt am Main: Suhrkamp.

Habermas, J. (2009), *Zwischen Naturalismus und Religion. Philosophische Aufsätze*, Frankfurt am Main: Suhrkamp.

Habermas, R. (2014), "Debates on Islam in Imperial Germany", in D. Motadel (ed.), *Islam and the European Empires*, 233–55, Oxford: Oxford University Press.

Haraway, D. (1988), "Situated Knowledges. The Science Question in Feminism and the Privilege of a Partial Perspective", *Feminist Studies*, 14 (3): 575–99.

Hamburger, F. (1984), "Erziehung in der Einwanderungsgesellschaft", in H. M. Griese (ed.), *Der gläserne Fremde. Bilanz und Kritik der Gastarbeiterforschung und der Ausländerpädagogik*, 59–70, Opladen: Leske + Budrich.

Hansen, R. (2010), "Citizenship Tests: an Unapologetic Defence", in C. Joppke and R. Bauböck (eds), *How Liberal Are Citizenship Tests? EUI Working Paper RSCAS* 2010/41, 25–7, Badia Fiesolana: European University Institute.

Hariri, A. (2005), *Das Paradigma der »islamischen Zivilisation« – oder die Begründung der deutschen Islamwissenschaft durch Carl Heinrich Becker (1876–1933)*, Würzburg: Ergon.

Haug, S., Müssig, S., and Stichs, A. (2009), *Muslimisches Leben in Deutschland. Im Auftrag der Deutschen Islam Konferenz*. Forschungsbericht, 6, Nürnberg: Bundesamt für Migration und Flüchtlinge.

Heckmann, F. (2014), *Integration von Migranten. Einwanderung und neue Nationenbildung*, Wiesbaden: Springer.

Henkel, H. (2008), "Turkish Islam in Germany: A Problematic Tradition in the Project of Constitutional Patriotism?", *Journal of Muslim Minority Affairs*, 28 (1): 113–23.

Hermani, G. (2010), *Die Deutsche Islamkonferenz 2006 bis 2009 – der Dialogprozess mit den Muslimen in Deutschland im öffentlichen Diskurs*, Berlin: Finckenstein & Salmuth.

Hess, S., Binder, J., and Moser, J. (eds) (2009), *No integration?! Kulturwissenschaftliche Beiträge zur Integrationsdebatte in Europa*, Bielefeld: transcript.

Hindess, B. (1977), *Philosophy and Methodology in the Social Sciences*, Stanford: The Harvester Press.

Hindess, B. (2001), "The Liberal Government of Unfreedom", *Alternatives: Global, Local, Political*, 26 (2): 93–111.

Hirschmann, N. (2003), *The Subject of Liberty. Toward a Feminist Theory of Freedom*, Princeton: Princeton University Press.

Hochberg, G. (2016), "'Remembering Semitism' or 'On the Prospect of Re-Membering the Semites'", *ReOrient*, 1 (2): 192–223.

Hoffmann, R. (1982), "Die katholische Missionsbewegung in Deutschland vom Anfang des 19. Jahrhunderts bis zum Ende der deutschen Kolonialgeschichte", in K. J. Bade (ed.), *Imperialismus und Kolonialismus. Kaiserliches Deutschland und koloniales Imperium*, 29–50, Wiesbaden: Steiner.

Jackson, P. (2019), "South East Asian Area Studies beyond Anglo-America: Geopolitical Transitions, the Neoliberal Academy and Spatialized Regimes of Knowledge", *South East Asia Research*, 27 (1): 49–73.

Jansen, Y. (2013), *Secularism, Assimilation and the Crisis of Multiculturalism: French Modernist Legacies*, Amsterdam: Amsterdam University Press.

Jansen, Y. and Meer, N. (2020), "Genealogies of 'Jews' and 'Muslims': Social Imaginaries in the Race–Religion nexus", *Patterns of Prejudice*, 54 (1–2): 1–14.

Jasch, H.-C. (2007), "State-Dialogue with Muslim Communities in Italy and Germany – The Political Context and the Legal Frameworks for Dialogue with Islamic Faith Communities in Both Countries", *German Law Journal*, 4 (8): 141–79.

Johansen, B. and Spielhaus, R. (2012), "Counting Deviance. Revisiting a Decade's Production of Surveys among Muslims in Western Europe", *Journal of Muslims in Europe*, 1 (1): 81–112.

Johansen, B. (2013), "Post-secular Sociology: Modes, Possibilities and Challenges", *Approaching Religion*, 3 (1): 4–15.

Joppke, C. (2010), *Citizenship and Immigration*, Cambridge and Malden: Polity.

Joppke, C. and Bauböck, R. (eds) (2010), "How Liberal Are Citizenship Tests?" *EUI Working Paper RSCAS 2010/41*, Badia Fiesolana: European University Institute.

Jouili, J. (2015), *Pious Practice and Secular Constrains. Women in the Islamic Revival*, Stanford: Stanford University Press.

Kalmar, I. (2016), "Jews, Cousins of Arabs: Orientalism, Race, Nation, and Pan-Nation in the Long Nineteenth Century", in E. Nathan and A. Topolski (eds), *Is There a Judeo Christian Tradition? A European Perspective*, 53–74, Berlin: De Gruyter.

Kelek, N. (2005), *Die fremde Braut. Ein Bericht aus dem Inneren des türkischen Lebens in Deutschland*, Köln: Kiepenheuer und Witsch.

Kelek, N. (2006), "Teilnahme von muslimischen Kindern, insbesondere Mädchen, am Sport-, Schwimm- und Sexualkundeunterricht an staatlichen Schulen,

Teilnahme an Klassenfahrten", in *Bundesamt für Migration und Flüchtlinge*, Berlin: Bundesamt für Migration und Flüchtlinge.

Keskinkılıç, O.Z. (2018), "Islam und 'Türkenfieber' im kolonialen Gefüge. Zum Verhältnis von Orient-, Kolonial-, und Islampolitik im Deutschen Reich", in I. Attia and M. Popal (eds), *BeDeutungen dekolonisieren. Spuren von antimuslimischem Rassismus*, 200–22, Berlin: Unrast.

Keskinkılıç, O.Z. (2019), *Die Islamdebatte gehört zu Deutschland. Rechtspopulismus und antimuslimischer Rassismus im (post-)kolonialen Kontext*, Berlin: AphorismA.

Kirchenamt der Evangelischen Kirche in Deutschland (ed.) (2006), *Klarheit und gute Nachbarschaft. Christen und Muslime in Deutschland. Eine Handreichung des Rates der EKD*, EKD Texte 86, Hannover: EKD.

Kirk, D. (1994), "Physical Education and Regimes of the Body", *Australian and New Zealand Journal of Sociology*, 30 (2): 165–77.

Kirk, D. and Spiller, B (1994), "Schooling the Docile Body. Physical Education, Schooling and the Myth of Oppression", *Australian Journal of Education*, 38 (1): 78–95.

Koenig, M. (2003), *Staatsbürgerschaft und religiöse Pluralität in post-nationalen Konstellationen. Zum institutionellen Wandel europäischer Religionspolitik am Beispiel der Inkorporation muslimischer Immigranten in Grossbritannien, Frankreich und Deutschland*, Dissertation, Phillips-Universität Marburg.

Koopmans, R. (2015), "Religious Fundamentalism and Hostility against Out-groups: A Comparison of Muslims and Christians in Western Europe", *Journal of Ethnic and Migration Studies*, 41 (1): 33–57.

Koopmans, R. (2017), *Assimilation oder Multikulturalismus? Bedingungen gelungener Integration*. Berlin/Münster: LIT Verlag.

Kostakopoulou, D. (2010), "The Anatomy of Civic Integration", *Modern Law Review*, 73 (6): 933–58.

Kostermann, G. (2000), *Der Öffentlichkeitsauftrag der Kirchen – Rechtsgrundlagen im kirchlichen und staatlichen Recht. Eine Untersuchung zum öffentlichen Wirken der Kirchen in der Bundesrepublik Deutschland*, Tübingen: Mohr Siebeck.

Kugelmann, C. (1986), *Koedukation im Sportunterricht*, Wiebelsheim: Limpert.

Kugelmann, C. (1999), "Koedukation im Sportunterricht oder: Mädchen und Jungen gemeinsam in Spiel, Sport und Bewegung unterrichten - ein altes Thema neu betrachtet Sportpädagogik", December 7, 2021, available online: http://www.sportpaedagogik-online.de/koedu.htm.

Kugelmann, C., Pfister, G., and Zipprich, C. (2004), *Geschlechterforschung im Sport: Differenz und/oder Gleichheit. Beiträge aus der dvs-Kommission Frauenforschung in der Sportwissenschaft*, Hamburg: Feldhaus Verlag.

Kühn, H. (1979), *Kühn-Memorandum. Stand und Weiterentwicklung der Integration der ausländischen Arbeitnehmer und ihrer Familien in der Bundesrepublik Deutschland*, Bonn: Memorandum im Auftrag der Bundesregierung.

Kundnani, A. (2015), *A Decade Lost: Rethinking Radicalisation and Extremism*, London: Claystone.

Kwaschik, A. (2018), *Der Griff nach dem Weltwissen. Zur Genealogie von Area Studies im 19. und 20. Jahrhundert*, Göttingen: Vandenhoeck & Ruprecht.

Kymlicka, W. (1995), *Multicultural Citizenship: A Liberal Theory of Minority Rights*, Oxford: Oxford University Press.

Langenfeld, C. (2011), "Religiöse Freiheit für Muslime – Gefahr oder Hilfe für die Integration?", in Martin Honecker (eds), *Gleichheit der Religionen im Grundgesetz*, 30–49, Paderborn: Ferdinand Schöningh.

Laurence, J. (2011), *Emancipation of Europe's Muslims: The State's Role in Minority Integration*, Princeton: Princeton University Press.

Lavi, S. (2009), "Unequal Rites: Jews, Muslims and the History of Ritual Slaughter in Germany", in S. Lavi and J. Brunner (eds), *Juden und Muslime in Deutschland: Recht*, Religion, *Identität*, 164–84, Göttingen: Wallstein Verlag.

Lemke, T. (2010), "Foucault's Hypothesis: From the Critique of the Juridico-discursive Concept of Power to an Analytics of Government", PARRHESIA, 9: 31–43.

Lemke, T. (2011), *Biopolitics: An Advanced Introduction*, New York: New York University Press.

Lewicki, A. (2014), *Social Justice through Citizenship? The Politics of Muslim Integration in Germany and Great Britain*, Basingstoke: Palgrave Macmillan.

Link, C. (2000), *Staat und Kirche in der neueren deutschen Geschichte*, Frankfurt am Main, Berlin, Bern, Bruxelles, New York, Oxford and Vienna: Peter Lang.

Linke, U. (1999), *German Bodies. Race and Representation after Hitler*, New York and London: Routledge.

Linke, U. (2006), "Contact Zones. Rethinking the Sensual Life of the State", *Anthropological Theory*, 6 (2): 205–25.

Löwenheim, O., and Gazit, O. (2009), "Power and Examination. A Critique of Citizenship Tests", *Security Dialogue*, 40 (2): 145–67.

Lyotard, F. (1978), *La condition postmoderne*, Paris: Les éditions de minuit.

Mahmood, S. (2005), *Politics of Piety. The Islamic Revival and the Feminist Subject*, Princeton: Princeton University Press.

Mahmood, S. (2015), *Religious Difference in a Secular Age: A Minority Report*, Princeton: Princeton University Press.

Mangold, S. (2004), *Eine weltbürgerliche Wissenschat. Die deutsche Orientalistik im 19. Jahrhundert*, Stuttgart: Franz Steiner Verlag.

Mandel, R. (2008), *Cosmopolitan Anxieties. Turkish Challenges to Citizenship and Belonging in Germany*, Duke: Duke University Press.

Marchand, S. (2010), *German Orientalism in the Age of Empire: Religion, Race, and Scholarship*, Cambridge: Cambridge University Press.

Markell, P. (2003), *Bound by Recognition*, Princeton and Oxford: Princeton University Press.

Mas, R. (2006), "Compelling the Muslim Subject. Memory as Post-colonial Violence and the Public Performativity of 'Secular and Cultural Islam'", *The Muslim World*, 96 (4): 585–616.

Mas, R. (2011), "On the Apocalyptic Tones of Islam in Secular Time", in M. Dressler and A. S. Mandair (eds), *Secularism and Religion-Making*, 87–103, Oxford: Oxford University Press.

Massad, J. (2015), *Islam in Liberalism*, Chicago and London: Chicago University Press.

Masuzawa, T. (2005), *The Invention of World Religions: Or, How European Universalism Was Preserved in the Language of Pluralism*, Chicago, IL: Chicago University Press.

Mavelli, L. (2012), *Europe's Encounter with Islam: The Secular and the Postsecular*, Abingdon and New York: Routledge.

Meer, N. (2013), "Racialization and Religion: Race, Culture and Difference in the Study of Antisemitism and Islamophobia", *Ethnic and Racial Studies*, 36 (3): 385–98.

Meer, N., Mouritsen, P., Faas, D., and De Witte, N. (eds) (2015), "Examining 'Postmulticultural' and Civic Turns in the Netherlands, Britain, Germany and Denmark", *American Behavioural Scientist*, 59 (6): 619–36.

Meier-Braun, K.-H. (2002), *Deutschland, Einwanderungsland*, Frankfurt am Main: Suhrkamp.

Merolli, J. L. (2015), *Feeling like a Citizen: Integration Exams, Expertise and Sites of Resistance in the United Kingdom and the Netherlands*, Ontario, Canada, Dissertation, December 7, 2021, available online:https://macsphere.mcmaster.ca/bitstream/11375/18342/2/J.Merolli%20-%20Thesis%20-%20Final%20Submission.pdf.

Mignolo, W. D. (2009), "Epistemic Disobedience, Independent Thought and Decolonial Freedom", *Theory, Culture & Society*, 26 (7–8): 159–81.

Michalowski, I. (2009), "Citizenship Tests in Five Countries – An Expression of Political Liberalism?", *WZB Discussion Paper*, SP IV 2009-702, Berlin: WZB.

Michalowski, I. (2011), "Required to Assimilate? The Content of Citizenship Tests in Five Countries", *Citizenship Studies*, 15 (6–7): 749–68.

Mittmann, T. (2011), "Säkularisierungsvorstellungen und religiöse Identitätsstiftung im Migrationsdiskurs", *Archiv für Sozialgeschichte*, 51: 267–89.

Modood, T. (2012), "Differenz und Integration", *Forschungsjournal Soziale Bewegungen*, 25 (1): 5–20.

Morsi, Y. (2017), *Radical Skin, Moderate Masks*, London and New York: Rowman Littlefield.

Müller, T. (2018), "Sicherheitswissen und Extremismus. Definitionsdynamiken in der deutschen Islampolitik", in S. Amir-Moazami (ed.), *Der inspizierte Muslim. Zur Politisierung der Islamforschung in Deutschland*, 185–214, Bielefeld: transcript.

Muckel, S. (2012), "Antworten des staatlichen Religionsrechts auf Herausforderungen durch den Islam", in L. Häberle and J. Hattler (eds), *Islam – Säkularismus – Religionsrecht. Aspekte und Gefährdungen der Religionsfreiheit*, 61–78, Berlin: Springer.

Nathan, E. and Topolski, A. (2016), *Is There a Judeo-Christian Tradition? A European Perspective*, Berlin: De Gruyter.

Neumann, U. (1980), *Erziehung ausländischer Kinder. Erziehungsziele und Bildungsvorstellungen in türkischen Arbeiterfamilien*, Düsseldorf: Pädagogischer Verlag.

Nikolinakos, M. (1973), *Die Politische Ökonomie der Gastarbeiterfrage. Migration und Kapitalismus*, Hamburg: Rohwolt.

Nirenberg, D. (2013), *"Jüdisch" als politisches Konzept. Eine Kritik der Politischen Theologie*, Göttingen: Wallstein.

Nirenberg, D. (2014), *Anti-Judaism. The Western Tradition*, New York: Norton and Company.

O'Brian, P. (1996), *Beyond the Swastika*, London and New York: Routledge.

Orgad, L. (2010), "Illiberal Liberalism. Cultural Restrictions on Migration and Access to Citzenship in Europe", *The American Journal of Comparative Law*, 58 (1): 53–105.

Pateman, C. (1988), *The Sexual Contract*, Cambridge: Cambridge University Press.

Peter, F. (2008), "Political Rationalities, Counter-Terrorism and Policies on Islam in the United Kingdom and France", in J. Eckert (ed.), *The Social Life of Anti-Terrorism Laws*, 79–108, Bielefeld: transcript.

Peter, F. (2010), "Welcoming Muslims into the Nation: Tolerance Politics and Integration in Germany", in J Cesari (ed.), *Muslims in Europe and the United States since 9/11*, 119–44, London and New York: Routledge.

Peter, F. (2021), *Islam and the Governing of Muslims in France. Secularism without Religion*, London, New York, Oxford, New Dehli, and Sidney: Bloomsbury Academic.

Pfister, G. (1998), „Historische Entwicklung des Schulsports und der Koedukation", in Landesinstitut für Schule und Weiterbildung (ed.), *Mädchen und Jungen im Schulsport*, 59–82, Bönen: Kettler.

Pfündel, K., Stichs, A, and Tanis, K. (2021), *Muslimisches Leben in Deutschland. Studie im Auftrag der Deutschen Islam Konferenz*, Berlin: Bundesamt für Migration und Flüchtlinge.

Plessner, H. (1974), *Die verspätete Nation*, Frankfurt am Main: Suhrkamp.

Polaschegg, A. (2005), *Der andere Orientalismus. Regeln deutsch-morgenländischer Imagination im 19. Jahrhundert*, Berlin and New York: de Gruyter.

Povinelli, E. (2002), *The Cunning of Recognition. Indigenous Alterities and the Making of Australian Multiculturalism*, Durham and London: Duke University Press.

Purtschert, P., Meyer, K., and Winter, Y. (2007), *Gouvernementalität und Sicherheit: Zeitdiagnostische Beiträge im Anschluss an Foucault*, Bielefeld: transcript.

Qasem, S. (2020), "MuslimInnen unter Generalverdacht: Perspektiven auf die Prävention von sogenanntem islamistischem Extremismus", in F Hafez and S. Qasem (eds), *Jahrbuch Islamophobieforschung/Islamophobia Studies Yearbook*, Vol. 11, 15–34, Wien: New Academic Press.

Reuter, A. (2014), *Religion in der verrechtlichten Gesellschaft: Rechtskonflikte und öffentliche Kontroversen um Religion als Grenzarbeiten am religiösen Feld*, Göttingen: Vandenhoeck & Ruprecht.

Rommelspacher, B. (2017), *Wie christlich ist unsere Gesellschaft? Das Christentum im Zeitalter von Säkularität und Multireligiosität*, Bielefeld: transcript.

Rose, N. (1999a), *Powers of Freedom. Reframing Political Thought*, Cambridge: Cambridge University Press.

Rose, N. (1999b), *Governing the Soul. The Shaping of Private Life*, 2nd ed. London: Free Assn Books.

Rütten, A. (2013), "Die Erfindung der Integrationspolitik", in D. Huneke (ed.), *Ziemlich Deutsch. Betrachtungen aus dem Einwanderungsland*, 31–42, Bonn: Bundeszentrale für Politische Bildung.

Saar, M. (2007), "Macht, Staat, Subjektivität. Foucaults ‚Geschichte der Gouvernementalität im Werkkontext", in S. Krasmann and M Volkmer (eds), *Michel Foucaults "Geschichte der Gouvernementalität" in den Sozialwissenschaften. Internationale Beiträge*, 23–45, Bielefeld: transcript.

Salvatore, A. (1999), *Islam and the Political Discourse of Modernity*, Reading: Ithaca.

Santner, E. (2011), *The Royal Remains: The People's Two Bodies and the Endgarnes of Sovereignty*, Chicago: University of Chicago Press.

Sayyid, S. (2014), *Recalling the Caliphate. Decolonisation and World Order*, London: Hurst.

Schlerka, S.M. (2021), *Islamdebatten im Deutschen Bundestag 1990–2009. Eine Habitusanalyse zur Formierungsphase deutscher Islampolitik*, Wiesbaden: Springer.

Schmolze, C. (2007), *Koedukation im Sportunterricht: Notwendigkeiten und Möglichkeiten der Differenzierung*, Saarbrücken: VDM Verlag Dr. Müller.

Shooman, Y. (2014), » … weil ihre Kultur so ist«: Narrative des antimuslimischen Rassismus, Bielefeld: transcript.
Shooman, Y. (2015), "Zur Debatte über das Verhältnis von Antisemitismus, Rassismus und Islamfeindlichkeit", Jahrbuch zur Geschichte und Wirkung des Holocaust, 19: 125–56.
Schachtschneider, K. A. (2011), Grenzen der Religionsfreiheit am Beispiel des Islam, Berlin: Dunker und Humblot.
Schaffer, J. (2007), Ambivalenzen der Sichtbarkeit. Über die visuellen Strukturen der Anerkennung, Bielefeld: transcript.
Schäuble, W. (2006a), "Muslime in Deutschland", Faz-net, September 27, 2006, available online:http://www.wolfgang-schaeuble.de/einheit-in-der-vielfalt-integration-in-deutschland/ (accessed December 7, 2021).
Schäuble, W. (2006b), "Einheit in der Vielfalt: Integration in Deutschland. Zugehörigkeit und Zusammengehörigkeit sind das Ziel von Integration", public lecture given at: Evangelische Akademie Tutzing, July 1, 2006, available online:http://www.deutsche-islam-konferenz.de/DIK/DE/Service/Bottom/RedenInterviews/Reden/20060701-einheitindervielfalt.html
Schäuble, W. (2008), "Staat und Religion in der pluralen Gesellschaft", "Heidelberger Hochschulrede" von Bundesminister Dr. Wolfgang Schäuble: "Staat und Religion in der pluralen Gesellschaft", October 29, 2008, available online:http://www.uni-heidelberg.de/presse/news08/pm2810303hfjs.html
Schäuble, W. (2009), "Zusammen in Deutschland - Zum Dialog zwischen Christen und Muslimen", Speech held at Theologischen Forums Christentum-Islam, 6. März 2009, Hohenheim, available online:http://www.deutsche-islam-konferenz.de/DIK/DE/Service/Bottom/RedenInterviews/Reden/20090306-theologisches-forum.html
Scheer, M. (2012), "Protestantisch fühlen lernen. Überlegungen zur emotionalen Praxis der Innerlichkeit", Zeitschrift für Erziehungswissenschaft, 15 (1): 179–93.
Scheffel, H. (1996), MädchenSport und Koedukation. Aspekte einer feministischen Sport-praxis, Butzbach-Griedel: Afra-Verlag.
Schiffauer, W. (2008a), "Zur Konstruktion von Sicherheitspartnerschaften", in M. Bommes and M. Krüger-Potratz (eds), Migrationsreport 2008. Fakten, Analysen, Perspektiven, 205–38, Frankfurt/M.: Campus.
Schiffauer, W. (2008b), Parallelgesellschaften: Wie viel Wertekonsens braucht unsere Gesellschaft? Für eine kluge Politik der Differenz, Bielefeld: transcript.
Schiffauer, W. (2010), Nach dem Islamismus. Eine Ethnographie der Islamischen Gemeinschaft Milli Görüş, Frankfurt am Main: Suhrkamp.
Schiffauer, W. (2015), "Sicherheitswissen und Prävention", in Friedrich-Ebert-Stiftung (ed.), Handlungsempfehlungen zur Auseinandersetzung mit islamistischem

Extremismus und Islamfeindlichkeit, Arbeitsergebnisse eines Expertengremiums der Friedrich-Ebert Stiftung, Berlin: Friedrich-Ebert-Stiftung, 217–43, Berlin: Friedrich-Ebert-Stiftung.

Schinkel, W. (2017), *Imagined Soceities. A Critique of Immigrant Integration in Western Europe*, Cambridge: Cambridge University Press.

Scott Wallach, J. (1997), *Only Paradoxes to Offer: French Feminists and the Rights of Man*, Harvard: Harvard University Press.

Scott Wallach, J. (2019), *Sex and Secularism*, Princeton: Princeton University Press.

Silverstein, P. (2004), *Algeria in France: Transpolitics, Race, and Nation*, Bloomington: Indiana University Press.

Sorkin, D. (2019), *Jewish Emancipation. A History across Five Centuries*, Chicago: Chicago University Press.

Spielhaus, R. (2011a), *Wer ist hier Muslim? Die Entwicklung eines islamischen Bewusstseins in Deutschland zwischen Selbstidentifikation und Fremdzuschreibung*, Würzburg: Ergon.

Spielhaus, R. (2011b), "Measuring the Muslim: About Statistical Obsessions, Categorisations and the Quantification of Religion", *Yearbook of Muslims in Europe*, 3: 695–715.

Spielhaus, R. (2013), "Vom Migranten zum Muslim und wieder zurück – Die Vermengung von Integrations- und Islamthemen in Medien, Politik und Forschung", in H.Meyer et al, (eds), *Islam und die deutsche Gesellschaft*, 169–94, Wiesbaden: VS-Verlag.

Spielhaus, R. (2020), "10 Jahre nach ‚Der Islam gehört zu Deutschland'. Wie steht es um die rechtliche Anerkennung des Islams?", Eine Expertise für den Mediendienst Integration, December 7, 2021, available online: https://mediendienstintegration.de/fileadmin/Dateien/Expertise_Rechtliche_Anerkennung_des_Islams.pdf.

Stauth, G. (1993), *Islam und westlicher Rationalismus. Der Beitrag des Orientalismus zur Entstehung der Soziologie*, Frankfurt am Main: Campus.

Stein, T. (2008), "Gibt es eine multikulturelle Leitkultur als Verfassungspatriotismus? Zur Integrationsdebatte in Deutschland", *Leviathan*, 36 (1): 33–53.

Stevens, J. (1990), *Reproducing the State*, Princeton and New Jersey: Princeton University Press.

Stoler, S. (1997), "Racial Histories and Their Regimes of Truth", *Political Power and Social Theory*, 11: 183–206.

Stoler, A. L. (2008), "Epistemic Politics: Ontologies of the Colonial Common Sense", *Philosophical Forum*, 39 (3): 349–69.

Stoler, A. L. (2016), *Duress: Imperial Durabilities in Our Times*, Durham and London: Duke University Press.

Sullivan, W. (2005), *The Impossibility of Religious Freedom*, Princeton: Princeton University Press.

Supik, L. (2014), *Statistik und Rassismus. Das Dilemma der Erfassung von Ethnizität*, Frankfurt am Main: Campus.

Seth, S. (2008), "Which Past? Whose Transcendental Presupposition?", *Postcolonial Studies*, 11 (2): 215–26.

Taylor, C. (1992), *Multiculturalism and the Politics of Recognition. An Essay by Charles Taylor*, Princeton: Princeton University Press.

Tezcan, L. (2006), "Interreligiöser Dialog und politische Religionen". Aus Politik und Zeitgeschichte: Beilage zur Wochenzeitung Das Parlament.

Tezcan, L. (2007), "Kultur, Gouvernementalität der Religion und der Integrationsdiskurs", in M. Wohlrab-Sahr and L. Tezcan (eds), *Konfliktfeld Islam in Europa*, Special Issue, *Soziale Welt*, 51–74, Baden-Baden: Nomos.

Tezcan, L. (2012), *Das muslimische Subjekt. Verfangen im Dialog der Deutschen Islam Konferenz*, Konstanz: Konstanz University Press.

Thomä-Venske, H. (1981), *Islam und Integration. Zur Bedeutung des Islam im Prozeß der Integration türkischer Arbeiterfamilien in die Gesellschaft der Bundesrepublik*, Hamburg: Rissen.

Tibi, B. (1998), *Europa ohne Identität? Die Krise der multikulturellen Gesellschaft*, München: Bertelsmann.

Tibi, B. (2000), *Der Islam in Deutschland. Muslime in Deutschland*, Stuttgart and München: Deutsche Verlagsanstalt.

Tibi, B. (2009), *Euro-Islam: Die Lösung eines Zivilisationskonfliktes*, Darmstadt: WBG academic.

Topolski, A. (2018), "Good Jew, bad Jew … good Muslim, bad Muslim: 'managing' Europe's others", *Ethnic and Racial Studies*, 41 (12): 2179–96.

Turner, B.S. (1993), *Max Weber: From History to Modernity*, London and New York: Routledge.

Tyrer, D. (2013), *The Politics of Islamophobia Race, Power and Fantasy*, London: Pluto.

Van Bijsterveld, S. (2015), "Religion and Law in the Netherlands", *Insight Turkey*, 17 (1): 121–42.

Van Oers, R. (2010), "Citizenship Tests in the Netherlands, Germany and the Uk", in R.Van Oers, E. Ersbøoll, and D. Kostakopoulo (eds), *A Re-Definition of Belonging? Language and Integration Tests in Europe*, 50–104, Leiden: Brill.

Verkaaik, O. (2010), "The Cachet Dilemma: Ritual and Agency in New Dutch Nationalism", *American Ethnologist*, 37 (1): 69–82.

Vial, T. (2016), *Modern Race, Modern Religion*, Oxford: Oxford University Press.

Westerduin, M. (2020), "Questioning Religio-Secular Temporalities: Mediaeval Formations of Nation, Europe and Race", *Patterns of Prejudice,* 54 (1–2): 136–49.

Wiese, K. (2008), *Lehrerinnen mit Kopftuch: Zur Zulässigkeit eines religiösen und geschlechtsspezifischen Symbols im Staatsdienst*, Berlin: Dunker und Humblot.

Winkler, J. (2017), "Freunde führen einander – Der kommunalpolitische Dialog mit dem 'Islam' im Modus einer Gouvernementalität der Freundschaft", *Geogr. Helv.,* 72 (303): 316.

Yuval-Davis, N. (1997), *Gender and Nation*, London: Sage.

Zimmermann, A. (2013), "From Internal Colonization to Overseas Colonization", in G. Steinmetz (ed.), *Sociology and Empire. The Imperial Entanglements of a Discipline*, 166–87, Durham and London: Duke University Press.

Žižek, S. (1998), *Ein Plädoyer für die Intoleranz*, Wien: Passagen.

Index

acculturation 157 n.9. *See also* culture
Ahmadiyya Muslim Jamaat 156 n.8
Anidjar, Gil 38, 58–9
   Semitic hypothesis 39
anthropos 78–9. *See also* humanitas
anti-Semitism 7, 44, 57, 124
Arab 39, 158 n.19
Arendt, Hannah 16, 154 n.9
   Jewish question 153 n.8
   race thinking 40
Aryan/Aryan language 37–8
Asad, Talal 22–3, 158 n.16
Asia/Asian language 37
assimilation 5, 31, 39–47, 52, 59, 67, 74, 83, 107, 110–11, 120, 154 n.9, 157 n.6, 157 n.9
Aumüller, Jutta 43, 45
Austin's speech act theory 122

Bade, Klaus 151 n.4
Batnitzky, Leora 154 n.13
   How Judaism Become a Religion: An Introduction to Modern Jewish Thought 43
Baubӧck, Rainer 112
Bauman, Zygmunt 5
   arbitrating power 146
   on assimilation 40–1, 44, 74
   on Jewish intellectuals in Germany 42
   Modernity and Ambivalence 31
Bazian, Hatem 62
Becher, Inna 157 n.8
Becker, Carl Heinrich 7, 32–3, 35, 37–8, 122, 152 nn.2–3, 153 n.6
   on problem of Islam 33–4, 39
Bergunder, Michael 81
Berlin, Isaiah 152 n.8, 160 n.3
Berlin Social Science Center (*Wissenschaftszentrum Berlin*) 67
Bertrams, Michael 118, 166 n.12
biocracy 15–17

biopolitics 15, 51, 69, 74
Bӧhmer, Maria 97–8, 100–1, 103–5, 107, 132–3
Bracke, Sarah 159 n.23
Brettfeld, Katrin, *Muslims in Germany: Integration, barriers to integration, religion and attitudes towards democracy, the rule of law, and politically-religiously motivated violence* 65
Brown, Wendy 160 n.3
   tolerance discourses 13–14
Brubaker, Rogers 115, 164 n.2
Buddhism 37, 43, 134
Bundesamt für Migration und Flüchtinge (BAMF) 64, 137, 168 n.23
bureaucrats/bureaucracy 10, 15–17, 72, 118, 125, 127–30, 132, 142–4, 154 n.10
Butler, Judith 122–3, 131

Cartesian body-mind split 77–8, 158 n.15
Chin, Rita 51
Christian/Christianity 7, 12, 33–9, 43–4, 56–7, 67–8, 79, 81–4, 90–5, 122, 134, 147–8, 154 n.9, 154 n.13, 158 n.15, 158 n.18, 159 n.22, 165 n.5. *See also* Budhism; Islam; Jews/Jewish; Judaism; non-Christian
   Catholicism 43, 100, 152 n.3
   Christian churches 53–5, 58, 93–4, 114, 155 n.7
   Christian Reformation 166 n.14
   missionary movements 55
   missionaries in African colonies 152 n.3
   political theology 94
   Western European 34–5, 38
churchification (*Verkirchlichung*) of Islam 94

Index

citizens/citizenship 6, 15, 17–18, 26, 41–2, 96, 112–14, 116, 154 n.10, 167 n.15
   citizenship laws 47, 49, 165 n.4
   citizenship tests 15, 17–18, 111–14, 132, 144, 149, 165 n.5
   across Europe 137
   BW-test 116–17, 121–2, 125, 127, 131–3, 166 n.11
   confession by civil servants (*Beamte*) 117–21
   knowledge-based 133–9
   loyalty 123–7, 132, 144
   membership speech acts 121–3
   criterion of birth 164 n.2
   formal 111
   institutionalization of 136
   moral 111
   and nationhood 114–16
civilization 16, 33, 36–7, 42, 158 n.19
civil society 6, 13–14, 23, 29, 53, 56–7, 76, 105, 121, 142, 148, 155 n.2
coercion 18–19, 108
Cohen, Arthur 73
colonialism 36, 92, 145, 153 n.5
commodification 51
Community of German Values (*deutsche Wertegemeinschaft*) 104
Connolly, William E. 102
Conseil français du culte musulman (CFCM) 152 n.9, 161 n.6
Constitution Plus (*Grundgesetz Plus*) 26, 104–7, 125, 132, 143
Coran Schools' (*Koranschulen*) 49
corporeal practices, Muslim 25, 41, 77–8, 102, 126, 149, 154 n.11
criminology 11, 66–7, 80
critical migration studies (scholarship) 3, 21, 111
critics of Islam (*Islamkritiker*) 96, 109, 162 n.13
culture 4–5, 9, 45, 49–60, 69, 77, 146
   conflict of culture (*Kulturkonflikt*) 50
   cultural diversity 50, 97–8
   cultural identity 50, 88, 161 n.5
   cultural plurality 14, 21, 29, 47–8, 51, 98 (*see also* religion, religious plurality)
   cultural racism 51
   cultures of origin (*Heimatkulturen*) 49
   German 50, 64, 66, 70, 73–5, 134

Dean, Mitchell 17
   on dividing practices 20
demarcations 8, 25–6, 40, 45, 56, 58, 85, 98, 103, 116, 138
democracy 63, 66, 69, 75, 91, 116, 166 n.13
   democratic state 12, 15, 93
   liberal 25–6, 90–3, 95, 105–6, 112, 116, 118–20, 128, 133–4, 145, 148, 166 n.14, 167 n.18
Descartes, René 159 n.24
descent (*Herkunft*) 48, 80–1, 114, 119, 126, 165 n.3, 167 n.14
Deutsche Islam Konferenz (DIK) 25–6, 30, 55, 61, 64, 68, 87, 90, 94–8, 103–6, 109, 158 n.14, 160 n.1, 161 n.6, 161 n.8, 162 n.13, 162 n.16, 164 n.25
diaspora 36
Diner, Dan 74
discrimination 51, 66, 75, 108
discursive explosion on Muslims 59

education/educational system 33–4, 48, 53, 66–7, 101, 151 n.7, 155 n.2
   Becker on 33
   civic 138
   coeducation/coeducational sports 96–7, 99, 101, 161 n.12, 162 n.15, 163 n.21 (*see also* sports)
   physical 98–9
Elias, Norbert 19
emancipation 7, 34, 43–5, 88, 108, 154 n.12
Enlightenment 33, 41, 76, 81, 92, 159 n.22
   Enlightenment-Protestant 81
epistemology 8, 12–13, 24–5, 32–4, 40, 63–4, 71, 73, 76, 79, 147, 156 n.4
Erdsiek-Rave, Ute 97
Esser, Hartmut 157 n.9
ethnic/ethnicity 35, 43, 51, 59, 65, 67, 69, 75, 77, 80, 102, 113–15, 126, 142, 157 n.13
   ethnic background 64–5
   ethnic minorities 75
Eurocentric epistemology 78
Europe/European 2–4, 6–7, 9, 14, 21, 23–5, 33–9, 67–8, 76, 87, 92, 111–12, 123, 151 n.5, 152 n.9, 160 n.24
   citizenship tests across 137
   Euro-Islam 1, 33, 119–20, 122–3, 152 n.1, 166 n.14

European Enlightenment 33
Islamization of 163 n.22
sociological knowledge in 8
survey data on Muslim 62–3
Western 34–5, 38, 45, 109, 153 n.8
Evangelischer Kirchenrat Deutschlands (EKD) 55–7
"Clarity and Good Neighborliness" (*Klarheit und gute Nachbarschaft*) 55–6, 93
extremism 49, 165 n.8

Fadil, Nadia 159 n.23
Federal Office of Migration and Refugees 133
First World War 32–3
foreign co-citizens (*ausländische Mitbürger*) 48, 50
foreign workers 48–9
Foucault, Michel 15, 17–19, 63, 159 n.24
 on governmentality 10
 regimes of truth 69–70, 77, 89
France 6, 19, 152 n.9, 162 n.14
 French Muslims 1
Franke, Patrick 152 n.1
Franz, Julia 50
Friedländer, Samuel 154 n.11
fundamentalism/fundamentalist 66–8, 82, 120, 142

Gazit, Orit 137
Geiger, Abraham 154 n.11
gender 50, 53, 63, 96, 124, 161 n.12
 equality 93–4, 96–8, 100–1, 126, 136–7
 gender-segregation 97, 99, 149 (*see also* segregation)
 hierarchies 99
 inequality 57, 101, 104
genealogy 6, 81, 85, 160 n.3
German basic law (*Religionsverfassungsrecht*) 53
German/Germany 2–3, 5, 7, 9, 17, 19–21, 26, 51, 59
 anti-Muslim racism in 7
 Baden-Württemberg 100
  BW-test 116–17, 121–2, 125, 127, 131–3, 166 n.11
 Bauman on Jewish intellectuals in 42
 Bavaria 100

Berlin 50
 Christian authorities in 54
 citizenship (*see* citizens/citizenship)
 constitutional loyalty of Muslims 17, 20, 26, 64, 92–3, 102, 113–14, 116–17, 119, 121–3, 125, 132–3, 143–4
 constitutional principles 103–5, 112, 117, 123, 126–8, 138, 155 n.7, 163 n.22
 ethical impregnation 105–6
 culture 50, 64–5, 70, 73–5, 134
 Day of the Foreigner (*Tag des ausländischen Mitbürgers*) 50
 Demand and Support (*Fördern und Fordern*) slogan 3, 48, 50, 52, 108, 145, 151 n.3
 East Germans 155 n.4
 education (*see* education/educational system)
 employment in 1, 156 n.9
 foreign co-citizens (*ausländische Mitbürger*) 50 (*see also* immigration/immigrants)
 German Empire (1884–1914) 38, 152 n.3, 153 n.5
 Germanness 42, 65, 113, 119
 guest-worker system in 47–8, 50
 Hamburg 156 n.8, 161 n.12
 Hessen 156 n.8
 Immigration Act of 2005 3, 151 n.3
 immigration policy (laissez-faire) of 29, 46–8, 51, 151 n.4, 154 n.1
 imperialism 7, 39, 92, 115, 123, 153 nn.5–6
 interfaith dialogue initiatives in 55
 Islampolitik (*see Islampolitik*)
 Jewish assimilation 41
 learning the nation 133–9
 marriages in 96, 121, 135–6, 168 n.25
 multiculturalism (*Multikulti*) 51, 53, 90, 164 n.28
 Münster 118, 161 n.12
 Muslims in Germany into German Muslims (integration) 6–8, 12–13, 22–5, 30–2, 34, 45, 60–1, 71, 90–3, 105–6, 146
 nationality code 49, 114, 116, 119
 nationality/nationality law 49, 113–15, 117, 126, 165 nn.3–4, 166 n.13

nationhood 18, 41, 95, 114–16
Orientalist scholarship 32–3
politico-theological structure 59, 109, 158 n.15
public mission (*Öffentlichkeitsauftrag*) 54
radicalization of Muslims 62, 67
survey data on Muslim (*see* surveys on Muslims)
German Islam Conference. *See Deutsche Islam Konferenz* (DIK)
German Youth Institute 48
Goll, Ulrich 167 n.15
Gosewinkel, Dieter 114–15
governance 3, 6, 9–11, 14, 19, 21, 25, 38, 63, 71, 75, 82, 91, 100, 145
governmentality *(gouvernementalité)* 9–21, 61, 69, 106, 114, 130–2, 141–4
secular 9, 22, 71, 80–5
and state sovereignty 13–14
governmentalization of state 10–11
Grell, Rainer 117–23, 128–30, 166 n.9, 166 n.11, 167 n.15, 167 n.18
on Euro-Islam 166 n.14
Imagination and Truth. The Story of the "Muslim Test" in Baden-Württemberg 117
on nationality 166 n.13
guest workers/guest-worker system 3, 47
culture of 50
in Germany 47–8, 50

Habermas, J. 54, 106, 112, 164 n.27
constitutional patriotism 112
Habermas, Rebekka 152 n.3
Hacking, Ian 71–3
Haraway, Donna 76–7, 79
headscarf 57, 103, 159 n.23, 165 n.5
hegemony/hegemonic 78–81, 98, 103, 130, 147, 162 n.14
hierarchical/hierarchizations 9–10, 17, 31–2, 34–5, 37, 52, 57, 73, 99, 120, 122, 137, 156 n.4
Hindess, Barry 151 n.7
homo-Islamicus 91
homosexual/homosexuality 68, 134–7, 166 n.8
Huber, Wolfgang 56
humanitas 78–9, 83. *See also* anthropos

Iberian Peninsula 152 n.1
illiberal politics 18, 112, 114
immigration/immigrants 1–5, 7, 29–30, 46, 48–51, 53–5, 59, 112–13, 115–17, 137–9, 145, 155 n.5, 160 n.2. *See also* migration/migrants
cultural difference 52, 55
culture of 50, 166 n.14
German nationality for 165 n.4
immigration policy of Germany (*laissez-faire*) 29, 46–8, 51, 151 n.4, 154 n.1
immigration societies 1–3, 47
integration of 8, 45, 48, 61, 157 n.12
knowledge testing of 133
and minority 8
Polish 115
postwar 47, 51
imperialism 7, 39, 92, 115, 123, 153 nn.5–6
individual freedoms 15, 17–18, 21
integration 1–3, 5–8, 27, 31, 46–52, 58, 87, 98, 105, 109, 127, 141–2
deficient/deficits of 1, 49, 52–3, 66–7, 125
of immigrants 8, 45, 48, 61, 157 n.12
law on integration (*Integrationsgesetz*) 2
as liberal governmentality 9–21
measuring 64–8
of Muslims 6–8, 12–15, 21–5, 29–32, 34, 45–6, 56, 60, 63, 71, 76, 79, 84, 90, 94, 103
proactive 52–3
Schinkel on 4, 8, 111
social 6, 52, 67
state-led integration programs 3, 55, 57, 85, 89, 98, 126
traps of integration as recognition 106–10
interpellation 24, 104, 122–3, 127, 132
Investiture Controversy 92
Islam 4, 6–8, 12, 35–6, 39, 43, 47, 52–7, 61, 65, 83–4, 110, 142, 155 n.5, 158 n.18, 159 n.21. *See also* Buddhism; Christian/Christianity; Jews/Jewish; Judaism
European (Euro-Islam) 1, 33, 119–20, 122–3, 152 n.1, 166 n.14 (*see also* Europe/European)

inner-Islamic theology 93
institutionalization of 1, 6, 13, 29–30, 53, 90, 145
Islamic classes in state schools 49, 53
Islamic Revolution in Iran 52
Islamic Studies 32, 35, 37, 152 n.2, 153 n.6, 158 n.19
Islamic Theology 53
Islamization 59, 118, 163 n.22
Muslim mosque movements 55
naturalizing 1
politics of 30–1, 152 n.1, 158 n.19
legacies of (see Islampolitik)
ritual slaughter 103, 163 n.21
Islamic organization Milli Görüş (IGMG) 104, 163 n.21
Islamophobia 7, 62, 87
Islampolitik 8, 30–40, 46–7, 52, 55, 59, 81, 83, 90, 145
Italy 152 n.9

Jews/Jewish 5, 31, 39, 41–4, 53, 55, 73–4, 109, 115, 120, 153–4 nn.8–12. See also Buddhism; Christian/Christianity; Islam; Judaism
Johansen, Scheperlen 68–9, 80
Joppke, Christian 112
Judaism 30, 35–6, 39, 43–4, 57, 158 n.15, 158 n.18. See also Buddhism; Christian/Christianity; Islam; Jews/Jewish
Judeo-Christian 57–8

Kant, Immanuel 43, 159 n.24
Karneval der Kulturen 50
Kelek, Necla 96, 121, 162 n.15
The Foreign Bride (Die fremde Braut) 121
knowledge 4, 8–11, 31, 35, 38, 70, 112–13, 122, 133, 143, 149
academic 39, 61, 68, 80, 120
geo- and body-politics of 76–9
knowledge-based citizenship tests 133–9
Orientalist 38, 153 n.5
production 4, 8, 10, 12–13, 15, 20, 31, 37, 39, 50, 61–4, 68, 70–1, 74–7, 79–81, 83–5, 103, 108, 110–11, 120, 129, 138, 144, 153 n.5, 156 n.4

scientific 10–11, 33, 118, 129
sociological 4, 8
Köhler, Axel Ayyub 97, 100–1, 103, 148
Koopmans, Ruud, Multiculturalism or assimilation? Conditions for a successful integration" (Multikulturalismus oder Assimilation. Bedingungen gelungener Integration) 68
Kühn, Heinz 49, 52, 155 n.3
Kühn-Memorandum 49–50, 52
Kulturnation (nation by culture) 115
Kulturprotestantismus for Muslims 34
Kymlicka, Will 90, 161 n.5, 164 n.28

labor market 1, 3, 47–9, 151 n.4
Langenfeld, Christine 163 n.22
legacy/legacies 5, 8, 12, 24, 30–1, 34, 45, 57, 82, 84, 127
of Cartesian body-mind split 158 n.15
Christian 79, 82, 84, 158 n.15
of knowledge production 83
of politics of Islam 32–40
premodern 158 n.18
racial/racist 18, 113–14
spatialized knowledge regime 7
legality 133–4
legal loyalty 57
legitimate/legitimacy 6–7, 13–14, 17, 23, 35, 85, 94, 101–4, 108, 112, 132–3, 149
Lemke, Thomas 11
liberal/liberalism 7, 11, 17–19, 22, 42, 46, 48, 52, 83, 103, 105, 112–13, 125, 134, 155 n.2
human rights 43–4
integration as liberal governmentality 9–21
liberal-democratic 25–6, 90–3, 95, 105–6, 112, 116, 118–20, 128, 133–4, 145, 148, 166 n.14, 167 n.18
liberal freedoms 8, 10, 19–21, 25, 31, 46, 79, 84, 106, 119
liberal-Protestant 43
liberal-secular matrix 2, 6, 8–9, 14–15, 21–7, 80, 82–4, 88, 102, 105–6, 111, 123–4, 129, 138–9, 141, 146–50
liberal state 10, 14, 76, 104, 112, 126, 134, 136, 139, 143, 163 n.22

politics/political 18, 20–1, 41, 113, 149
  technocratic 155 n.2, 155 n.4
Linke, Uli 116
  contact zones 129–30
Löwenheim, Oded 137

Al-Mafaalani, Aladin 8
Mahmood, Saba 25, 149, 151 n.6
majorities/majoritarian 1, 30–1, 79, 101, 103, 107, 149–50. *See also* minorities/minoritarian
Marchand, Suzanne 34, 153 nn.5–6
Markell, Patchen 26, 95, 160 n.3, 161 n.5, 164 n.28
  on Jewish emancipation 44
  on recognition 88–9, 107–8
Mas, Ruth 125, 162 n.14
Masuzawa, Tomoko 35–6, 57, 153 n.4
Mavelli, Luca 159–60 n.24
McCutcheon, Russel, *Critics Not Caretakers: Redescribing the Public Study of Religion* 159 n.20
Mendelsohn, Moses 154 n.11
El-Menouar, Yasemin 157 n.8
Merkel, Angela 53, 155 n.6
Mignolo, Walter M. 78–9
migration/migrants 3, 7, 45, 47–8, 52, 59, 64, 80, 90, 116, 151 n.4. *See also* immigration/immigrants
  culture of 50
  migration background (*Migrationshintergrund*) 64, 69, 119, 136, 156 n.5, 157 n.9
  postwar 51, 62
  Turkish 49
minorities/minoritarian 1–2, 5, 7, 9, 12, 15, 25, 30–1, 39–40, 42, 44–5, 49, 53, 63, 69, 71, 74–6, 79, 85, 87, 96, 100, 105, 141, 150, 158 n.13, 164 n.28. *See also* majorities/majoritarian
  ethnic 75
  and immigration 8
  inclusion of 44–5
  minority management 31, 109
  non-Muslim 57
  politics 59
  recognition of 107–8
  religious 2, 5–6, 26–7, 80, 82, 88, 95, 111, 148

Mittmann, Thomas, re-coding of foreigners 54–5, 59
modernity 14, 23, 34, 40–1
modernization 34
  of Christianity 37
modern-state 5, 10–11, 15–16, 22–3, 32, 40–2, 44, 127
Modood, Tariq 161 n.6
monotheism 56
multiculturalism 51, 53, 90, 164 n.28

Nagel, Tilman 118
national body (*Volkskörper*) 5, 40, 45, 102, 106–7, 114
national constitutionalism 112
National Integration Congress (*Integrationsgipfel*) 53
national integration forum (*Nationaler Integrationsplan*) 30
The National Office of Statistics (*Bundesamt für Statistik*) 137
nation-states 5–6, 10, 15, 26, 31–2, 35, 38–40, 44–5, 59–60, 69, 71–2, 74, 78–9, 81, 87, 109, 113–14, 116, 132, 151 n.4, 153 n.8
  German 31, 35, 39, 46, 108, 114–15, 122
  modern 5, 10, 15–16, 22–3, 32, 40–3, 127
  secular 2, 6, 8–9, 22, 24, 39, 45
  Western-European 73
naturalization 12, 15, 79, 112, 114, 137, 165 nn.4–5
natural sciences 40, 71, 74
Nazi/Nazism 48, 51, 55, 74–5, 120, 154 n.2, 156 n.10
neoliberal 10, 12. *See also* liberal/liberalism
neo-nationalization 111
The Netherlands 152 n.9, 156 n.3
Nikolinakos, Marios 48
9/11 attack 6–7, 13, 30, 62
non-Christian 35, 37, 39, 42. *See also* Christian/Christianity
non-Muslim 57, 70, 125, 127, 142
Norddeutscher Staatenbund constitution (1869) 154 n.10

objectivism 71, 76–9
O'Brian, Peter 48, 52
  Beyond the Swastika 154 n.2
  technocratic liberalism 155 n.2, 155 n.4
Occident/Occidentalism 57, 78

Office for Migration and Refugees. *See Bundesamt für Migration und Flüchtinge* (BAMF)
Orgad, Liav 112
Orient/Orientalism/Orientalists 7, 36, 38, 153 n.6
  knowledge/knowledge production 38, 153 n.5
  Oriental Studies 35, 37
Orthodox 43, 66, 109, 119–20, 142
The Other 108, 145
  antiseptic Other 98
  concrete Other 98
  internal Other 152 n.3
  transcendental Other/God 159–60 n.24
Ottoman Empire 32, 34, 153 n.5
Özdemir, Cem 162 n.13

paradox 8, 42, 55, 74, 130
  paradoxes of assimilation 5, 47, 59, 74
  Bauman's analysis of 40, 44
Pateman, Carole, sexual contract 136, 168 n.25
paternalistic approach 34, 55–6, 58, 79, 103, 106, 120
pedagogy 11, 34–5, 38, 99
  civic 18–20, 98, 142
  culture conflict thesis 50
  pedagogical-civilizational approach 39
perlocutionary acts 122
Pfeiderer, Otto 36
pilots of integration (*Integrationslotsen*) 57
politics 27, 102
  illiberal 18
  of Islam 30–40, 152 n.1, 158 n.18 (*see also Islampolitik*)
  multicultural 87, 98, 161 n.6
  political economy 151 n.5
  political liberalism 18, 20–1, 41, 113, 149
  political rationalities 10, 17–18, 27, 30, 59, 61, 134, 142
  political secularism 7, 23, 25, 59, 92, 102, 149
  of population (*Bevölkerungspolitik*) 91
  and religion 22, 92, 102, 148, 162 n.13
  of religion (*Religionspolitik*) 91
  state-recognition 87

power 2–3, 5, 7, 9–15, 19, 21, 23–4, 45, 71, 76–8, 83–4, 87–8, 94, 108, 131, 137, 141, 144, 150, 151 n.5
  biocratic 17
  of freedom 18
  governmental 11–12, 14, 131
  political and pastoral 11, 13
  sovereign 12, 16, 131–2
  state 2, 10, 12–13, 17, 25, 120, 126, 129
principle of right of blood (*jus sanguinis*) 114–16, 126, 165 n.4
proletariat 48
Protestant 43–4, 57, 154 n.11, 154 n.13, 156 n.9
  Protestant church 56, 93
Protestant Council of Germany. *See Evangelischer Kirchenrat Deutschlands* (EKD)
Prussia 43, 152 n.3
  Prussian civil code (*Preußisches Untertanengesetz*) 165 n.3
  Prussian Edict of 1812 154 n.12

Qur'an 65, 104, 119. *See also* Islam

race/racism/racialization 7, 9, 17, 31–2, 36–9, 41–2, 44–5, 48, 50–60, 63, 71, 74–5, 78, 80, 158 n.17
  anti-Muslim racism in Germany 7
  biological 51
  Chin on 51
  critical race scholarship 51
  cultural 51
  institutional 67
  race thinking 40, 42, 51
  racial markers 38
  racial purity 17, 115
  and statistics 73
  tabooing of 51
rationality/rationalities 17, 40–1, 90, 125, 131–2, 137
  juridical 18, 132
  pedagogical 138
  political 10, 17–18, 27, 30, 59, 61, 111, 134, 142
realism 71
Rech, Heribert 127–8, 132
recognition 1, 15, 26, 30, 45, 87, 90–2, 105, 126
  conditionality of 93–5, 111

Markell on 88–9, 107–8
minority 107–8
political 111
secular embodiments of conditional 95–104
state-managed 96, 106
traps of integration as 106–10
Reformation 35, 92, 159 n.22, 166 n.14
refugee crises 1–2
religion 8–9, 12, 23, 31, 34, 36, 38–9, 42–3, 45, 48–60, 63, 66, 71, 80–3, 85, 94, 102, 111, 146. *See also* world-religions; *specific religions*
  corporeal practices 25, 41, 77–8, 102, 126, 149, 154 n.11
  politics (*Religionspolitik*) of 22, 91–2, 102, 148, 162 n.13
  problematization of 80–5
  prototypes of 12
  religiosity 8, 17, 23, 26, 34, 43, 59, 63–5, 70, 77, 79–80, 82–3, 87, 96, 105, 110
  religious attitudes 66–7
  religious classes 49, 53
  religious freedom 58, 92, 97, 103, 155 n.7, 163 n.16, 163 n.22
  religious fundamentalism 67
  religious minority 2, 5–6, 26–7, 82, 88, 95, 148
  religious orientations 66–7
  religious plurality 1, 3, 7, 9, 14–15, 21–2, 24, 26, 29, 47, 53, 82, 87, 98, 103 (*see also* culture, cultural plurality)
  religious practices 1, 9, 12, 21–4, 26, 44, 59, 62–3, 71, 74, 77, 83–5, 90–1, 101–2, 105, 107–8, 130, 137, 146–9, 152 n.3, 153 n.5
  religious sensibility 6, 9, 19–20, 22, 24–5, 79, 83–4, 87, 91, 94–6, 100–2, 107, 124, 128–30, 132, 145, 149
Roman law 114
Rose, Nikolas 18–19
  civilized sensibilities 20
  on liberal freedoms 20
  pedagogy of civility 19–20
Rusdhie Affair 53, 61

Salvatore, Armando 158 n.19
Santner, Eric 15–16

Schachtschneider, K. A. 163 n.22
Schäuble, Wolfgang 29 n.1, 30, 47, 67, 90–6, 104–5, 161 n.8
Schiffauer, Werner 163 n.21
Schily, Otto 157 n.6
Schinkel, Willem
  on culture 4, 163 n.20
  Imagined Soceities. A Critique of Immigrant Integration in Western Europe 4
  on integration 4, 8, 111, 156 n.3, 157 n.12
  on secularism 6
  virtualization of citizenship 138
Schlerka, Sebastian Matthias 155 n.5
Schmidt, Helmut 49
Schmitt, Carl 131
Secular Islam (*Säkularer Islam*) 96, 121, 162 n.13
secular/secularism 5–8, 21–6, 59, 81, 84, 87, 93–4, 96, 102, 113, 147, 149, 153 n.4
  governmentality 9, 22, 25, 71, 80–5
  political 7, 23, 25, 59, 92, 102
  secular episteme 78, 83, 85
  secularity 25, 92, 102, 149
  secularization 23, 34–5, 92, 95, 148, 159 n.22
  secular Muslims 96, 109–10, 162 n.14
securitization 1, 62, 87, 130, 148, 157 n.6
security studies program 62
segregation 1, 7, 27, 40, 44, 52, 99–100, 108, 149
self-conduct 11
selfhood 20
Semitic language/religion 36–7, 39
sexuality 20, 63, 84, 96, 99–100, 102, 124–6, 136, 161 n.12
Sharia law 56–7
Social Democratic Party (Sozaildemokratische Partei Deutschlands, SPD) 49, 97
social science 4, 71, 74, 80
social theory 4, 45
society 4, 6, 45, 157 n.12
  civil 13–14, 23, 29, 53, 56–7, 76, 105, 121, 142, 148, 155 n.2
  German 3, 7–8, 29, 33, 46, 51, 65–6, 70, 75, 84, 90–1, 93, 101, 105, 108, 128, 136, 142, 144–5, 168 n.24
  secular 21, 23, 142

Sociology of Religion 35, 37, 158 n.19, 159 n.22, 159 n.24
sovereign state (state sovereignty) 6, 13, 15–16, 26, 43, 88–9, 105, 130–2, 141–4
Spielhaus, Riem 68–9, 80
sports 99–101, 161 n.12, 162 n.15, 163 n.21, 167 n.15
   swimming classes 25, 96–8, 101, 104, 125, 161 n.12, 162 n.15, 163 n.21, 167 n.15
state neutrality 15, 23, 93, 105, 110, 145
status of a statutory body under public law (*Körperschaft des öffentlichen Rechts*) 53–4
Stein, Tine 112
Stevens, Jacqueline 164 n.2
Stoler, Ann L. 5, 46, 145, 156 n.4
subjectivity 9, 14, 19, 23–5, 76, 130
Sullivan, Winnifred, *The Impossibility of Religious Freedom* 163 n.16
Supik, Linda 73, 75
surveys on Muslims 61–3, 65–8, 82, 156 n.3
   Muslimisches Leben in Deutschland 68, 157 nn.8–9
   statistics 72–5
   surveying and surveilling 68–76
Süssmuth, Rita (Süssmuth Commission) 155 n.3

taxonomy 73, 75, 80
Taylor, Charles 90, 161 n.5
terrorism. *See* 9/11 attack
Tezcan, Levent 32, 55, 90–1
Theologisches Forum (2009) 91
think tanks 48, 62

Tibi, Bassam 166 n.14
Topolski, Anya 109, 156 n.10
totalitarianism 92
traditional-conservative Muslims 66, 142
transcendent 22, 81, 84
   transcendental Other (God) 159–60 n.24
transgressions 85, 99, 102
Troeltsch, Ernst 153 n.4
truth 58, 69–73, 84, 92–4, 144, 160 n.24
   regimes of truth 69–71, 77, 89

The United States 13, 62, 160 n.4
universalism 130, 153 n.4

Van Gogh, Theo 53, 61, 152 n.9
Varnhagen, Rahel 154 n.9
Verkaaik, Oskar 168 n.19
Vial, Theodore 12, 81–2, 159 n.20

Weber, Max 37, 158 n.19
Weimar Constitution 155 n.7
Western Allies 155 n.2
Western European Christianity 34–5, 38. *See also* Christian/Christianity
Wetzels, Peter, *Muslims in Germany: Integration, barriers to integration, religion and attitudes towards democracy, the rule of law, and politically-religiously motivated violence* 65
Widmann-Mauz, Annette 98
Wieck, Michael 120
world-religions 31, 35–7, 43, 57, 81, 153 n.4. *See also* religion

Žižek, Slavoj 98

www.ingramcontent.com/pod-product-compliance
Lightning Source LLC
Chambersburg PA
CBHW061831300426
44115CB00013B/2337